The Visual Is Political

The Visual Is Political

Feminist Photography and Countercultural Activity in 1970s Britain

NA'AMA KLORMAN-ERAQI

Rutgers University Press

New Brunswick, Camden, and Newark, New Jersey, and London

Library of Congress Cataloging-in-Publication Data

Names: Klorman-Eraqi, Na'ama, 1979– author.
Title: The visual is political : feminist photography and countercultural activity in 1970s Britain / Na'ama Klorman-Eraqi.
Description: New Brunswick : Rutgers University Press, 2019.
Identifiers: LCCN 2018046487 | ISBN 9781978800311 (paperback) | ISBN 9781978800328 (hardcover)
Subjects: LCSH: Feminism—Great Britain—History—20th century. | Feminism and art—Great Britain—History—20th century. | Women photographers—Great Britain—History—20th century. | Great Britain—Economic conditions—20th century. | BISAC: PHOTOGRAPHY / History. | SOCIAL SCIENCE / Feminism & Feminist Theory. | ART / History / Contemporary (1945–). | SOCIAL SCIENCE / Women's Studies. | ART / Art & Politics.
Classification: LCC HQ1593 .K56 2019 | DDC 305.420941/09047—dc23
LC record available at https://lccn.loc.gov/2018046487

A British Cataloging-in-Publication record for this book is available from the British Library.

∞ The paper used in this publication meets the requirements of the American National Standard for Information Sciences—Permanence of Paper for Printed Library Materials, ANSI Z39.48-1992.

www.rutgersuniversitypress.org

Manufactured in the United States of America

Dedicated with love to Mika and Kadya

Contents

Illustrations

The Visual Is Political

1

Introduction

This book examines feminist photography as it unfolded in Britain during the 1970s.[1] This period was marked by instability due to the collapse of the welfare state, massive unemployment, race riots, and workers' strikes. However, it was also a time in which various forms of social activism thrived. This surge of political activity continued a transnational manifestation of social resistance that had begun in the 1960s, which included the struggle for civil rights and protests against the war in Vietnam in the United States, the May 1968 student riots in Paris and the subsequent formation of revolutionary student organizations in Europe, and the formation of women's liberation movements across North America and Europe.[2]

This book follows feminist photography from its emergence outside the institutional spaces of the museum and academia to its later incorporation into the fine arts museum toward the end of the 1970s. Although women and feminist photographers worked in various British cities, this book focuses on feminist photography produced in London and Leeds.[3] I chose to focus on London since it was a major cultural and feminist center where diverse forms of feminist photography developed during the 1970s, and I chose to focus on Leeds because it fostered unique forms of radical and revolutionary feminist activism that had distinct intersections with photography.

British feminist photography from this era has often been overlooked in research. In recent years, however, interest in the subject has increased. This newfound enthusiasm is manifested in a growing body of scholarly research, as well as by the National Museum Reina Sofia Center of Art's recent acquisition of British feminist photography for the "Feminist Revolution" section of its collection *From Revolt to Postmodernity 1962–82*, housed in Madrid.[4]

In this book, I will show that photography and feminist activity in 1970s Britain were considered institutionally unrestricted since they both took shape outside such spaces as academia or the museum, and this noninstitutionalized development contributed to the diversity of their arguments and forms of organization and activity. It should be noted that feminists, like other politicized photographers, increasingly turned to photography and photographic documentation as part of their activism and were informed by the era's politicized debates about photography.

The photography theory that emerged in Britain in the mid-1970s had political underpinnings and initially developed outside academia, as did other forms of politicized photographic activity. Among photography theory's contributions were its employment of psychoanalytic, semiotic, and Marxist theories to explore photography's political and ideological functions. Prominent photography theorists such as Victor Burgin, John Tagg, and Allan Sekula did not assume the existence of a photographic essence or aim to articulate a narrow, art-historical account of photography. Rather, they focused on photography's capacity to produce and disseminate meaning and explored how this meaning is reproduced within the contexts in which photographs appear.[5] Thus, photography theory marked a breakaway from the then-prevailing models of photography criticism that analyzed photographs on the basis of personal thoughts and feelings and emphasized the significance of the photographer's biography.[6] *Thinking Photography* (1982), edited by Burgin, is a key anthology that brought together theoretical texts and illustrated their main influences and political engagements. In this anthology, which has become a canonical text, Burgin lays out photography theory's goals and closes with the following puzzling assertions:

> It remains for me to explain an absence. There are no essays by women in the anthology. This is a matter neither of oversight nor prejudice. . . . Much of

> the work by women on representation occupies different theoretical registers and/or engages different practical projects. . . . On the one hand, the sort of writing associated with . . . the journal *m/f* is too general . . . to *appear* to engage the particular histories of art and photography addressed here; on the other hand the work specifically on photography of, say, Jo Spence has had its own quite distinct cultural political project. . . . Writing by women which would otherwise fit very happily into this present book is not specifically about photographs. . . . Nevertheless I wish to emphasize that . . . the theoretical project to which this book is a contribution owes itself to the initial and continuing insistence of the women's movement on the politics of representation.[7]

Burgin's omission of texts by women writers and essays engaging with feminist issues deserves further attention. Did women writers really engage with different practical projects? Why is the journal *m/f*, a prominent site for the development of feminist theory, considered not to engage with the histories of art and photography, when feminist theory turned to semiotic, psychoanalytic, and Marxist theories, the same discourses employed by photography theory?[8] Moreover, why did writing by Spence, alleged by Burgin to be the *only* woman who wrote about photography, not fit in with *Thinking Photography*'s cultural project?[9] Also, if the insistence of the women's movement on "the politics of representation" was so crucial to photography theory, why are no feminist texts addressing this issue in the anthology?

Burgin's exclusion of women writers and feminist concerns reflects a glaring lacuna in his volume. As Elspeth H. Brown and Thy Phu observed in a recent critique of 1970s photography theory, Burgin's advocacy of *thinking* photography (as opposed to modes of criticism rooted in personal feelings) reflects a condescending rejection of feminist perspectives prevalent at that time. Whereas feminist authors of the 1970s espoused the view that "the personal is political," Burgin dismissed this stance as intellectually inferior.[10] However, Burgin's dismissal of feminism was not exclusively his own but rather a manifestation of a broader marginalization of women and feminist concerns in the field of photography at the time. Therefore, it is necessary to trace historically how, in contrast with Burgin's view, the fields of feminism and photography intersected, influenced each other, and were articulated around their shared political engagement with the politics of representation.

Feminist Photography's Diversity

Despite the large body of scholarship on feminism and on photography from this period, their distinctive intersections remain insufficiently explored. As I began this book, I found that feminist photography produced in Britain in the 1970s was a vibrant, rich, and diverse field and that its study would add greatly to the understanding of feminist countercultural practices produced in this particular moment of upheaval. Moreover, an exploration of the intersection of feminism and photography in the context of the social conflict and theoretical debates of the time can enrich our perspective on photography's political uses.

Feminist photography of the era was informed by the diverse and conflicting feminist factions of the women's movement. This influence could be seen in the decision of several feminist photographers to work collectively, a strategy that correlated with other decentralized forms of organization in the women's movement that set out to challenge "male" structures of leadership and permanence.[11] Indeed, although heterogeneous feminist photographic interventions belonged to different feminist "camps," I argue that their practical concerns and theoretical perspectives were interrelated in manifold ways. For instance, the centrality of media politics to debates at the time can be seen in feminist theoretical writings, in socialist feminist photography practices, in photography practices oriented to consciousness raising, and in revolutionary feminist militant direct action. Additionally, as I will discuss later, certain crucial points in the historical development of the women's movement illustrate the numerous ways in which feminism intersected with photography. Among these are the disruption of the Miss World competition by women's movement demonstrators in 1970, the launch of the feminist magazine *Spare Rib* in 1972 as an accessible alternative to commercial women's magazines, the Reclaim the Night marches in 1977 that protested male violence against women, the unionization strike by Asian and Asian British women workers against the Grunwick film-processing factory in North London in 1976–1978, and the *Three Perspectives on Photography* exhibition at the Hayward Gallery in London in 1979, which marked the entry of feminist photography into the space of the public museum.

The structure of this book reflects the plurality of intersections between feminism and photography during this period. Chapters are structured around thematic points of focus rather than around specific feminist narratives, around careers of particular feminist photographers, or as a chronological survey of feminist photography. Thus, chapter 2 examines the influence of the media and the myriad ways in which media images became a central focus for feminist photographic practices and debates. The chapter notes that, despite political conflicts among the differing feminist factions, media representation was a shared political concern and a necessary target of feminist politics. In chapter 3 I turn to the political role of street photography and the feminist critique of the numerous gender, sexual, racial, and class tensions that surrounded it. I show that the camera was perceived as a powerful political tool capable of capturing the "truth" of events otherwise misrepresented in the media. Chapter 4 explores the debate surrounding the entry of feminist photography into the space of the art museum at the end of the 1970s and the perception of photography's institutionalization as a compromise of its political edge. This moment marks a significant turning point since, like other forms of politicized photography, feminist photography did not initially aspire to be recognized first and foremost as an "art" practice. Chapter 5 looks back at the book's main themes from the perspective of the present day and explores their ramifications.

The Centrality of "Representation"

Feminist photographic engagements with "representation" are not presented in this book as mere effects of representation in term of ideology and power but are, rather, historicized in terms of the distinct feminist arguments, photography debates, and photography practices in the period under study.[12] It should be noted that photography theory has, since the 1970s, begun to break away from its earlier emphasis on representation and shift toward an exploration of themes such as memory, affect, performativity,[13] the photograph's materiality, and transmission.[14] Thus, while I relate to and historicize the centrality of representation during the period under study, my analysis also employs photography theory's contemporary engagements in order to further explore and situate the political aspects of 1970s British feminist photography.

In my analysis, I approach photographs' representational content, but, drawing on Elizabeth Edwards's work and Tagg's Foucauldian approach, I also locate photographic meaning within the photographs' spaces of production and circulation, the feminist value of their networks of exchange, and the social, cultural, and political conflicts of their moment.[15] Furthermore,

I seek to explore the affective aspects of their processes of production and viewing. My analyses are rooted in a variety of primary sources uncovered in archives of photographs and other materials gathered from public archives, personal collections, libraries, newspapers, journals, and magazines from the period. These sources have been supplemented by the interviews I conducted with people who were key protagonists in the field of feminism and photography in the 1970s. These primary sources, here brought together for the first time, open up a critical space for reflection on feminism and photography produced in 1970s Britain.

Shaping Feminist Photography History

It is curious that although feminist art history took shape in the 1970s in Britain alongside other critical discourses, such as cultural studies and the social history of art, it largely overlooked feminist photography as a rich and distinct field.[16] Nevertheless, those feminist photography practices informed by feminist theory were the first to be seen as exemplars of British feminist photography.[17] Among such works is Mary Kelly's *Post-partum Document* (1973–1979). This work recorded the first several years of the relationship between Kelly and her infant son and the work, as it was completed by that time, was exhibited in 1976 at the Institute of Contemporary Arts in London. Informed by conceptual art practices, the piece included photographs, feeding charts, and diapers, as well as Kelly's theoretical notes, which drew on psychoanalytic and linguistic theory.[18] Kelly's work, which was invested in feminist theory, was only one articulation of feminist photography's conceptions of feminist politics, organizational strategies, methods of intervention, and spaces of circulation. Thus, while feminist photography practices informed by theory made significant contributions to the field of photography, I offer a further exploration of the plural forms of such practices and their political meaning. My research reveals that these practices, which initially received little scholarly attention, were predominantly informed by "woman-centered" perspectives and often sought to use the camera as a "consciousness-raising" tool for exploring and defining a collective sense of women's identity.[19] This perspective was nevertheless often critiqued by photographers engaged with feminist theory such as Kelly, who challenged the category "woman" and analyzed it as constituted by various oppressive social structures. Thus, in order to capture the diversity of the feminist perspectives informing photography practices, I avoid the theoretical terms used by the contending sides to conceptualize the category "woman"; instead, I define womanhood as a foundation of these groups' feminist politics, and I approach the political implications of the category "woman" in its historic and geographic contexts.[20] Additionally, I find it necessary to avoid advocating a feminist narrative of "progression" from grassroots feminist activism to the feminist theory that took shape in the 1980s.[21] Instead, I historicize this process in an effort to shed light on the various conflicts and ruptures produced by this issue of alleged "progression" in relation to feminist photography. Such narratives of progression from grassroots activity to theory also existed in the field of photography. As I will discuss later, this view was manifested in Burgin's refusal to have his work, which was informed by photography theory, hung opposite that of the socialist feminist community photography collective the Hackney Flashers at the *Three Perspectives on Photography* exhibition.[22]

Oversights in 1970s Feminist Debates

Prevailing 1970s feminist debates had their own oversights. While class was a prominent issue in British feminist debates due to the advent of socialist feminism, it was only toward the end of the decade that the relationship between photographic representation and race began to be examined. It should be noted that in 1970s Britain, the term *black* was used by African Caribbean and South Asian activists to denote a political position of unity against white British racism. I thusly make similar use of this term in this book. It was during the late 1970s that a number of black feminist organizations began to address issues such as immigration policy, stop-and-search laws, police violence, and domestic violence against women within black communities.[23] The marginalization of black women's experience in women's movement debates and the absence of a feminist analysis exploring the interconnections of class and gender were also becoming evident at the time. Notably, Hazel V. Carby's 1982 essay "White Woman Listen! Black Feminism and the Boundaries of Sisterhood" stressed that the lack of accounts of black women's experiences in feminist history needed to be addressed by analyzing how black women's femininity and sexuality were represented differently from those of white women.[24] Sexual difference was another concern that gained visibility between the late 1970s and early 1980s. Thus, the lack of feminist focus on these issues and its possible implications for feminist photography deserve further attention.

Although racial tension increased in Britain in the late 1970s as black youths were criminalized by state racism, there were nevertheless earlier landmark events in British sociopolitical history that fractured race relations, such as the Notting Hill race riots in 1958 and Enoch Powell's "Rivers of Blood" speech in 1968.[25] In this context, the term *black activism* should be understood as referring not only to people of African descent but also to people from India and Pakistan.[26] During the late 1970s, the term *black art* was politically used within the visual arts to describe the work of black artists—both those who arrived in Britain in the postwar period and those who were born there—who studied in British art schools.[27] The contributions of black women artists were nevertheless often marginalized within the then-emerging narratives of black art.[28] Decades later, photography initiatives such as Autograph ABP (Association of Black Photographers) emerged with the mission of raising the profile of black photography within photographic practice. Among the speakers at Autograph's 1988 launch was revolutionary black lesbian feminist Linda Bellos, whose presence highlighted the intersectionality between gendered, raced, classed, and sexed experiences in relation to photography. While the connections between intersectional experiences and photography had been acknowledged before, they began to attain greater visibility at this time.[29] For instance, despite the increasing prevalence of antiracism discourse in the late 1970s, the issue of race was not prominent in the early volumes of *m/f*, which focused instead on articulating a feminist theory informed by Lacanian and semiotic theories. Also, feminist theorist Laura Mulvey wrote a hugely influential essay titled "Visual Pleasure and Narrative Cinema" in 1975, which used Freudian psychoanalytic theory to analyze how representations of women in classic Hollywood cinema function as objects for the desiring male gaze. This essay made no distinctions in terms of racial or sexual differences.[30]

Such racial and sexual oversights figure in my discussion in chapter 3, where I consider how these issues influenced feminist photography and its analysis. I will focus on a group of photographs that documented street events such as the Grunwick strike and the Battle of Lewisham, both of which erupted as a result of racial tensions. I will show how the photography practices related to these particular events had feminist underpinnings, and I explore how they intersected with historical issues pertaining to race.

Feminist Cultural Activity Revisited

My interest in the intersections between feminism and photography in 1970s and early 1980s Britain adds to recent publications dealing with feminist cultural activity at the time. Like my book, Siona Wilson's *Art Labor, Sex Politics: Feminist Effects in 1970s British Art and Performance* examines the implications of class and sexual difference for aesthetics debates, and it also explores the feminist and queer aspects of the experimental art group COUM Transmissions' performances and Mary Kelly's early socialist feminist engagements, exemplified by her participation in producing the film *The Night Cleaners* (1975). The impact of the theme of sexual difference on feminist art practice is also prominent in Kathy Battista's book *Renegotiating the Body: Feminist Art in 1970s London*, which locates feminist art practices produced in 1970s London within the broader context of contemporary art, as well as the women's movement.[31] My book's distinct contribution is its focus on the unique intersection between feminism and photography produced in 1970s Britain in light of the time's social and historical events, feminist and photography debates, and political expectations invested in cultural activity.

Recent years have also seen a resurgence of interest in British political movements of the 1970s, and these historical studies have provided an important context for my study in this book. For example, Andy Beckett's *When the Lights Went Out: What Really Happened to Britain in the Seventies* focuses on both the official and the grassroots politics of the era, and John A. Walker's *Left Shift: Radical Art in 1970s Britain* looks at the countercultural manifestations of radical art practice at the time.[32] I draw on these books and other recent publications on British history for a broad background to situate my study of feminism, feminist countercultural practices, and photography. The present book nevertheless centers on a select group of conjunctures and interventions in order to unpack the political engagements of feminist photography in the period under study. I strive to engage the competing views of the goals of feminist photographic practice without claiming to be exhaustive. Additionally, like any archive, the one I have assembled is fragmented and far from complete. My historical review no doubt remains limited by the very selective inclusions, exclusions, and ways of making sense that shaped the organizations and institutions from which this archive came.[33] Even so, the book's close and critical analysis of feminist photography practices, the primary materials it draws on, and the form of organization given to them open a space for a new critical reflection on feminism and photography in Britain that leads to a deeper understanding of the correlations between political movements, cultural practices, and their social implications.

Time Frame and Contemporary Resonance

This book's historical timeline begins in the early 1970s and concludes in the early 1980s. I chose this endpoint because the early 1980s saw the culmination of the earlier surge of politicization, the diminishing of social and political activism, and the waning of countercultural photographic practices. The early 1980s were also marked by a shift to the right in the politics of the British state, which was exacerbated by the election of Margaret Thatcher's Conservative government in 1979. A similar shift took place in the United States, where Ronald Reagan's 1980 election is often seen as marking an end to progressive American politics. In Britain, Thatcher's government promoted privatization and imposed cuts on public bodies that, as I will discuss, resulted in marked changes to cultural institutions that affected the production, circulation, and reception of feminist photography practices. The early 1980s also witnessed an increasing media and social backlash in response to some of the achievements attained in the previous decade by the second wave feminist movement. It was during this time that the term *post-feminist* originated in the media and was repeatedly used until the early 2000s to signal "liberation" from outdated feminist ideologies that were perceived as making women miserable.[34] Nevertheless, the twenty-first century has thus far seen a revival of feminist debates and activism. A parallel might be drawn between the period of unrest in the 1970s and the economic crisis of 2008, which made debates about feminism and photography relevant again in new ways. Additionally, feminist demands for equal pay and arguments about sexual violence, the social effects of media images, and immigrant rights have begun to reemerge in new forms of feminist social, virtual, and cultural activism.[35]

Furthermore, the advent of mobile-phone cameras, the speed of digital photography's image processing, and the immediacy of sharing images on social networks have made it possible for photography to continue to be employed as a political tool. This has been evident in politically conflicted areas, most notably in Egypt during the Arab Spring in 2010, but also in contemporary feminist street events such as the 2011 Slut Walk, feminist selfie representations on social media, the Me Too movement's campaign, and feminist Twitter campaigns such as #NotBuyingIt that challenge brands that rely on misrepresentations of gender and sexual objectification to sell their products.[36]

Thus, the feminist revival following the aftershocks of the 2008 recession, the current feminist critiques of media images, and the contemporary reconceptualization of the street as a gendered site suggest the ongoing significance of 1970s feminist debates. Additionally, the continuing feminist politicization of photographic production and circulation has further shed light on the relevance of this earlier contentious, creative, and perhaps more politicized moment of feminism and photography, before it was institutionalized academically and incorporated into the fine arts museum.

2

Feminist Photography and the Media

Beginning in the early 1970s, and continuing well into the 1980s, media representation was a key issue for the majority of the feminist factions within the British women's liberation movement.[1] Though they had political differences, these groups all felt that media images had a significant impact on the socialization of women and were thus a necessary target of feminist politics. In this chapter I show that photography was a significant activist tool for intervening in the media's portrayal of women and for cultivating a shared sense of feminist identification. Such feminist photography practices primarily circulated outside the institutionalized spaces of academia and art museums and were diverse in their strategies and feminist positions. Moreover, the majority of these works were products of collaborative forms of feminist organization that in themselves were significant manifestations of feminist activism and mobilization. Feminist photography that responded to images in the media was a continuation of early forms of feminist activism, such as the Miss World beauty contest protest at the Royal Albert Hall on November 20, 1970.[2] In this event, approximately one hundred women disrupted the televised broadcast by throwing smoke bombs and flour bombs on the stage. The women also used noise as an element of their disruption by blowing whistles and waving rattles.[3] The Miss World protest—and the arrest of some of the women involved—garnered headlines and media attention. The publication of the London Women's Liberation Workshop, *Shrew* (1969–1978), portrayed the subsequent trial of the protesters as the first women's liberation trial since those of the suffragettes and called on women to come to the courthouse and show their support.[4] The disruptive character of the Miss World protest also brought to mind political strategies employed by the suffragettes who, on the eve of the general election in 1905, interrupted a Liberal Party meeting in Manchester by repeatedly asking whether the party's representatives would give women the right to vote if they were elected. Ultimately, the suffragettes' actions led to their ejection from the hall and their being charged with obstruction, an incident that, like the Miss World protest, attracted newspaper coverage.[5] Additionally, the Miss World protesters' use of rattles and whistles evokes the suffragettes' use of noise in their public demonstrations. The suffragettes, as suggested by Mary Chapman, used their voices in public to signal a shift from their earlier, quiet assemblies in domestic spaces and to appropriate the "shrieking sisterhood" stereotype perpetuated by men.[6] The Miss World protesters similarly used noise to voice feminist arguments that had earlier been articulated in spaces removed from the public eye, such as consciousness-raising groups.

In an anonymous essay, several of the protesters at Miss World explained that they had aimed to dispute and disrupt the public celebration of the traditional female road to success: good looks and marriage. The essay's authors suggested that one of the demonstration's achievements was that it had received extensive media coverage, which pushed the women's movement further into the public eye.[7] Finally, the authors added that the Miss World demonstration revealed the political potential of such actions and suggested that even a seemingly impenetrable spectacle such as the Miss World competition could be disrupted easily.[8] Thus, this event and the attention it drew became an invitation to develop further disruptive feminist strategies for challenging images and their social stereotyping of women.

The Miss World protest used guerilla strategies to disrupt the media event, but it also employed them to transmit feminist ideas. Similar disruptive tactics were also used by several contemporaneous radical political groups that operated in Europe at that time, such as the Baader-Meinhof Group in Germany, the Red Brigade in Italy, and the urban guerilla group the Angry Brigade in Britain.[9] For instance, the Angry Brigade placed a bomb in a BBC broadcast van outside Albert Hall on the morning of the 1970 Miss World competition.[10] Nonetheless, despite the Miss World protest's connection with various contemporary radical groups, which were often patriarchal, it was primarily embedded in the development of the second-wave feminist movement and focused on highlighting the ramifications of media images for gender roles. Thus, the feminist arguments posed in the Miss World demonstration suggested that media images of women were politically significant for understanding women's social positioning, and as will be shown, these arguments were central to feminist countermedia photography practices.

The Personal Is Political and Feminist Photography

The feminist arguments posed in the Miss World demonstration and in other feminist countermedia activities no doubt resonated with early women's liberation movement politics, which explored women's personal experiences and asserted that they were not "natural" but rather political and could be transformed by feminist collective action. The position that "the personal is political" prevailed among the politically diverse feminist factions in Britain and the United States, particularly in their attitudes toward media images. This viewpoint was manifested early on, for example, in Betty Friedan's groundbreaking *Feminine Mystique* (1963), which demystified the blissful image of the lives of middle-class housewives in the postwar United States. Such feminists also argued that advertising and media images offered women a glossy model of femininity that targeted their uncertainty regarding who they were and what they should become.[11] Socialist feminists, the predominant force in the British women's movement particularly during the early 1970s, argued for women's rights within the context of class exploitation, as well as against the underrepresentation of working-class women's experience in the media. Socialist feminists also set out to relate working-class women's experience to other political struggles.[12]

In the mid-1970s, however, predominantly under the influence of feminism in the United States, radical feminism began to gain ground in Britain. This faction asserted that women were a class within itself that was oppressed by men, and radical feminists focused on the personal and social impact of the relationship between the sexes.[13] One of the then leading American radical feminist texts to influence British feminism was Kate Millett's *Sexual Politics*,[14] which asserted that "sex" is a political category that constructs relationships between men and women based on power differences.[15]

Similarly, radical feminists often viewed sexualized representations of women in the media as patriarchal structures that generate and sustain the power relations between the sexes. Canadian-American Shulamith Firestone's *Dialectics of Sex* was another influential text that theorized that the primary social and political contradiction in all societies is that between men and women, and that women's subordination arises from male power.[16] *The Female Eunuch*, by Germain Greer, an Australian feminist living in Britain, was another significant book that argued that women were sexually repressed by men and that sex should therefore be re-defined for women as desire and creation.[17]

The feminist stance that the personal is political corresponded with distinct feminist strategies and forms of organization such as consciousness raising and a range of collective activity manifested in feminist countermedia production.[18] The majority of the feminist media interventions addressed in this chapter hinged on the conviction that the personal is political and on articulating a certain shared affective experience distinct to women's lives. Nonetheless, it should be noted that feminist theory that developed in the mid-1970s drew on Marxist, linguistic, and psychoanalytic theory and argued that a coherent "woman" identity did not exist. Developing feminist theory moved away from collective and so-called emotive feminist strategies such as consciousness raising that had prevailed in the women's movement from early on. Furthermore, one of feminist theory's key concerns, informed by Jacques Lacan's psychoanalytic writings, was questioning how femininity was constructed. Feminist theorist Juliet Mitchell, for example, recognized an emphasis in Lacan's writing—which she established through her reading of Louis Althusser—that "woman" was not an essentialist category but rather a product of the social and economic structures within which the concept of "woman" was constructed.[19] Nevertheless, despite feminist theory's polemical and analytical approach toward women's identities, it should be emphasized that like other feminist factions, its proponents regarded the media and its representations as a central concern. Griselda Pollock, for example, in "What's Wrong with 'Images of Women'?" (1977), took issue with prevalent feminist views of images as "reflecting" or "not reflecting" "real women" by taking a more language-inspired approach that focused on signs and signification. Thus, she suggested that there are no inherently bad or good "images of women" but that these images instead function as signifiers in an ideological discourse in which meaning is constructed in relation to other signifiers. For instance, she argued that women's bodies signify sexuality and sale, whereas men's bodies signal activity and autonomy.[20] Similarly, Laura Mulvey, in her now canonical essay "Visual Pleasure and Narrative Cinema" (1975), used Freudian psychoanalytic theory to articulate an argument concerning gendered power relations and visual pleasure. She examined how classic Hollywood narrative cinema represents women as fetish objects for the desiring male gaze and suggested that these representations reinforce sexual differences in the social field. It should be noted that although centering on film, this essay's insights were germane to feminist debates in other cultural fields as well.[21] Feminist theory, like a range of other feminist practices, was largely shaped outside the academic institution, such as at women's liberation movement conferences, in film and media journals such as *Screen* and *Screen Education*, and in feminist theory publications like *m/f* (1978–1986). In 1976 one of the first conferences to present arguments in feminist theory was entitled Papers on Patriarchy and was held in London. This conference raised a number of claims in favor of feminist theory, among them its potential for methodically uncovering the basis for women's oppression and for articulating a theoretical common ground for the women's movement.[22] Nevertheless, at Papers on Patriarchy, there were participants who criticized feminist theory, indicating another growing divide within the women's movement. The Dalston Study Group, for instance, claimed that feminist theory's methods that employed structuralism and Lacanian psychoanalysis were alienating and, therefore, reminiscent of oppressive male academic structures that mystified knowledge. In response, the Dalston Study Group organized a spontaneous conference workshop for women who did not understand or agree with the feminist theory papers and opposed their nonconversationalist form of delivery.[23]

The photography practices that I address in this chapter largely subscribed to the feminist perception that aimed to express and define a particular experience of the world perceived to be distinctive to women. While feminist photographers active during the 1970s (e.g., Mary Kelly, Marie Yates, and Yve Lomax) incorporated feminist theory into their work, I instead focus on photographic work that was often interconnected with collective forms of production and organization and that have received less attention in research.

The desire to articulate and politicize women's personal experiences was shared by those who employed the art practices that took shape in the United States. One of the earliest manifestations of these practices was the art project

Woman House (1971–1972) initiated by Judy Chicago, Miriam Schapiro, and their students from the feminist art program at the California Institute of the Arts in Los Angeles. Over the course of this project, they converted an old mansion into a feminist art space in which they exhibited their artwork and performance pieces that addressed issues such as domestic labor, menstruation, sexuality, and childhood.[24] Consciousness raising was one of the techniques used to develop this project.[25] *Woman House* is believed to have served as a model for various British feminist art projects. For example, in the early 1970s, the Women's Workshop of the Artists Union, a subgroup of the British Artists Union, planned to take over an abandoned house, decorate it with art expressive of women's lives, and use it as a studio and meeting place.[26]

Feminists' use of photography to counter media representations and their creation of feminist platforms for circulating photographs correspond with earlier uses of photography by social movements.[27] Moreover, drawing on social movement theory, cultural production, like photography, was employed to create a collective feminist identity that supported political protest and mobilized feminists into action.[28] In addition, countermedia practices, which often corresponded with the feminist notion that the personal is political, constructed "frame alignments" that enabled women to identify events in their lives and render them meaningful. Thus, these countermedia practices organized experience as politically significant, a process that further guided individual and collective action.[29]

Photography and the Politics of Representation

Feminist countermedia practices produced in 1970s Britain and their correlated debates were locally and historically specific. Representation, for instance, was a major target for feminist countercultural intervention. This focus can be situated in the changing debates of the period; it was during this time that the British Left broke away from traditional trade unionism and Marxism.[30] This ideological shift made room for new political forces and discourses;[31] under the influence of Althusser, the concept of representation took on a new centrality within Marxism. Althusser broke away from expressive and economic deterministic readings of Marx and argued that "ideology" had to be understood as a material practice located in "ideological state apparatuses" (e.g., religious, educational, and cultural institutions). He suggested that these were the sites in which ideological representations were produced, and that they constituted social subjects and organized social relations.[32] Furthermore, John Tagg, a theorist and historian of photography, has recalled that Althusser's theories served as the basis for new forms of cultural activism and legitimized the idea of cultural struggle as political struggle. Thus, within this context, photography was perceived as a politically potent practice that could produce counterideological forms of representation that would intervene in the social field. Although it is uncertain whether feminist photographers of the time engaged directly with Althusser's texts, his ideas regarding the role of cultural apparatuses in the production of ideology and the interpolation of subjects resonated in some feminist photography texts. For instance, feminist photographer Jo Spence's essay "The Politics of Photography" (1976) suggested that television, cinema, and magazines convey hidden and explicit ideological messages that shape our concepts of what is "normal," construct social roles, and shape our perception of sexual and racial stereotypes.[33] Thus, Spence's position, which recalls Althusserian notions, informed her own feminist practice, as well as that of others, such as the socialist feminist collective the Hackney Flashers (soon to be discussed), of which she was a member.

Engaging with the political aspect of photographic representation was a significant theme in photography theory, a burgeoning field in 1970s Britain. Among photography theory's engagements was challenging the truth value associated with photography and various documentary traditions. One of the central photography theory texts published in Britain was Victor Burgin's anthology *Thinking Photography*, whose essays drew on theories from outside photography practice, such as semiotics, Marxism, and psychoanalysis, in order to focus on the social, historical, and ideological functions of photography as a specific practice of signification.[34] Similar engagements were explored in an issue of the film and media journal *Screen Education*, whose theme was "the politics of representation." The journal editors emphasized that this issue addressed the political significance of power relations in and among the institutions in which representation is produced, as well as the way in which theoretical work could inform political action. Its essays drew, for example, on the works of Antonio Gramsci, Michel Foucault, and Althusser in asking, What is representation? How does it work? And what effects does it produce? Also evident in this issue was that the journal's deconstruction of the category "representation" was influenced by feminist theory, which held that "woman" was a constructed signifier that derived its meaning from its relation to other signifiers within an ideological discourse.[35] It should be noted that feminist theory developed alongside photography theory in various publications, such as *Screen Education* and *Screen*, and mobilized similar theoretical tools for developing its various arguments. For instance, one of the essays by Tagg, "Power and Photography," drew on Foucault's notions of "power" and "knowledge" to examine how institutions such as law enforcement endowed photography with the function of evidence and used it as an instrument of surveillance over the social field.[36]

Comparable politicized engagements with photography and representation were manifested in the United States, particularly in the early 1980s. Photographer and photography theorist Allan Sekula, for instance, argued that photography was contingent on forces residing outside the photograph and attached to various discourses of power that give it meaning and social value. Moreover, drawing on nineteenth-century American philosopher and semiotician Charles Sanders Peirce, Sekula argued that photographs are indexical signs and therefore merely a physical trace of light, rather than of a photographic "essence."[37] Similarly, feminist photographer Martha Rosler criticized early documentary traditions and positioned them within the ideological climate of state liberalism and reform in the United States. Furthermore, in her photographic work *The Bowery in Two Inadequate Descriptive Systems*, she challenged documentary representations of the Bowery in New York as a slumming spectacle by avoiding photographing Bowery "bums" and by juxtaposing her photographs of the Bowery to texts alluding to drunkenness.[38]

Since the 1980s, however, photography debates have increasingly moved away from questions of realism, photographic truth, and representation and toward such concerns as memory, ethics, personal identity, and affect.[39] Nonetheless, the previously mentioned issues remain pertinent to my discussion and my analysis of the discursive climate in which feminist countermedia photographic practices emerged.

Photography and Political Intervention

As I argued earlier, during the period under study in Britain, cultural production was perceived as capable of intervening in the sphere of representation and its structures of power. Moreover, photography in particular was considered to belong to a broad category of activism that was not restricted to an academic or other institutional arena and was therefore capable of intervening in the social sphere and of forming powerful political arguments.[40] The time's photography practices often developed in sites such as community centers, alternative presses, photography-related publications, and galleries. Thus, a number of photography education initiatives emerged at that time, many of which set out to "democratize" photography skills as a way to foster its perceived interventionist potential. One such initiative was the Photography Workshop collective (1974–1992) formed by socialist photographer Terry Dennett and feminist photographer Jo Spence. Photography Workshop held free photography workshops on children's adventure playgrounds; they used an old ambulance that had a mobile darkroom and exhibition space.[41] Spence and Dennett also gave lectures and seminars on photography and were involved in various community photography projects, such as the Hackney Flashers.[42] Additionally, Spence and Dennett were members of the Half Moon Photography Workshop gallery.[43] This gallery was one of the first photographic exhibition spaces in Britain to include a darkroom for public use, and it exhibited photography that addressed social and political issues.[44] The gallery published the photography journal *Camerawork* (1976–1986), which served as a significant platform for developing critical discussions concerning photography and political as well as feminist photographic practices.[45]

During the 1970s, various photography workshops were publicly funded and supported as a state service. For example, photographer Trisha Ziff, who worked for Social Services in Southwark—a predominantly working-class area of London—ran photography workshops for groups of women, the elderly, youths, and the disabled. She believed these classes presented an opportunity for democratizing photography skills and for her students to use photographic representation for telling their stories, depicting their experiences, and uniting their communities.[46]

Photography was also used frequently by feminists and various women's groups, such as the Hackney Flashers, the Leeds Women Fight Back Campaign, and the Pavilion Feminist Photography Centre in Leeds.[47] Women were a marginalized minority in the field of photography; therefore, making the medium accessible to women, undoing its image as a "masculine" technology, forming feminist photography initiatives, and appropriating photography as a feminist political tool were discernible feminist concerns.[48] This position was also noticeable in articles such as "Developing Your Own Film" by Stephanie Gilbert, published in the feminist magazine *Spare Rib* in its Spare Parts section, which was dedicated to demystifying gendered tasks, such as changing fuses or fixing a broken faucet. Gilbert introduced basic photography equipment and recommended joining a photography class but warned that she was unaware of any classes run by women. She whimsically suggested that these classes could be helpful because male instructors "love expounding all their knowledge" to women.[49]

Moreover, during this time, several polytechnics began offering degree courses in photography. One of these was the Polytechnic of Central London, where Burgin and Tagg began teaching in the mid-1970s; it offered a strong model of a theoretical approach to photography and set out to politicize this practice.[50] Feminist ideas and debates were present in this photography program; for instance, feminist photographer Maggie Murray taught courses that addressed concerns about representation. Additionally, photography students such as Spence and Brenda Prince engaged in feminist projects that challenged mainstream depictions of the nuclear family and confronted issues such as breast cancer and lesbian motherhood.[51] Nonetheless, despite this photography program's political edge, feminism was often considered a controversial form of politics and was often marginalized. Murray, for instance, recalled that in the late 1970s, feminism was still a new concept and was often met with resistance. She also suggested that feminist strategies of personalizing the political were often marginalized in the program and labeled as purely "personal" and therefore inferior to theory.[52]

Thus, it can be argued that feminists used photography not only to pose political arguments but also to claim a feminist presence within the predominantly masculine field of photography education and photography theory.

Feminist Photography Practices Challenging Media Images

Feminist countermedia practices were often in dialog with then emerging feminist and photography debates, and they also corresponded with other cultural products, such as advertising images, photojournalism, photomontages, and punk aesthetics. These feminist countermedia strategies posed a variety of arguments; for example, some challenged the limited portrayal of women by producing what they perceived to be alternative feminist images. Some images represented women performing tasks associated with nontraditional female occupations or defying the codes of femininity that were often portrayed in the media. The special visual issue of *Spare Rib*, "Pictures Talk" (1978), produced by several feminist photographers, illustrates this trend.[53] *Spare Rib* was itself a feminist intervention in the media. This magazine, founded by feminists Marsha Rowe and Rosie Boycott, had a strong visual component and was modeled after women's magazines sold at newsstands, but it aimed to present a feminist alternative. *Spare Rib* initially operated as a collective and was written for women by women, many of whom had previously worked in the underground press that flourished in the 1960s, which was considered radical and controversial.[54] Although the underground press dealt with issues such as ecology, sexuality, communal living, drugs, and civil rights, the issue of women's rights was absent. Thus, many of these women criticized the exclusively male point of view of the underground press, which they experienced as exploitative. They noted that in the underground press, women made tea, typed, and handled production and distribution, but they rarely had the opportunity to write or edit.[55] Thus, one of *Spare Rib*'s feminist interventions was to be a magazine that centered on women's experience of patriarchy in a range of issues pertaining to advertising, work, health, violence, and sexuality.[56] The *Spare Rib* visual issue aimed to focus on the power that images have to shape women's lives and to challenge existing views of women. It also focused on how women were seen and contrasted this perspective with how women might see themselves.[57] Photography was used as a key tool for exploring these concerns in this particular issue of *Spare Rib*. For instance, Ruth Wallsgrove, in her photo-essay "Who Do I Think I Am?," challenged the representation of women in a Sea Witch hair-color ad by contrasting it with photographs and drawings of herself (figure 1).[58] The images appear to be pasted or drawn, which gives it a handmade, do-it-yourself quality reminiscent of punk zine and feminist punk zine aesthetics. This punk-like visual strategy further differentiated Wallsgrove's images from those of the slick pages of women's magazines (see chapter 3). Furthermore, the Sea Witch ad depicts a woman with a stereotypically feminine hairstyle who is wearing makeup, tilting her head, and looking dreamily at the viewer. In the text accompanying the image, Wallsgrove proposes that the model's appearance is an artificial depiction of what a "real" woman is supposed to look like. Additionally, she suggests that, although the model is represented as oblivious to her own good looks, in reality she must worry about her appearance in order to be employed. By contrast, in one of the photo-

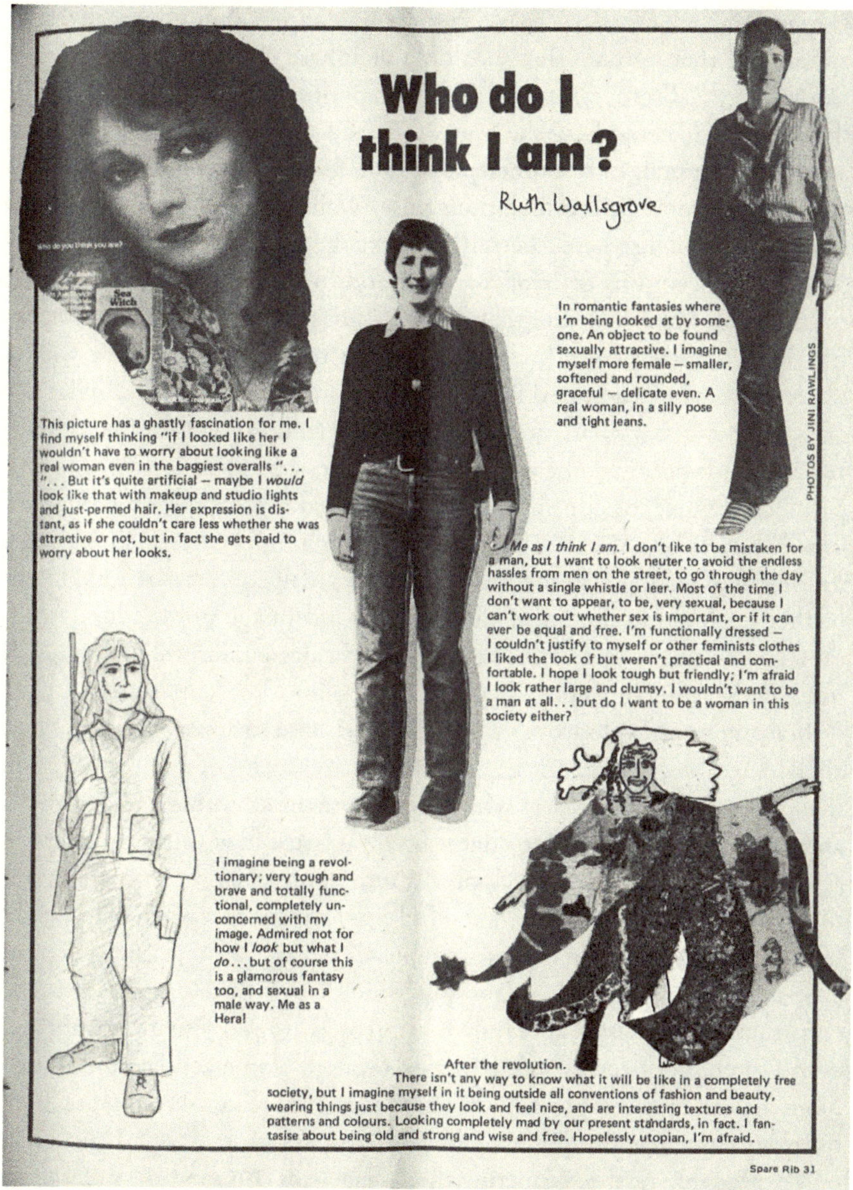

Who do I think I am?

Ruth Wallsgrove

Who do you think you are?

Sea Witch

This picture has a ghastly fascination for me. I find myself thinking "if I looked like her I wouldn't have to worry about looking like a real woman even in the baggiest overalls"... "... But it's quite artificial – maybe I *would* look like that with makeup and studio lights and just-permed hair. Her expression is distant, as if she couldn't care less whether she was attractive or not, but in fact she gets paid to worry about her looks.

In romantic fantasies where I'm being looked at by someone. An object to be found sexually attractive. I imagine myself more female – smaller, softened and rounded, graceful – delicate even. A real woman, in a silly pose and tight jeans.

PHOTOS BY JINI RAWLINGS

Me as I think I am. I don't like to be mistaken for a man, but I want to look neuter to avoid the endless hassles from men on the street, to go through the day without a single whistle or leer. Most of the time I don't want to appear, to be, very sexual, because I can't work out whether sex is important, or if it can ever be equal and free. I'm functionally dressed – I couldn't justify to myself or other feminists clothes I liked the look of but weren't practical and comfortable. I hope I look tough but friendly; I'm afraid I look rather large and clumsy. I wouldn't want to be a man at all... but do I want to be a woman in this society either?

I imagine being a revolutionary; very tough and brave and totally functional, completely unconcerned with my image. Admired not for how I *look* but what I *do*... but of course this is a glamorous fantasy too, and sexual in a male way. Me as a Hera!

After the revolution.
There isn't any way to know what it will be like in a completely free society, but I imagine myself in it being outside all conventions of fashion and beauty, wearing things just because they look and feel nice, and are interesting textures and patterns and colours. Looking completely mad by our present standards, in fact. I fantasise about being old and strong and wise and free. Hopelessly utopian, I'm afraid.

Spare Rib 31

FIG. 1 Photo of Ruth Wallsgrove by Jini Rawlings (*center*); Sea Witch hair-color ad (*top left*); photo of Ruth Wallsgrove by Jini Rawlings (*top right*); drawing by Ruth Wallsgrove (*bottom left*); drawing by Ruth Wallsgrove (*bottom right*); all from Ruth Wallsgrove, "Who Do I Think I Am?," in "Pictures Talk: Special Visual Issue," *Spare Rib*, July 1978, 31, courtesy of Ruth Wallsgrove.

graphs, Wallsgrove is depicted with short hair and in a functional dress, an appearance that signifies that she does not adhere to the expected codes of femininity. Wallsgrove suggests that her photograph presents what she thinks she is like and how she wants to look—tough and friendly but not particularly sexual. In the other photo, she appears in soft lighting, self-consciously mimicking a flirtatious pose. Wallsgrove explains that in this image she has constructed herself as a sexually attractive object that conforms to conceptions of "real" womanhood in that she is smaller, softer, rounder, and more delicate than in the other photo.[59] Her drawings portray what she labels her imagined selves: a tough revolutionary with a scarred face who is admired not for how she looks but rather for what she does, and an old woman after the feminist revolution who is free of conventions of fashion and beauty. Thus, Wallsgrove poses alternatives to and parodies of what she considers to be the limited representation of women in ads such as Sea Witch. Her work therefore implies that such ads are a distortion of women's "authentic" identities, which could be "revealed" and further explored by feminist photography and image production. Additionally, the torn edges of the Sea Witch ad can be interpreted as a visual strategy that interrupts the ad's perceived illusion.[60]

In many ways, Wallsgrove's work was a response to an advertising image. Such images were common targets for numerous forms of feminist activism that criticized the manner in which they represented women. Wallsgrove's and other feminists' focus on advertising was situated within a broader critique of Britain's postwar development into a consumer society, which was the result of a buoyant economy and full employment that reached its height in the 1960s. Media and advertising images played an increasingly significant role in this process.[61] One outcome of this development was the construction of a visual economy that pivoted around visual pleasure and desire, often produced by seductive portrayals of women and commodities. Nonetheless, in the 1970s Britain experienced an economic collapse, high inflation rates, and rising unemployment. These factors affected consumer power, arguably further rendering the spectacle of commodities and advertisements as an unattainable fantasy. Not surprisingly, it was during this time that advertising and media images of women became a central issue within the feminist movement and for feminist photographers. In parallel, critical debates on advertisements and their ideological function became common. Politically engaged scholarship, such as Judith Williamson's *Decoding Advertisements* (1978), analyzed the ideological function of advertisements by drawing on semiotics and psychoanalysis to expose the operation of their signifying structures. Williamson suggested that advertising structures create a symbolic exchange between people and the connoted meaning of objects and, in so doing, produce a desire for the commodity in the viewer.[62]

Perhaps the earliest of these analyses was offered by Burgin, whose 1975 essay entitled "Photographic Practice and Art Theory" used the theoretical tools of Marxism, semiotics, and psychoanalysis to unravel the rhetorical structures of advertisements and use them as models for constructing counterideological messages.[63] Burgin also applied this notion to his photographic practice; for example, his work on class consciousness from 1973 to 1976 used sleek visual codes and catchy textual language associated with advertising to convey a political message that signified class consciousness raising. This strategy was also used in his 1976 poster captioned, "What does possession mean to you? 7% of our population owns 84% of our wealth." The poster featured a slick image of an embracing upper-class couple. Thus, Burgin's work employed rhetorical tools of advertising to challenge property relationships and to depict heterosexual relationships as property relationships.[64] Although Wallsgrove did not employ similar theoretical tools in her critique of the Sea Witch advertisement, she nevertheless addressed advertising's rhetorical structures and presented them as ideological and patriarchal constructions with implications for social life. Additionally, Wallsgrove aimed to counter advertising's ideological messages by juxtaposing them to images that she considered as alternatives.

Liz Heron's photo-essay "Getting on Top of the Job: Women in Manual Trades"—which also appeared in *Spare Rib*'s visual issue—similarly employed alternative representations of women as a means to pose a feminist argument. This essay consisted of photographs taken by Heron and interviews she conducted with British women working in so-called nontraditional professions, such as plumbing, carpentry, and construction.[65] In one photograph, Heron captured Sandy and Jill, who were electricians working for a community housing association in London (figure 2). Jill and Sandy are depicted in the midst of a training session with another woman. The camera is positioned across the table from where the women are working, thus engendering in the viewer a sense of participation. On the women's far left, a man is standing, gazing into the distance with his hand listlessly placed on his chest. Heron captioned this photo "Working together makes it a lot easier than working on your own," which, in line with the feminist climate

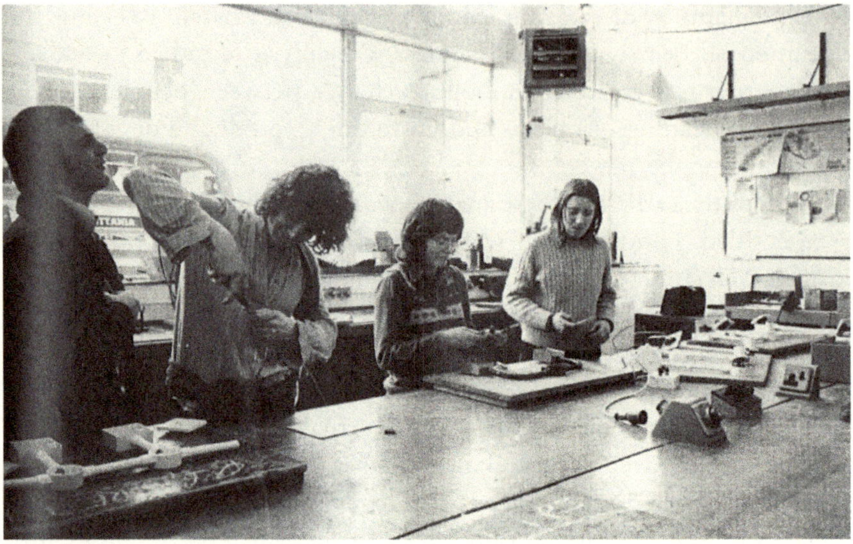

FIG. 2 Liz Heron, photo, ca. 1978, from Liz Heron, "Getting on Top of the Job: Women in Manual Trades," in "Pictures Talk: Special Visual Issue," *Spare Rib*, July 1978, 45, courtesy of Liz Heron.

of the time, stresses the significance of feminist collective action. Furthermore, this photograph and others in the essay imply that there is a broad range of occupations that women could hold, an idea that was reinforced by the photographic representation of possibilities that were not found in the mainstream media.

Producing alternative images and intervening in media representations were also among the goals of the Format Photography Agency collective (1983–1993), the first all-female photography agency in Britain.[66] Format performed commercial work but also covered various women-related and other social issues.[67] According to Format photographer Maggie Murray, some of the ways in which they attempted to influence the sphere of representation included picturing social groups that were underrepresented in the media, such as women, blacks, gays, lesbians, and the disabled. Additionally, she stated that a client requesting a photograph of a plumber or a midwife might receive from Format an image of a woman plumber or an image of a male midwife. In a similar vein, Format member Brenda Prince photographed Sue Batten, London's first firewoman, in an attempt to offer a representation of a woman who rejected traditional gender roles (figure 3).[68]

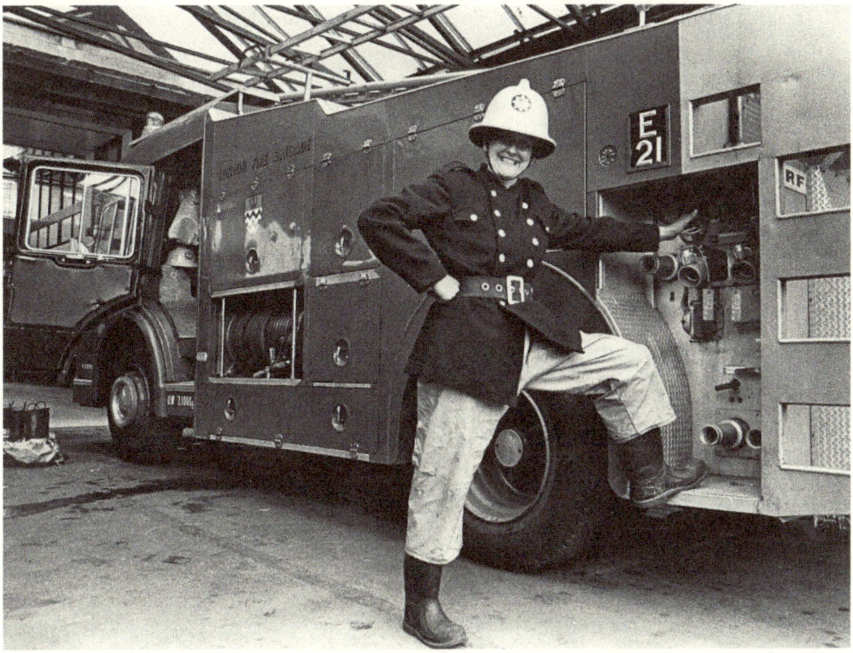

FIG. 3 Brenda Prince, *Sue Batten: London's First Woman Firefighter*, London, 1982. © Brenda Prince Format Archive, 1983.

Wallsgrove, Heron, and Format argued that the media disseminated false or limited representations of women and that "genuine" aspects of women's lives and identities could be better explored, captured, and articulated in feminist image production. These photographers claimed that their photographs would broaden the range of possibilities for the socialization of women and would successfully compete against the influence that media images wielded in the world. In many ways, Wallsgrove, Heron, and Format presented their feminist images as documents that could go beyond the language of photographic representation and offer immediate access to aspects of the real experiences of women and their genuine depiction. Thus, such feminist countermedia practices were in many ways making a claim for the real and positioning themselves in contrast to media images that they perceived as "distorted" patriarchal representations.[69] Additionally, such countermedia practices were tools for politicizing personal experience, engendering feminist identification, generating an empowered sense of feminist collectivity, and claiming a space within the predominantly masculine field of photography.

Format photographers were aware that the use of their photographs by their clients, which included leftists and feminist journals but also commercial entities and mainstream publications, would influence the process of their signification.[70] Consequently, Format developed strategies that attempted to control the meaning of its images. This included maintaining copyrights and monitoring the use of Format's photographs by refusing to sell clients an image if the collective did not approve of its intended use.[71] However, Format's intention to control the meaning of its photographs is questionable, because it implies that there was a fixed signification in its photographs that could be guarded and kept in place with the "correct" strategy. Nonetheless, despite the limited ability of the collective to control and "genuinely" capture photographic signification, its arguments indicate the central role that media politics had in the women's movement and the extent to which images were perceived to influence women's lives. This point will be further illustrated later in my discussion of additional feminist photographic practices; such practices posed different political arguments, but they shared similar positions regarding the ideological distortions of media images, the transparency of feminist media interventions and their immediate access to the "real," and the claim to a certain truth in women's experience and the fixity of its photographic meaning.

For instance, media images were also a concern for the socialist feminist photography collective the Hackney Flashers (1974–1980), whose members criticized the portrayal of women in the media but used the rhetoric of media advertising to address local social issues. Members of the collective lived and worked in Hackney, a traditionally working-class area that was a center of the low-wage clothing industry.[72]

Their first show was the documentary exhibition *Woman and Work* (1975), which was designed for the Hackney Union's seventy-fifth anniversary celebrations.[73] The black-and-white photographs depicted women in Hackney working in offices, manual jobs, and other forms of low-paid and unskilled work.[74] The photos were displayed alongside statistics regarding women's work and working hours to shed light on their exploitation as women and as workers.[75] According to the Hackney Flashers, the photographs in this exhibition served as a transparent "window to the world" that enabled working women from Hackney to encounter images of themselves that were otherwise absent in the media.[76] Thus, the collective's argument about the interventionist potential of their photography was similar to the convictions of the feminist photographers discussed earlier.

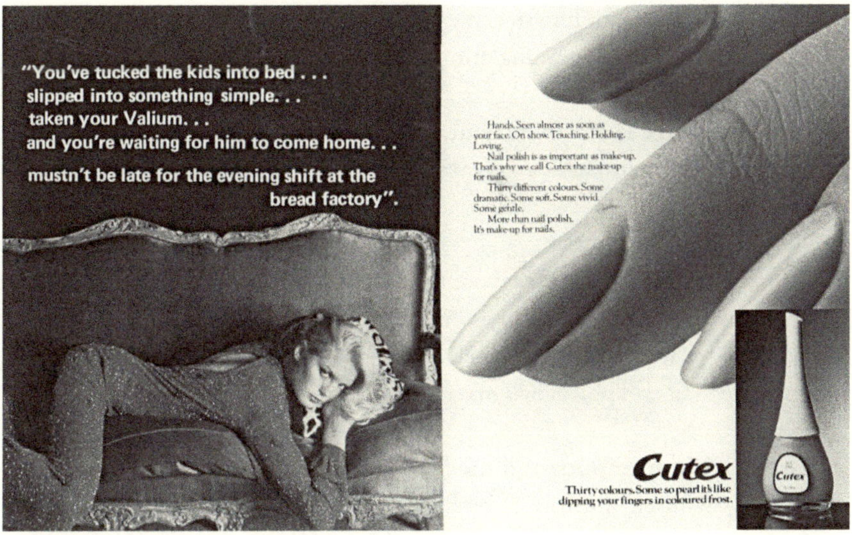

FIG. 4 Hackney Flashers, panel from *Who's Holding the Baby*, with Cutex ad, 1978, slide 20 from Liz Heron, *Domestic Labour and Visual Representation*, slide packet prepared by the Hackney Flashers, 1980, private collection of Michael Ann Mullen, courtesy of the Hackney Flashers.

The Hackney Flashers' second project, *Who's Holding the Baby*, was first exhibited at the Centerprise Community Project in Hackney in 1978. This project predominantly set out to criticize the unavailability of state-funded nurseries for working-class women in Hackney and demanded a return to the World War II policy that made nurseries available so women could work in factories.[77] Additionally, this project criticized what the Hackney Flashers understood to be the limited portrayal of women in media advertisements. Juxtaposing advertising images to text or photographs that the Hackney Flashers took of women in Hackney was the collective's typical strategy for illustrating the contradiction between media images of women and what they perceived as the "real" experience of working-class women.[78] This strategy can be viewed in a panel the collective created that consists of two juxtaposed images (figure 4). One is an advertising image of a woman in an evening dress who is seductively sprawled on a couch, above which appears a humorous caption by the group:

> You've tucked the kids into bed . . .
> slipped into something simple . . .
> taken your Valium . . .

> and you're waiting for him to come home . . .
> mustn't be late for the evening shift at the bread factory.

The second image is an advertisement for Cutex nail polish that features a photograph of a woman's fingers with pink nail polish. The following captions the ad:

> Hands. Seen almost as soon as your face. On show. Touching. Holding. Loving.
> Nail polish is as important as make-up. That is why they call Cutex make-up for nails. . . .
> More than nail polish it is make-up for nails.

Thus, these juxtapositions and the humorous use of text disrupt the advertisement's assumed illusion of reality and criticize the limited availability of media representations of women as either glamorous sex objects or caring mothers. Additionally, this technique highlights the contradiction between advertising's representations of women and the lived experience of working-class mothers who are not represented in advertisements.[79] Thus, the Hackney Flashers suggested that one method of intervening in the structures of advertising was to "reveal" how they produced ideological messages.

Another montage from the project *Who's Holding the Baby*, titled "Don't Take Drugs, Take Action," consists of a drug advertisement that was initially aimed to appeal to doctors and encourage them to prescribe certain medications (figure 5). The ad depicts a working-class woman next to a baby carriage, angrily grabbing her other child's shoulder. An enlarged image of the woman's agitated face is superimposed on the ad, emphasizing her distressed and anxious expression. The ad is captioned, "Struggling against impossible odds, surrounded by children with poor housing and facilities and little money." To the right of the image is text stating, "Adverse circumstances such as too many children and too little money are recognized as causes of neurotic depression or anxiety neurosis in persons with a low stress. These are prime indication for Triptafen-DA or Triptafen-minor." Below the ad is a Hackney Flashers photograph of a group of women and children taking action and marching with placards bearing slogans such as "Parents must unite and fight" and " A nursery is my right." These two images were combined to disrupt the advertisement's message and its condescending portrayal of women as passive victims of their own problems. The Hackney

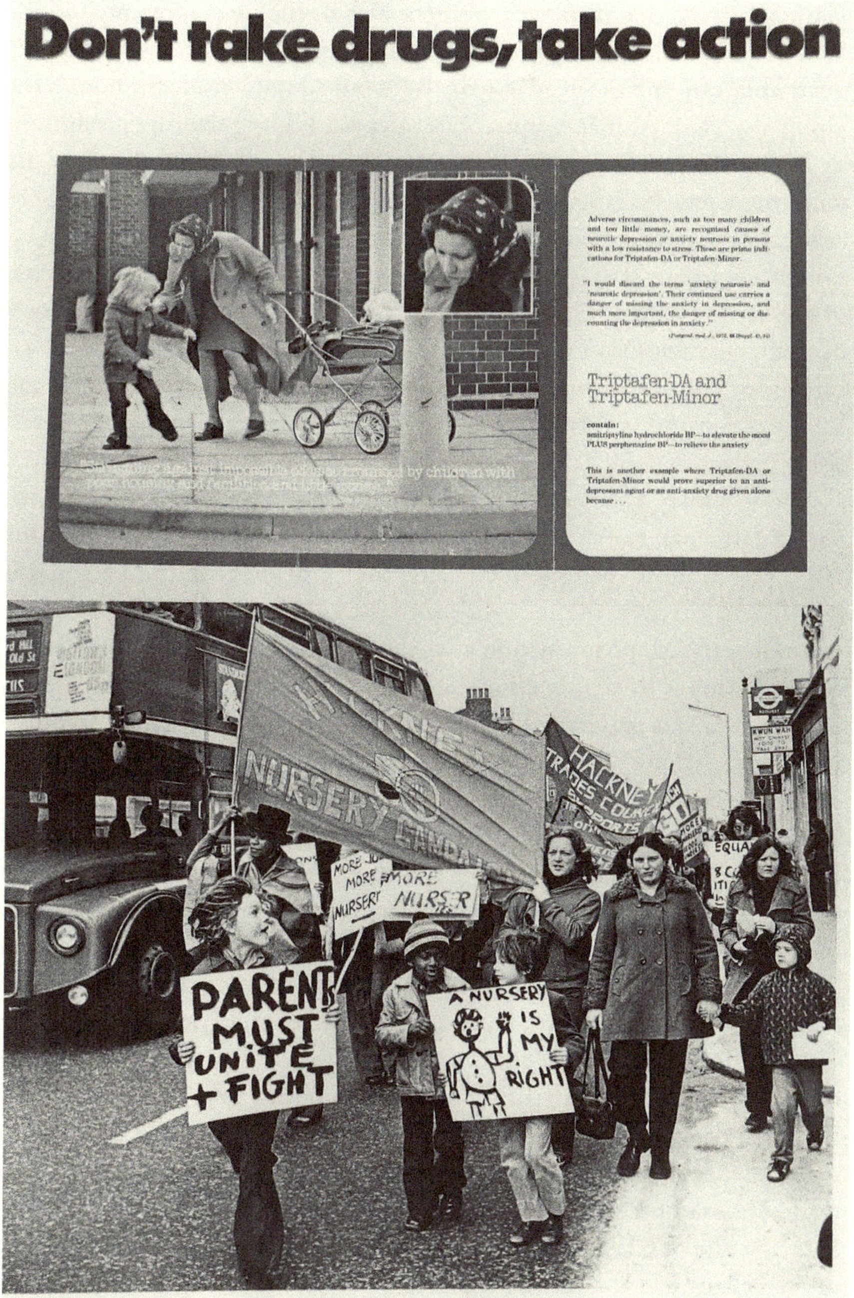

FIG. 5 Hackney Flashers, "Don't Take Drugs, Take Action," 1978, slide 23 from Liz Heron, *Domestic Labour and Visual Representation*, slide packet prepared by the Hackney Flashers, 1980, private collection of Michael Ann Mullen, courtesy of the Hackney Flashers.

Flashers argued that distressed women, such as the one represented in the ad, were made that way by social conditions, including the absence of adequate childcare and the need to work both outside and inside the home. The group also claimed that women were adept at finding their own solutions by taking collective action instead of taking drugs.[80] Thus, as others did with the practices discussed earlier, the Hackney Flashers used montage to argue that advertising images offered an ideologically distorted representation of a working-class woman's experience and that their own photograph of the demonstrating Hackney women documented a "real" event. Moreover, this juxtaposition implied that the image of the demonstration was capable of politically mobilizing working-class women to take similar collective action and in this way compete with the socializing impact of advertising images.[81]

The Hackney Flashers used the camera to explore and articulate the particularities of the shared experience of working-class women. In many ways, this notion corresponded with the position that the personal is political. Moreover, the motivation to articulate a collective experience resembled the Marxist position advocated in the then developing field of cultural studies by scholars such as Stuart Hall and Dick Hebdige, who regarded various patterns of living and cultural manifestations as expressing class positions.[82]

The Hackney Flashers' visual strategies of juxtaposition also bear resemblances to earlier uses of montage, such as Sergei Eisenstein's and Bertolt Brecht's film and theater practices, which set out to shock the viewer into attaining new understandings with regard to the social field.[83] Furthermore, the Hackney Flashers' choice of visual strategy appears to be in dialog with John Heartfield's photomontage practices, which criticized capitalism, the rise of fascism in Germany, and the work of art as an aesthetic object.[84] Heartfield's works from the 1920s and 1930s, as well as Brechtian ideas, were increasingly resurrected in the 1970s in photomontages by other politicized British photographers, such as Peter Kennard, Peter Dunn, and Lorain Leeson. Heartfield's work was also referenced in various photography publications. For example, Hackney Flashers member Jo Spence, in her essay "The Sign as a Site of Class Struggle: Reflections on Works by John Heartfield," praised Heartfield's photomontages for their agitational use of photography against fascism and capitalism. Spence also offered a feminist reading of some of his works and addressed his representations of women in the context of women's class status in Germany at that time.[85] Nevertheless, despite the Hackney Flashers' feminist engagement with class, racial difference was an overlooked issue. Though they represented black working women and mothers in their projects, race was universalized by the collective within the broader context of working-class women's experience.[86]

The Hackney Flashers, Format, and other all-female photography collectives at the time were making a feminist statement in the manner in which they operated. As mentioned earlier, women photographers were a marginalized minority within the field of photography. Thus, the decision to operate as a group of all-female photographers had substantial feminist underpinnings. For instance, the manner in which the Hackney Flashers worked was consciously geared to cultivate an egalitarian and accessible climate for women interested in photography.[87] This was achieved in part by opening the group to professional as well as less experienced photographers. For example, Maggie Murray and Sally Greenhill were professional photographers, whereas Heron, a writer for various feminist and leftist publications who had little experience with photography, joined the group to gain technical photographic knowledge. Furthermore, the members collectively shared their various skills. Spence recalled that one person would often start working on a project and later have a more skilled member take over.[88] The Hackney Flashers also held photography workshops where they taught darkroom techniques and design and layout methods to the group's members, as well as other interested women. The sense of egalitarianism and equal access was also manifested in the decision of the group to credit their works to the Hackney Flashers Collective rather than to individual photographers.[89] Similarly, Format, although producing works by individual photographers, initially operated as a collective in which each member had an equal vote on various production and administrative issues.[90]

Feminist Media Politics and the Street

In the late 1970s and early 1980s in Britain, billboard advertisements' sexualized representations increasingly attracted feminist criticism that corresponded with radical feminist ideas from the United States. Such sexualized images became the particular target of radical feminists who viewed them not only as depicting women in a limited number of roles or in an artificial way but also as encouraging abuse. According to social movement theorists Suzanne Staggenborg and Amy Lang, social movements such as the women's movement often engage in cultural activity to communicate emotions and convey meaning to movement supporters in an attempt to directly or indirectly change power structures and public policies. I similarly argue that feminist countermedia practices that primarily focused on the issue of violence and sexual violence against women became tools for generating and interpreting emotions such as anger, communicating feminist ideas, and developing a sense of radical feminist identity and collectivity, all of which were geared toward radically altering patriarchal power structures.[91]

A particular billboard that elicited repeated feminist criticism was a late 1970s advertisement for Gigi underwear that appeared on British streets and in subway stations. This advertisement depicted a woman walking at night on an unlit street and glaring at the camera as if expressing that she did not want to be approached. In a second image, the woman has undone her coat to reveal her underwear. A caption reads, "Underneath they're all Lovable in Gigi."

One ardent response to this ad was Rosalind Coward's essay "Underneath We're Angry," which was written as an open letter to the Advertising Standards Authority[92] and published in 1980 in *Time Out*—a leading London underground magazine at the time.[93] In this letter, Coward asserted that the Advertising Standards Authority should obliterate sexist representations of women. She added that the Gigi ad and others like it are an invitation to rape and that they create an oppressive and intimidating environment for women.[94]

This ad was also addressed in Jill Nicholls and Pat Moan's essay "'What Offends One of Us Won't Offend the Next Chap,'" published in *Spare Rib*'s special visual issue mentioned earlier. Nicholls and Moan's essay opened, "I am alone in the underground . . . All around me are huge images of female parts. . . . I don't know where to look that doesn't make me feel . . . vulnerable. A man comes into the tunnel and looks me up and down. All these ads are like his gang—telling him . . . that I am waiting for him. . . . (The Lovable bra ad, his hand resting lightly . . . on her naked waist—his territory)."[95] This essay included an illustration of a muscular man in underwear holding a bag of nuts, followed by the caption, "Hunky, Chunky, Big & Crunchy, Stuart's Nutz Are Best." This illustration utilizes advertisement structures to humorously disrupt their modes of operation while also indicating that advertisements sexualize women but avoid similarly sexualized representations of men (figure 6).

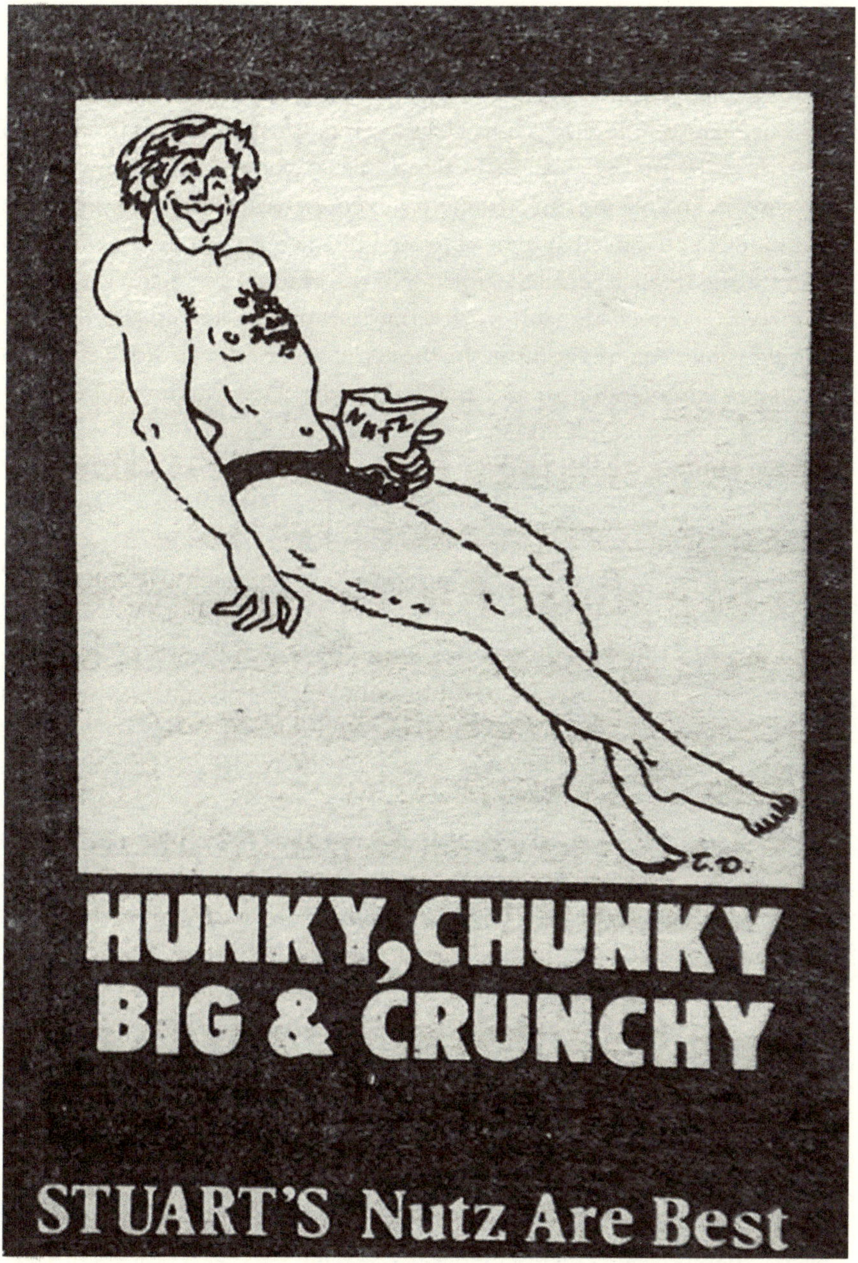

FIG. 6 T. O., "Hunky, Chunky, Big & Crunchy, Stuart's Nutz Are Best," 1978, from Jill Nicholls and Pat Moan, "'What Offends One of Us Won't Offend the Next Chap': The Advertising Standards Authority's Line on Sexism," in "Pictures Talk: Special Visual Issue," *Spare Rib*, July 1978, 18.

Feminist Graffiti Countering Media Images

Feminist graffiti was another form of angry response to sexualized portrayals of women in billboard advertising. Such graffiti often mobilized sharp wit in order to direct the viewer's attention to its feminist argument, evoke amusement, and counter an ad's offensive representations. The feminist use of humor can be viewed in light of Jo Anna Isaak's understanding of laughter in the medieval carnival as a form of transgression that defies the dominant ideology, which arguably further frames humor as a political strategy.[96] Photography had a pivotal role in these practices because it was used to document feminist graffiti and enabled its circulation in feminist publications. For instance, Jill Posener's photography book *Spray It Loud* (1982) depicted feminist graffiti made in London and other cities between 1978 and 1982.[97] In one example, a photograph featured a Pretty Polly ad in Blackfriars, London, that depicted an illuminated pair of women's legs in stockings. The ad was captioned, "Where would fashion be without pins?" and thus incorporated working-class slang for *legs* to imply that they should be on display. This ad was spray-painted "Free of Little Pricks . . . (stop needling us)."[98] Similarly, another photograph showed a Fiat billboard in Farrington, London, with a caption that read, "If it were a lady it would get its bottom pinched," and bore the graffiti, "If this lady was a car she'd run you down."[99]

Some feminist billboard graffiti found in Leeds was undertaken by the Leeds Women Fight Back Campaign, a group of approximately twenty-five women who organized to graffiti sexist billboard advertisements in their area. The group explained that in preparation for their project, they took photographs of advertisements that they found offensive to women and made a detailed map of their locations. They then set out at night and plastered these ads with large sheets of paper sprayed with their responses and photographed the results.[100] One of their pieces of graffiti from 1984 targeted a billboard for Harp beer, and the photograph of the graffiti, seemingly captured by the group, was published on the cover of *Outwrite*, a women's newspaper.[101] The Harp beer ad depicted two beer glasses alongside the slogan "We are talking tastier than a pair of page of 3's," referencing the topless page 3 of the popular daily tabloid the *Sun*, which used sex and sensationalism as key organizing elements.[102] The ad was graffitied with the text, "We are talking nastier than a pair of nutcrackers," which set out to humorously turn the reference on its head (figure 7).[103] The Leeds Women Fight

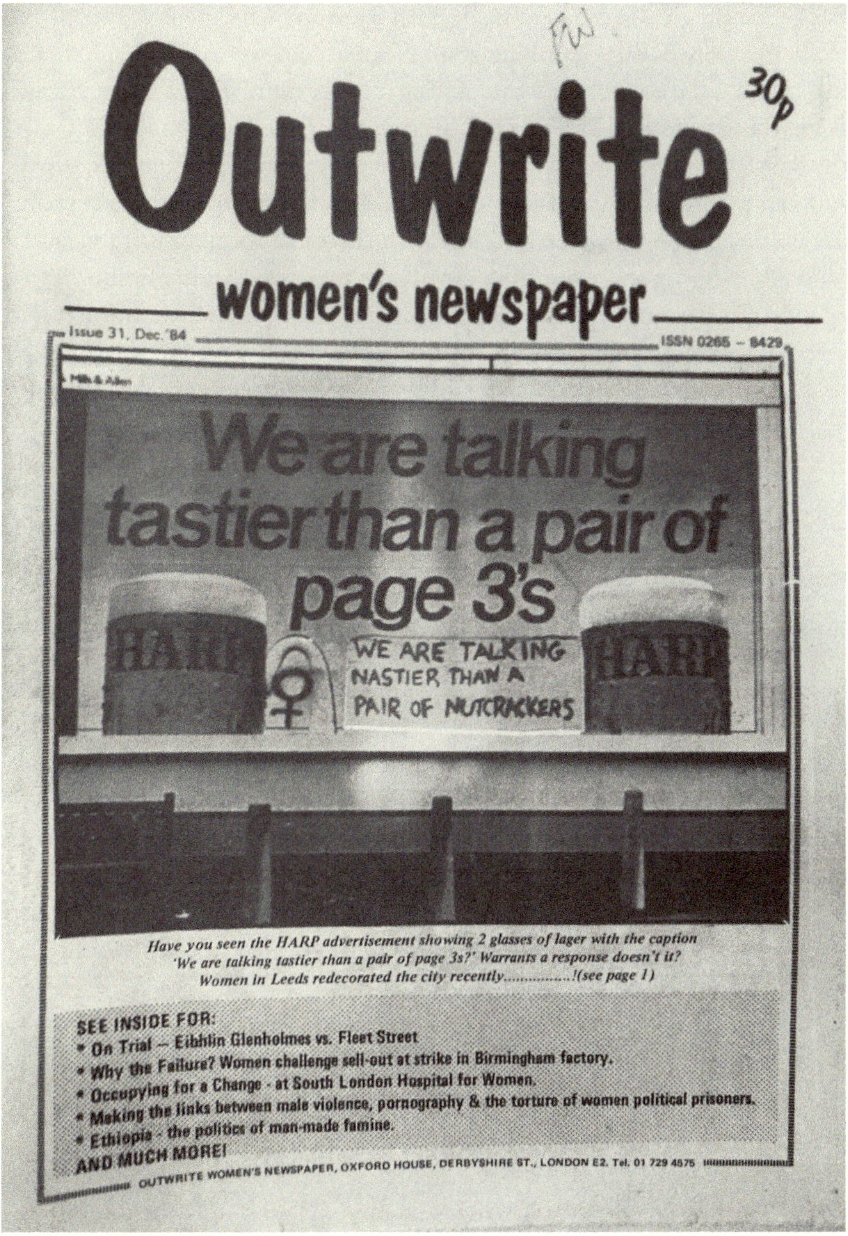

FIG. 7 Leeds Women Fight Back Campaign, graffiti on Harp Beer advertisement, December 1984, from *Outwrite*, December 1984, cover.

Back Campaign also plastered a Bacardi Rum advertisement that depicted the actor Telly Savalas drinking rum. Next to him were a bowl of tropical fruits and a dark-skinned woman. The ad was captioned, "With Bacardi Rum, there is no forbidden fruit." This was plastered with "Hope He Gets the Shits."[104]

Such graffiti practices asserted that women were active subjects capable of resisting billboard advertising's limited representations of women and of radically altering their signification. These practices could also be viewed as a type of détournement, a term coined by the French Situationists that referred to the practice of appropriating signs in the sphere of the spectacle to divert their meanings and control their range of references.[105] The Situationist practice of détournement, however, was primarily invested in reusing artistic and mass-produced elements to create new combinations that would take a different contextual direction and restructure cultural experience.[106] Thus, rather than communicating a distinct social argument, détournement was based on a politics of appropriation and contextual transformation.[107] In contrast, although it restructured the cultural experience of viewing ads, the feminist appropriation of billboard graffiti through biting humor became a strategy for delivering a social message that positioned men and advertisers as exploitative aggressors and women as their victims.

Moreover, a number of feminist graffiti practitioners argued that sexualized billboard representations were similar to actual acts of violence against women. For example, members of the Leeds Women Fight Back Campaign explained that they viewed advertisements that objectified women's bodies to be a form of violence against women that gave men license to abuse women and girls. They claimed that redecorating such billboard ads would help women fight against these images.[108]

Violence against Women and Reclaiming the Street

The Leeds Women Fight Back Campaign's sexual politics—and Coward's and Nicholls and Moan's challenges to the Gigi ad—must be understood in the context of the threat of Peter Sutcliffe, nicknamed the Yorkshire Ripper by the media and police. This man committed thirteen murders and seven attempted murders between 1976 and 1981 in Yorkshire and Leeds. His victims were attacked on the street, raped, beaten, and mutilated.[109] The threat of his crimes had a significant impact on feminists from Leeds as well as elsewhere, generating a vast feminist political reaction.

In light of these events, a network of rape crisis centers was formed and the Women against Rape movement was created, modeled on an American precedent. These crisis centers set out to provide women with support that was not offered by the state.[110] The increasing criticism of sexualized images of women in the media in Britain spurred additional forms of feminist reaction. For instance, revolutionary feminism—a militant version of radical feminism that advocated separatism and withdrawing from contact with men as a means to resist sexism—was gaining ground, particularly in Leeds. This feminist faction's emergence and its assertions were prompted by various events, including Sheila Jeffreys's paper "The Need for Revolutionary Feminism," which was delivered at the National Women's Liberation Conference in London in 1977. In this paper, Jeffreys expressed her dissatisfaction with feminist strategies of campaigning and theory, referenced socialist feminism and feminist theory, and called for more militant feminist politics.[111] She proposed that women were a class that was socially and financially oppressed by men and questioned the efficacy of socialist feminism's analysis of capitalism and its political alliances with men. She ended her talk with a plea to form a network of women interested in advancing her ideas.[112] Soon after, the group Women against Violence against Women (WAVAW) was formed in Leeds by several revolutionary feminists, and another branch was later established in London by Jeffreys and other feminists, such as Linda Bellos.[113] WAVAW's activities included raising consciousness regarding male violence and sexual violence against women and opposing pornography, goals that the Leeds Women Fight Back Campaign also had.

A feminist group called Women against Violence against Women, which was separate from the British group, was also formed as early as 1976 in Los Angeles. It was founded by feminist activist and former United Farm Workers organizer Julia London in response to the Los Angeles debut of the film *Snuff*, which featured a sexually explicit scene of a woman being brutally murdered. The group was formed in the Woman's Building, a cultural center founded in downtown Los Angeles in 1973 to promote feminist visual art and social activism. It was soon after joined by other national American groups such as Women against Violence in Pornography and Media in San Francisco and Women against Pornography in New York.[114] As did the British group, the WAVAW group in Los Angeles took action against sexualized billboards. In 1976, for instance, a billboard promoting the Rolling Stones album *Black and Blue* was the focal point of the group's outrage. This poster, installed on the Sunset Strip of Los Angeles, depicted a bound and bruised young woman and was captioned, "I'm Black and Blue from the Rolling Stones and I Like It." WAVAW's resistance to this representation ultimately led to a national consumer boycott of Warner Brothers. Graffiti were also used to resist this billboard, which was spray-painted, "This is a Crime against Women!"[115]

In Britain, WAVAW organized a series of Reclaim the Night marches (further discussed in chapter 3), among other activities. The first demonstrations in 1977 took place simultaneously in a number of British cities (Leeds, London, Manchester, York, Newcastle, and Bristol).[116] In Leeds, 130 women participated, while hundreds of women marched through Soho, the sex industry's location in London, carrying banners that read, "All women should be free to walk down any street, night or day without fear," among others. The women chanted and slapped stickers on massage parlor windows, strip joints, and porn shops. They also glued sex shop locks and smashed the windows of strip clubs.[117] The concept for Reclaim the Night seems to have been borrowed from a similar march that took place in a number of towns in West Germany in 1977. Participants in the West German march traveled through bleak train stations and areas with sex shops and nightclubs to protest the rape and abuse of women by men. The coverage of the German march by *Spare Rib* perhaps prompted Leeds feminists to organize a similar march.[118] Similar marches named Take Back the Night took place in the United States. Among the earliest of these marches was one in Philadelphia in 1975 in response to the violence and sexual assault that women face in the public and domestic spheres.[119]

The marches in Britain were in part a result of the climate caused by Sutcliffe's crimes. It is notable that both the Reclaim the Night marches and the feminist billboard graffiti were strategies that responded to representations of women on the street, a site that had particular significance for feminists. In the period during which Sutcliffe was active, WAVAW challenged the advice from police that women stay home after dark and demanded instead that a curfew be imposed on men.[120] Photographs of other forms of feminist graffiti found in Posener's book addressed these concerns. In 1981, for example, Posener photographed a wall in Oxford spray-painted with the slogan "Men off the Streets." The graffiti in other photographs taken in London areas near this time read, "WOMEN SAY NO TO MALE

VIOLENCE," in Battersea, "SUTCLIFFE—NOT MAD MALE" in Archway, and "RAPE IS AN OFFENSE" in Finsbury Park.

Thus, the impact of these feminist graffiti practices was not restricted to the surface of the billboard and the space of the street. The photographs of these practices that appeared in feminist publications were significant in that they increased awareness of such practices and exposed feminists' concerns regarding media images and representation.

Feminist Direct Action against Pornography and a Crisis in Feminist Consensus

As noted earlier, groups from the 1980s such as the Leeds Women Fight Back Campaign argued that sexualized portrayals of women in the media were actual acts of violence. Additionally, slogans such as "Pornography is the theory; rape is the practice" and "Pornography is violence against women" were associated with certain feminist revolutionary groups such as WAVAW.[121] These statements emerged from feminist antipornography debates and actions, which were gaining ground in Britain as well as in the United States and were splitting the feminist movement. It should be noted that most statistics and theories supporting antipornography activism in Britain came from the United States. Among the most influential texts was Kate Millett's *Sexual Politics*, mentioned earlier. Another was Andrea Dworkin's *Pornography: Men Possessing Women* (1981), which asserted that pornography was a male system for debasing women.[122] Lastly, Susan Griffin's *Pornography and Silence: Culture's Revenge against Nature* (1981) challenged the libertarian association of pornography and erotic liberation and claimed that pornography was a violent and silencing attack on women's bodies and souls.[123] All of these books had a substantial impact on the development of the antipornography debate in Britain.[124]

Feminist opposition to pornography was also manifest in Britain in a series of extreme direct actions, such as an event in 1984 in which five women in Leeds vandalized two windows and a number of sculptures at an exhibition at Leeds Polytechnic; as a result, they were charged with criminal damage. An article in *Outwrite* entitled "Porn Not Art" that reported on the incident highlighted that one of the exhibition's sculptures portrayed a woman's body wrapped in cling film and placed in a refrigerator with rotting fruit. Another sculpture depicted a woman on her back with stakes piercing her breasts and her vagina slashed. Attached to the stakes were porn magazines bunched into flowers.[125]

Other forms of feminist direct action were executed by a Leeds group called Angry Women (1978–1984), an extremist splinter group of WAVAW whose members shared WAVAW members' views on violence against women and pornography but differed from them in their choice of actions, which included setting fire to sex shops and acting against individual men who violated women.[126] According to an *Outwrite* interview with a former Angry Women member, approximately twenty-five sex shops were set on fire in Leeds and its vicinity during the period of the group's activity.[127] A photograph of a sex shop after it caught fire was included in the article and was captioned (possibly by the group members), "We have to make demands that pernicious propaganda of this nature has to be stopped. How can we do this politely?"[128]

After each attack, Angry Women would make an anonymous phone call to the *Yorkshire Evening Post* and report their actions. Additionally, they would send ashes of the burned pornographic materials with press releases to local and national papers.[129] The *Yorkshire Evening Post*, in covering two of their arson attacks in Leeds on the night of January 14, 1983, against J. T. and Son Video Film Club in New Road Side, Horsforth, and the Ultra Video club in Ivegate, Yeadon, indicated that these came a month after the director of J. T. and Son had pleaded guilty to handling unauthorized "pirate" cassettes.[130] Angry Women's contact with the *Yorkshire Evening Post* and other papers suggests that they set out to intervene in the space of the street but also to claim their space in the mainstream press.

Although Angry Women were successful in drawing public attention to their feminist arguments and antipornography interventions, and in attracting media interest, their activities were contested by some women within the feminist movement who objected to the group's illegal activity, its potential to endanger human life, and its censoring attitude. Furthermore, several Leeds feminists felt that Angry Women's activities exposed their community to the risk of constant police surveillance; in fact, after their attacks, the police would raid the houses of various feminist Leeds women and interrogate them.[131]

As can be seen, different factions of the British women's movement were in agreement regarding the effects of media images on women's socialization, but this sense of uniformity was ruptured as a result of internal struggles concerning pornography.[132] These developments consequently also complicated the movement's exploration of the possibility of portraying female sexuality in a nonexploitative manner.

As discussed earlier, some revolutionary feminist groups vehemently opposed the production and circulation of pornography, which they viewed as a form of actual violence against women. Other feminists challenged the growing predominance of the antipornography position within the women's movement and its ramifications. Rosalind Coward, for instance, who initially attacked the Gigi underwear ad for being an invitation to rape, would later criticize WAVAW in a special issue on sexuality in the feminist journal *Feminist Review* (1979–present) for targeting aggressive male sexuality as the group's primary feminist concern.[133] Moreover, several black feminists criticized the feminist antipornography debate for disregarding the issue of race and racist depictions in pornography.[134] Additionally, socialist feminists contended that the emphasis on pornography hindered the possibility of addressing a range of social policies relevant to women, such as wages and working conditions.[135]

Coward also opposed the implication that if something resembles pornography, it is pornography. She maintained that it was necessary to define the differences between a pornographic representation, an offensive media image, and "legitimate" erotic representation. She also expressed the need to analyze and revise sexist codes of representation so that feminist critiques of offensive advertisements would be taken more seriously by bodies such as the Advertising Standard Authority, to which she addressed her letter regarding the Gigi ad.[136] Similarly, Kathy Myers, in her essay "Towards a Feminist Erotica," argued that she saw the need to differentiate among types of sexualized representations. Her essay was written as a response to arguments that WAVAW's members made at the Camerawork gallery (previously named Half Moon Gallery and Half Moon Photography Workshop gallery) during a conference for women on pornography. She suggested that introducing the term *erotica* into feminist sexual politics might create a space for female sexual pleasure as an independent entity without confining it to a binary opposition between oppressive male sexuality and its passive reception by women.[137] Moreover, Myers—who drew on Foucault's notion of sexuality—suggested that sexual pleasure should not be addressed as a coercive power oppressing women but rather as a multifaceted and flexible force used to maintain social order.[138]

A similar divide with respect to the issue of pornography was forming in the women's movement in the United States. Feminist tensions around this issue were particularly explosive at "Towards a Politics of Sexuality," a feminist conference held at the women's center at Barnard College on April 24, 1982. The initial aim of the conference was to address the then emerging and conflicting feminist debates about sexuality and sex. While some papers addressed topics such as women's sexual autonomy and the exploration of pleasure in domains such as sadomasochism, other papers characterized sexuality as a dangerous domain for women that should be restricted.[139] Despite the conference holders' desire to provide a forum for a plurality of views, it was followed by rupture. In the days after the conference, individuals associated with feminist antipornography groups such as Women against Pornography, New York Radical Feminists, and WAVAW called on prominent feminists to denounce the conference for inviting advocates of "antifeminist" sexuality to participate. Moreover, the Barnard College administration confiscated 1,500 copies of the conference diary; a coalition leaflet distributed at the conference attacked individual participants by name and presented them as "morally unacceptable" and beyond the feminist pale; and the Helena Rubinstein Foundation withdrew its financial support for the women's center's future Scholar and Feminist series.[140]

Feminists in Britain were arguably aware of the events associated with this conference and the compilation of the conference's papers (*Pleasure and Danger: Exploring Female Sexuality*), which was simultaneously published in Britain and the United States in 1984.[141] Moreover, British feminist Elizabeth Wilson, who attended the conference, published her accounts in the British journal *Feminist Review*. Wilson observed that the feminist opposition to the antipornography argument in Britain, unlike in United States, focused on the antipornography argument's narrow political scope and on developing theoretical questions concerning the language of representation and the construction of sexuality and gender.[142]

The feminist antipornography stance was being attacked from within the feminist movement. In the United States, feminists like Catharine MacKinnon who viewed pornography as an assault on women's civil rights were aligning themselves with conservative bodies for this cause. MacKinnon's strategy was criticized because whereas she and other feminists wanted to ban pornography for its violence against women, conservative bodies were minimally concerned with women's rights and primarily mobilized antipornography rhetoric in order to support censorship and their own agendas. Similarly, in Britain the feminist antipornography argument was criticized for sharing its position with British conservative bodies and the moral Right, including Mary Whitehouse, who since the early 1970s had been an active campaigner against "moral collapse."[143] Whitehouse was also a leader of the social purity campaign against "promiscuity" in the media and helped organize an evangelical rally, the Festival of Light, at Westminster Central Hall in London. At this event, various "sins," such as homosexuality, were condemned. The Festival of Light was met with a counterdemonstration by the political activist group the Gay Liberation Front, whose members infiltrated the hall dressed as nuns, kissed each other, and released mice in the aisles. In 1977 Whitehouse also successfully sued the newspaper *Gay News* for blasphemous libel after it published a poem depicting a Roman centurion's love for Jesus and implying that Christ was homosexual. Whitehouse and events like the Festival of Light predicated their strong antipornography position on "moral majority" values.[144] Whitehouse also co-opted the feminist direct-action campaigns against sex shops in Leeds to indicate that there was a need for censorship and that there was support for her campaign against obscenity.[145] WAVAW disputed these allegations and argued that Whitehouse and other conservative groups attacked pornography for threatening the nuclear family, whereas the primary concern of groups such as WAVAW was how pornography portrayed women.[146]

In the United States, the opposition to the antipornography debate primarily centered on freedom of speech and censorship. Additionally, the arguments posed by American feminists were often more libertarian and focused on pleasure and diverse sexual practices.[147] One of the American writings that circulated in Britain and engaged with "propleasure" arguments was the essay "Talking Sex: A Conversation on Sexuality and Feminism," by Deirdre English, Amber Hollibaugh, and Gayle Rubin. The latter two had also participated in the Barnard conference. This essay argued that the feminist movement should not limit its discussion about sex to addressing power relations between men and women; instead, it should expand the feminist discourse by engaging in wider discussions on sexual expressions and desire. This essay was initially published in the American journal *Socialist Review* in 1981 and was reprinted in the British *Feminist Review* in 1982.[148] Similarly, in 1981, the American publication *Heresies* published an issue dedicated to sex that politicized various sexual practices such as lesbianism and sadomasochism.[149] This particular issue was heavily criticized in Britain by WAVAW. Jayne Egerton, for example, indicated in the *Revolutionary and Radical Feminist Newsletter* that the women who contributed to the *Heresies* issue were antifeminist and that all sexual desires were necessarily constructed under male power whose sole function was to oppress women.[150]

In spite of attempts to separate the two positions, the feminist and the Christian Right antipornography positions occupied the same space in a photograph of a sex shop in Oxford taken by Posener in 1981. This image featured the shop's facade, which was spray-painted with feminist "woman" symbols and the slogan "Porn is Sexual Hatred." It was also inscribed with images of the cross and the texts, "Porn Is the Opium of the People," "Jesus Christ Orders the Evil Spirits of Greed and Lust to Come Out," and "Mother of God and Joan of Arc Aid Our Cause." It should be emphasized that the end of the 1970s coincided with Britain's general political shift to the right. This political change was epitomized by the election in 1979 of Margaret Thatcher, whose social and economic policies, as described later, adversely impacted the public sector and threatened women's rights and the women's movement.[151] Ironically, without the social and political impact of feminism, Thatcher might not have not entered politics, let alone become prime minister. Nonetheless, her anti-working-class and anti-welfare-state politics curtailed political feminist aspirations.[152] Among the ramifications of Thatcher's policies for feminist accomplishments was the abolishment of the Greater London Council's Women's Committee, which was founded by Valerie Wise in 1982. The goals of the Women's Committee included ensuring that women's interests were politically recognized and that public money would be invested in services for women. This political body addressed a variety of social issues pertaining to women, including health, violence, and reproductive rights. It also developed childcare projects, offered resources for women's centers, and established various counseling and support services for women. In 1986 this body was abolished by Thatcher as part of her attempt to hinder local authorities that were dominated by the Labour Party. Although the Women's Committee was not Thatcher's primary target, conservative interests saw municipal feminism as a threat to the traditional family.[153]

During this period, divides also deepened in the women's movement. For instance, identity politics played a prominent role in the power relations within the women's movement, particularly concerning issues such as racial differences and lesbianism.[154] Although identity politics raised a range of significant questions and concerns that were earlier marginalized by the women's movement, it also prompted a ghettoization of different feminist groups rather than opening up a dialog to accommodate the diverse voices in the movement.

As can be seen, many of the feminist photography practices and interventions in the media in the 1970s circulated outside official cultural institutions such as museums and academia. Instead, they were dispersed throughout sites such as community centers, bookstores, feminist publications, and the street, where a feminist counterpublic was formed. Nonetheless, toward the end of this decade, some of these arguments entered the official political sphere. In 1979 there was a public debate at Conway Hall in Red Lion Square between feminist journalist Beatrix Campbell, who engaged with communist politics, and Arthur Scargill, president of the National Union of Mineworkers. The debate centered on whether the *Yorkshire Miner* should have a pinup of a topless woman on its page 3 similar to that of the tabloid daily the *Sun*.[155] While Scargill did not oppose the topless pinup, Campbell's critique corresponded with a broader feminist debate that was manifested in feminist writing and counterpractice that targeted the *Sun*'s topless depictions of women. Such arguments challenged the paper's seemingly lighthearted attitude toward sexuality and asserted that it was objectifying women's bodies for male visual pleasure and consumption.[156] Campbell and Scargill's debate can also be viewed in light of Campbell's critique of traditional organizations of the British Left for their failure to address and serve women's interests.[157]

Media representations also became a concern for official political bodies that operated at the margins of mainstream culture, such as the Greater London Council's Women's Committee, which included Bellos, a member of WAVAW.[158] In 1984, for example, the committee campaigned to change London Transport's advertising acceptance policies. The committee insisted that sexist advertising should be banned because it made women feel unsafe. Because the Greater London Council was the funding body of London Transport, the campaign was successful.[159]

Thus, by the end of the decade, despite its deepening divisions, the women's movement had become a substantial force in British society and some of its concerns had infiltrated official politics. Moreover, feminist photographic activity played a role in introducing feminist arguments about the significance of media images as a viable political struggle.

Feminist Photography and Affective Encounters

The feminist photography projects I have discussed functioned as tools for countermedia representations. Additionally, it can be argued that these projects were intended to further generate a form of political activism and a sense of feminist collectivity that was often organized around shared experiences. The women who advocated feminism and feminist photography were marginalized in the field of photography, but they nevertheless made an empowered claim for the presence and political significance of their work. Moreover, the indexical value of these photography practices as markers of original feminist photographic events and of the often unique collective forms of feminist organization producing them was high. Thus, drawing on photography theorists David Green and Joanna Lowry, I argue that these photographs were indexes not only of chemical traces of light on film but also of traces of a feminist photographic act that subverted media representations of women and their claim to the "real."[160] These works, which appeared in forums where they were encountered by feminist and potential feminist spectators, arguably encouraged similar forms of photographic intervention and brought attention to the feminist insistence on the generation of new images for feminist identification. As was mentioned earlier, the feminist countermedia practices addressed in this chapter related to the notion that the personal is political, and feminist countermedia practices therefore often became tools for articulating aspects of women's personal experiences, which feminists claimed were underrepresented in the media. Thus, these practices also functioned as objects that aimed to produce emotion and affect in their viewers and to encourage further feminist identifications and political mobilization.[161] It should be noted that during the 1970s and 1980s, feminist theory, photography theory, and other fields of political cultural analysis employing semiotics perceived "concrete" social experience to be a more adequate interpretive strategy than "feelings."[162] Furthermore, it can be argued that the association between emotion and feminism is still considered to be politically dangerous. The danger results from linking women with a "feminine" stereotype such as being reactive and closer to nature and therefore unable to transcend the body through stereotypically masculine attributes such as thought, will, and judgment, which feminists have fought hard to claim for themselves. Nonetheless, I argue that the affect evoked by feminist countermedia practices was far from "private" or idiosyncratic but rather corresponded with socially shared feelings among feminists and feminist photographers; these feelings were often produced, recognized, and interpreted by women viewing these practices. Thus, through the repetition of production and spectatorship, the affect generated by feminist countermedia practices arguably enhanced the feminist resistance to prevalent media representations,[163] as well as functioning as a political strategy that constructed meaning and allowed its producers and viewers to partake in a collective feminist identity.[164] Moreover, the collaborative feminist forms of activism that produced many of these practices were generating and sustaining the argument that media images were a shared feminist concern that deserved to be a political focus.

The process of viewing the products of these practices also enacted a sense of feminist identity and collective community that posed itself against its "other"—patriarchal forces that exclude or misrepresent women in the media.[165] Thus, drawing on feminist theorist Sara Ahmed, I maintain that the emotion and affect evoked by the encounter with feminist counterpractices became political modes of transmission between the viewing bodies and the images,[166] rendering such encounters politically significant for defining a collective and generating its mobilization.[167]

Additionally, feminist publications, which were one of the main sites in which these practices circulated, had a significant role in the production and framing of their photographic meaning. Like feminist countermedia practices, these publications set out to produce a sense of feminist community,[168] which was generated not only by the viewing process but also by the collaborative forms of production and organization that were often the backdrop for these practices.

Conclusion

The British women's movement, and its countercultural practices, asserted that media images were central to the socialization of women and a necessary target of feminist politics and practice, despite widening divisions among its feminist factions toward the end of the 1970s and early 1980s. The shared views were informed by the prevailing position that the sphere of representation interpellates social subjects and organizes social relationships. These concepts developed within the context of the wider transitions and discourses in British culture and society; they resulted from discursive shifts in the British left that had positioned cultural activity as a political statement and made room for the struggles against racism and women's oppression that fell outside the established political domain of work and economy.

The feminist countermedia practices discussed in this chapter also corresponded with the second-wave feminist argument that the personal is political, which suggested that the experience of being exposed to media images was politically significant and that these images should therefore be countered and criticized. This stance, as well as other feminist debates, also corresponded with feminist developments in the United States in the fields of art and politics. Additionally, feminist publications in Britain, where many of the addressed photography practices were published, became significant platforms for the production of feminist photographic meaning.

Partially a response to the re-evaluation of consumer culture spurred by Britain's economic crisis in the 1970s, several of the feminist photographic activities discussed were part of the critique of advertising and its strategies for producing consumer desire. Such feminist counterpractices also addressed the sexual-political aspects of representations in advertisements. Their rhetoric often positioned media and advertising representations as distorted portrayals of reality and asserted that their own interventions were "beyond" representation because they provided unmediated access to women's "real" experiences and "genuine" perspectives.

These practices in feminist photography were produced in a moment when cultural activity—and photography in particular—was understood to be capable of intervening in the social and political spheres and in the sexual politics of representation. These practices circulated outside official cultural institutions (in feminist publications, community centers, and the street), a factor that contributed to the diversity of their strategies and ideas and enabled them to be manifested in multiple forms. Thus, in the period under study, the plurality of images became a site of intense political struggle, a struggle that sheds light on the significant role that image production and circulation had in articulating feminist arguments.

This discussion has also shown the growing predominance of the feminist antipornography debate in the early 1980s, the emergence of identity politics, and a general shift to the right. These developments posed a crisis for the women's movement's sense of imaginary cohesion and its uniformity regarding the impact of images on women. Concurrently, feminist media politics in this period began to have an impact on the institutional spaces of official politics. This process exhibits the predominance of debates about media politics in the 1970s and its infiltration into institutionalized forms of feminist politics, which would begin at the end of the decade and continue into the 1980s.

Finally, as women and feminism were marginalized in the field of photography, the discussed photography practices, and the various collaborative feminist forms of their production, became forms of claiming as well as formulating a feminist presence in this field. Furthermore, those who engaged in these practices were perceived as participating in political activism, which also engendered a sense of feminist community, generated new forms for feminist identification, and positioned media images as a cause to mobilize around politically. Moreover, these images were designed to evoke among their female viewers emotive and affective responses that, through their repetition, organized experience as meaningful and politically significant.

3

Photography and the Street

Feminist Documentary

During the late 1970s and early 1980s, British streets became a charged site where various political movements and positions clashed and alliances were formed. Unlike now, at the time there were no laws requiring police permission for public assembly or marches.[1] Thus, the street became a powerful stage for demonstrations, marches, street riots, and picket lines. In this chapter I focus on three street events and their photographic documentation: the Battle of Lewisham, the Grunwick strike, and Reclaim the Night. The Grunwick strike and the Reclaim the Night marches advocated feminist concerns, whereas the Lewisham demonstration protested racism. Although the Battle of Lewisham was not directly associated with the women's movement, it attracted white women demonstrators who were arguably also women's movement supporters. Additionally, as will be discussed, the use of photography during this demonstration intersected with feminist mobilizations of street photography in other events. The aforementioned events and other street demonstrations became a focus for feminist and political street photographers, who regarded their photographs as capable of documenting the "truth." Street photographers also viewed their activity as posing a challenge to the misrepresentation of political street events in the national press and mainstream media. In this chapter I show that feminist and other political street photographers played an activist role. I also consider the various politically engaged photography journals and feminist publications that published politically motivated photographs and examine how these journals became platforms for "alternative" photojournalism.

Street photography in 1970s Britain took place in the context of the emergence of political photo libraries and photography agencies in Britain. Among these agencies were Network Photographers in London, formed in 1981 by a group of nine freelance photographers; the Photo Co-Op, a photo library that contributed to feminist-related projects; and Rent a Snap—a Socialist Photo Library, a resource center for trade unions and various political groups. Many of these agencies worked cooperatively and tended to document particular areas of conflict or social change. These agencies also insisted on having editorial control over their work and stopped collaborating with national newspapers.[2] These agencies' formation and goals were in some ways informed by photography cooperatives such as Magnum Photos, the international photography cooperative of photojournalists founded in New York by Henri Cartier-Bresson, Robert Capa, George Rodger, and David Seymour. Previously, magazine editors assigned stories to photographers and retained their negatives and associated copyrights. Magnum photographers, in contrast, chose their stories and kept the negatives and corresponding copyrights.[3] Another influential photography agency was Dephot, which was formed in Germany in 1929 by photographer Simon Guttman, who immigrated to London in the 1940s. Dephot aimed to challenge news photography, which it viewed as misinforming the public and concealing information. Guttman also encouraged photographers to capture lively pictures and the climax of events and to take physical risks. In London Guttman formed the photography agency Report, which similarly aimed to document politically significant events that were overlooked or misrepresented by the mainstream and national press. Report joined the cooperative group of photographers IFL (International Freelance Library) in 1970 and was renamed Report/IFL.[4]

Street Photographer as Activist and the Battle of Lewisham

The *Camerawork* issue "Lewisham: What Are You Taking Pictures For?" was dedicated to documenting the Battle of Lewisham.[5] This upheaval erupted in August 1977, when members of the National Front, the fascist political party, attempted to march through Lewisham, an area that was home to a large black population. Since the mid-1970s, groups such as the National Front were committed to opposing immigration, engaging in raw racial incitement in the form of incendiary marches through immigrant neighborhoods, holding intimidating street meetings, and occupying public space.[6] During the National Front's march in Lewisham, violence broke out between the police and antifascist protesters, who had organized a counterdemonstration.

The Lewisham *Camerawork* issue, which included several contributions from photographers associated with the aforementioned alternative photography agencies,[7] expressed some of the political aims of street photography in Britain.[8] It appears that *Camerawork* was the only photographic publication to dedicate an entire issue to the Battle of Lewisham. This magazine challenged the mainstream media's reluctance to relate this event to the rising racism in Britain and questioned their portrayal of the police as brave victims who supposedly mediated between the extreme British Right and Left.[9] Thus, *Camerawork* endeavored to use photography as a tool to counter racism. This position resonated with critiques of the intense police control over black communities following the 1958 Notting Hill race riots. These riots were sparked by attacks on members of a West Indian community by white teenagers.[10] After this event, the Victorian-era "sus" laws were revived, allowing the police to stop, search, and arrest without evidence those suspected of criminal intent.[11] These laws resulted in a nearly permanent police presence in black neighborhoods.[12]

The rise in racist attitudes was in many ways an outcome of the postwar period, when members of the former British colonies were encouraged to immigrate to Britain as a means of solving labor shortages.[13] Inner-city and industrial centers such as Lewisham, which had white working-class communities and a large black population, nevertheless experienced recession and unemployment during the 1970s.[14] These conditions prompted the racist perception that the black population was diminishing the "Britishness" of white working-class communities.[15]

The Lewisham issue of *Camerawork* urged photographers out in the street to act as political activists. Photographer Paul Trevor, for example, explained that as he was photographing the Battle of Lewisham, he was asked by a protesting woman, "What are you taking pictures for? Come down and give us a hand." Trevor responded, "Don't you understand what we are doing? We are also playing an important role in this."[16] Many of the photographers also described their difficulties with the police. Mike Abrahams and Tom Picton stressed that the police were generally hostile and violent toward the Left press. By contrast, at Lewisham the police were cooperative with the Fleet Street press, even cordoning off a small area for the BBC.[17] Picton added that it was easier for mainstream press photographers to take pictures, as they often captured their images by standing behind police lines and their subject matter consisted of the police making arrests or getting injured. Picton also asserted that his and his colleagues' photographs contradicted these portrayals.[18]

Drawing on queer theorist Michael Warner, I argue that street photographers and demonstrators in protests such as the Battle of Lewisham formed a counterpublic. According to Warner, a queer counterpublic is marked by gender and sexual differences, defined by its tension with a larger public, and structured by alternative dispositions that make different assumptions about what can be said or goes without saying. This counterpublic also subsumes a space consisting of exits, entrances, and unsystematized lines of acquaintance that generate a form of intimacy that requires no relationship to domestic space, property, or nation. The antiracism demonstrators and photographers in the Battle of Lewisham and other street events similarly formed a counterpublic. The coming together of demonstrators and photographers in the space of the street did not so much highlight the differences between the heteronormative and the queer as it allowed for interactions and political alliances supporting the interests of racial minorities, the lower classes, and women rather than those of the status quo.[19]

Furthermore, given the perceived political potential attributed to photography, the street presence of photographers and their cameras in political demonstrations had a performative function that mediated political arguments between those present on the street and the imagined viewers of the photographs.[20] That is to say, the street photographer's camera did not simply capture what was happening and convey it as a "truthful" form of knowledge; rather, the street photographer's presence and activity became part of the street action. Some of this action was performed for the camera and was evoked by an exchange between the photographer and the photographed subjects and their acknowledgment of one another's presence. Additionally, as indicated by photography theorist Ariella Azoulay, the camera's street presence, regardless of whether an actual photograph was taken, drew attention to the event taking place and its political underpinnings.[21] These dynamics were then represented by the photographers and shaped as evidence.[22]

The presence of street photographers and their perceived political capacity to "make the real visible" were considered "dangerous" by the police, who responded violently to them.[23] The police, for instance, tried to prevent Peter Marlow from photographing them brutally kicking a demonstrator. Chris Steele Perkins recalled Abrahams being punched in the face by the police while taking a photo of street protests. Likewise, a policeman removed the film from Trevor's camera to stop him from taking pictures.[24]

Police violence targeted street photographers in other political events during this period as well. In the Grunwick strike, the police arrested Marlow when he attempted to photograph two policemen gripping a young demonstrator by the collar and ramming his head against the side of a police van. The police also knocked Marlow's photography equipment to the ground.[25]

Thus, to a certain extent, state and police power were momentarily confronted during the Battle of Lewisham and similar street events. A similar dynamic between political demonstrators and the police is exposed in Judith Butler's analysis of recent street protests demanding safety for women, sexual minorities, and genderqueer individuals. According to Butler, the street presence of transsexuals is often met with violence by passersby as well as the police. Butler, however, suggests that the threat of police power is reduced and overcome during such demonstrations, especially when the demonstrators become too numerous and mobile. Butler suggests that such demonstrations engender anarchist moments when the legitimacy of a regime is called into question but is not replaced. Until order is restored, the assembled bodies and their actions create a new time and space for a shared will that demands a different future. Thus, the crowd exercises a performative power through bodily action, movement, congregation, and exposure to possible violence.[26] Although Butler's analysis addresses a moment that is historically and politically distant from the 1970s, the bodily presence of the assembled demonstrators and photographers in political street events in

1970s Britain also posed a threat to institutions such as the police. In fact, contrary to Butler's assumptions, given the rising racial tension in 1970s Lewisham, it was perhaps the black street demonstrators and photographers documenting the brutal escalation of the events who provoked violence from the police and the National Front. Nevertheless, the demonstrators and photographers confronted power structures, shaped a shared political will, and, in a way, reconfigured the space of politics.

Several of the photographs in *Camerawork*'s Lewisham issue portrayed police violence and violent clashes between the antifascism demonstrators and the National Front. The close proximity to the photographed subjects gives the impression that the street photographer intended to "reveal" socially significant events on the street and to actively participate in them.[27] Moreover, the photographs and their layout on the second and third pages of the *Camerawork* issue emphasize the volatile dynamics between the event's participants and, in this way, aimed to generate social and political concern (figure 8).

The photographic sequence on these pages illustrates the violent escalation of the conflict on the street. The sequence on page 2 begins with a photo by Chris Schwarz of attempts by the police to clear out the antiracism demonstrators before the National Front march, continues with photos of National Front members holding British flags and waiting to march, and ends with an image by Peter Marlow of the police protecting National Front members from antiracism demonstrators. The photographs by Marlow on page 3 document the escalation of the violence. For example, a photo captioned "New Cross Road. National Front supporters attack anti-racist demonstrator" portrays National Front members waving their flag and cheering as one of their members pounces on an antifascism demonstrator who is being carried away by the police. Another photo, captioned "Clifton Rise. Arrest," features policemen appearing amused while pulling a black demonstrator by the throat as they arrest him. The next photo, captioned "Achilles St. Arrest," shows these policemen holding the same demonstrator by his arms and legs and carrying him away. Police violence was also captured in a photograph by Abrahams on page 11 of this issue, captioned "Lewisham High St. Policeman throws a missile," which shows a group of policemen apparently throwing a missile toward demonstrators.

Thus, the Lewisham issue of *Camerawork* utilized photography to advocate specific views concerning politically charged issues, such as racism,

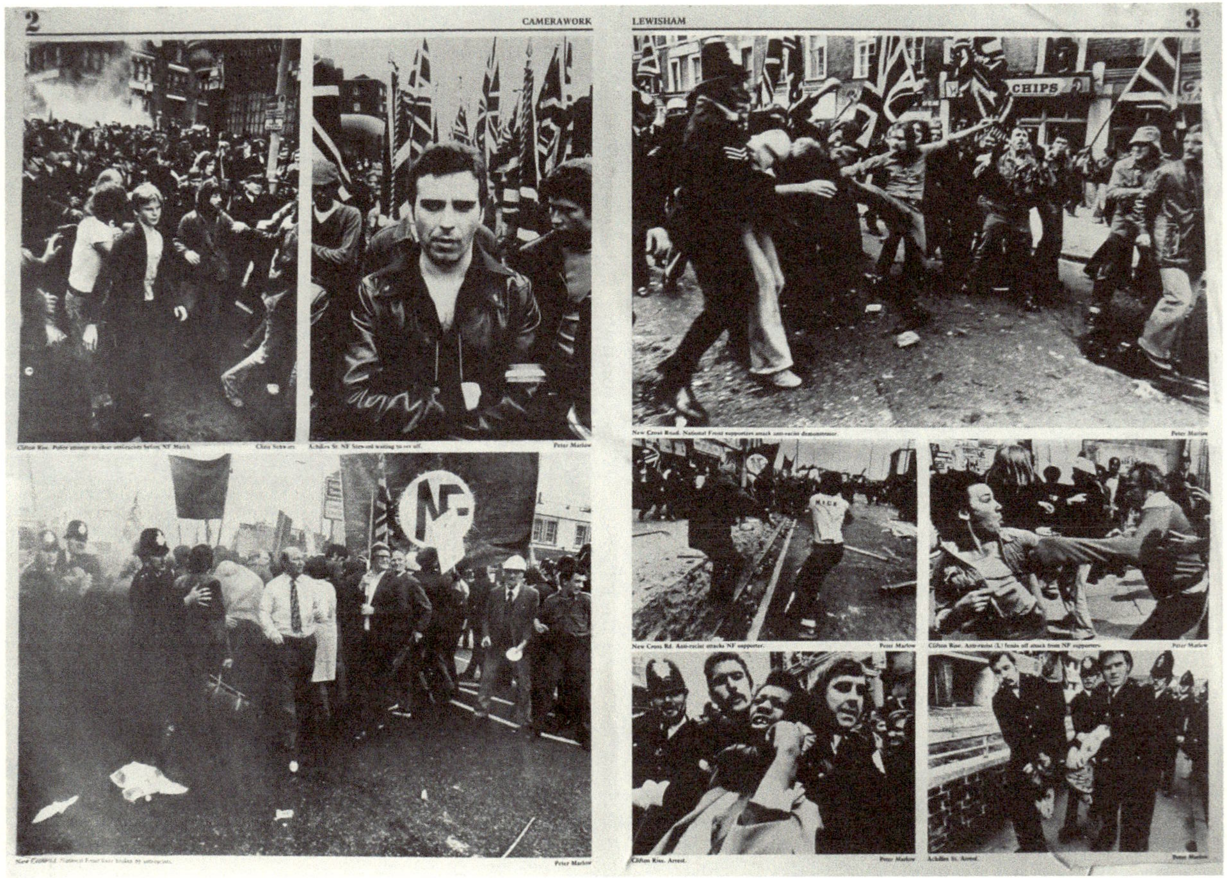

FIG. 8 Chris Schwarz, "Clifton Rise. Police attempt to clear anti-racists before NF march" (*page 2, top left*); Peter Marlow, "Achilles St. NF Steward waiting to set off" (*page 2, top right*); Peter Marlow, "New Cross Rd. National Front lines broken by anti-racists" (*page 2, bottom*); Peter Marlow, "New Cross Road. National Front supporters attack anti-racist demonstrator" (*page 3, top*); Peter Marlow, "New Cross Rd. Anti-racist attacks NF supporter" (*page 3, middle left*); Peter Marlow, "Clifton Rise. Anti-racist (L) fends off attack from NF supporters" (*page 3, middle right*); Peter Marlow, "Clifton Rise. Arrest" (*page 3, bottom left*); Peter Marlow, "Achilles St. Arrest" (*page 3, bottom right*); all from "Lewisham: What Are You Taking Pictures For?," special issue, *Camerawork*, November 1977, 2–3.

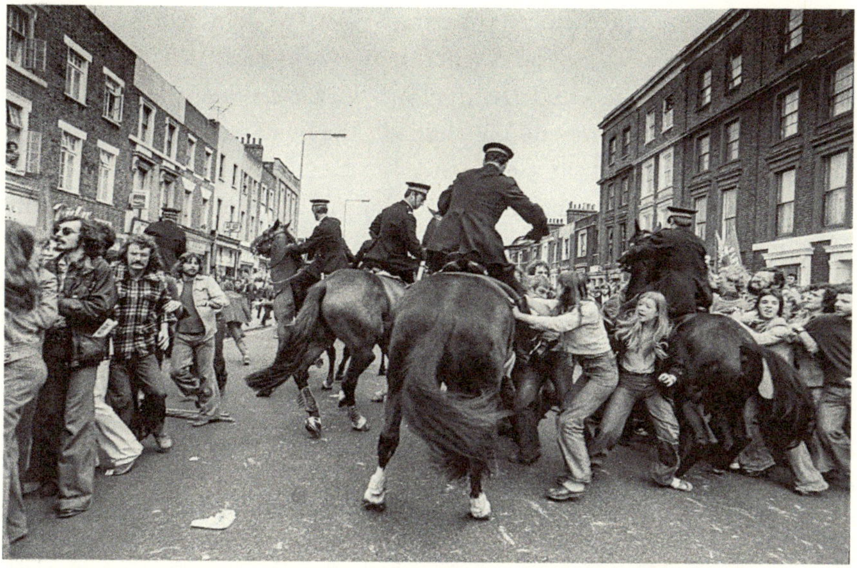

FIG. 9 Mike Abrahams, "New Cross Rd. Police charge anti-fascists," from "Lewisham: What Are You Taking Pictures For?," special issue, *Camerawork*, November 1977, 4, courtesy of Mike Abrahams.

and expose the state's violent attempts to assert control over the street. The Lewisham issue also prompted street photographers to assume a political role and use photographic representation to support that role.

Val Wilmer, one of the founding members of Format Photography Agency, was among the street photographers documenting the Lewisham events.[28] Additionally, given the visibility of protests organized by the women's movement and its members' support of a broad range of social issues, some of the white antiracism demonstrators and street photographers at Lewisham could have been feminists. Furthermore, black feminists, although they chose to be physically absent from the demonstration, viewed the Lewisham struggle as a crucial political issue.[29] Despite these factors, a feminist perspective was absent from *Camerawork*'s Lewisham issue. Additionally, all of the photographers included in the *Camerawork* issue were men, and the photographs of the violence on the Lewisham streets mostly captured encounters between men. Thus, these records represented the street and street photography as a predominantly masculine domain where women's political agency was absent or marginalized. Several women demonstrators were, however, captured in the photograph captioned "New Cross Rd. Police Charge Anti-Fascists" by Mike Abrahams (figure 9). This photograph portrays mounted policemen cornering a crowd of demonstrators, including a number of women. The absence of questions regarding gender might be explained by the recent departure from the *Camerawork* staff of feminist photographers Jo Spence and Liz Heron.[30] The Lewisham issue was the first installment assembled without Spence.[31]

In contrast, various feminist publications documented violent confrontations between the police and women demonstrators at the Grunwick strike and the Reclaim the Night marches, describing these protests as reflecting a women's movement issue. Moreover, a number of feminist photographers set out to document political street events. Among them was Maggie Murray, mentioned earlier, and photographer Joanne O'Brien, who recalled covering a political party conference in Ireland where she was the only woman photographer. When another woman photographer appeared on the site, one of the many male photographers exclaimed, "There are a lot of women photographers here!" According to O'Brien, this comment implied that women photographers not only were unusual but also posed a threat.[32] Wilmer recalled that when she was covering the Battle of Lewisham, she was "bruised and bloodied" like all the male photographers. However, she stated that when she worked for the *Times* of London, she received unsettling looks from her male colleagues, who were unaccustomed to seeing a woman photographer in their territory.[33]

Wilmer and Murray addressed the machismo in the field in their essay "Photography," published in 1982 in the London magazine *City Limits*. In this piece, they humorously suggested that for many men, photography equipment became a form of phallic jewelry. Noting the action television series *The Professionals*, the authors commented that photographers should be inconspicuous, put people at ease, and use minimal body movements rather than dramatically occupy the street.[34] This essay included a photograph by Murray of a woman being arrested at an abortion campaign demonstration in London's Trafalgar Square (figure 10). The photo depicts Wilmer swiftly moving across the frame in order to take a picture and Michael Ann Mullen, a former Hackney Flashers photographer, standing behind Wilmer and adjusting her camera; also shown is photographer John Sturrock, a member of Network Photographers, walking next to Wilmer.[35]

The inclusion of this photograph in the essay perhaps was an attempt to convey the presence of women street photographers, who, like their male colleagues, documented political events and took an active part in political action. As mentioned in the previous chapter, Murray and Wilmer were

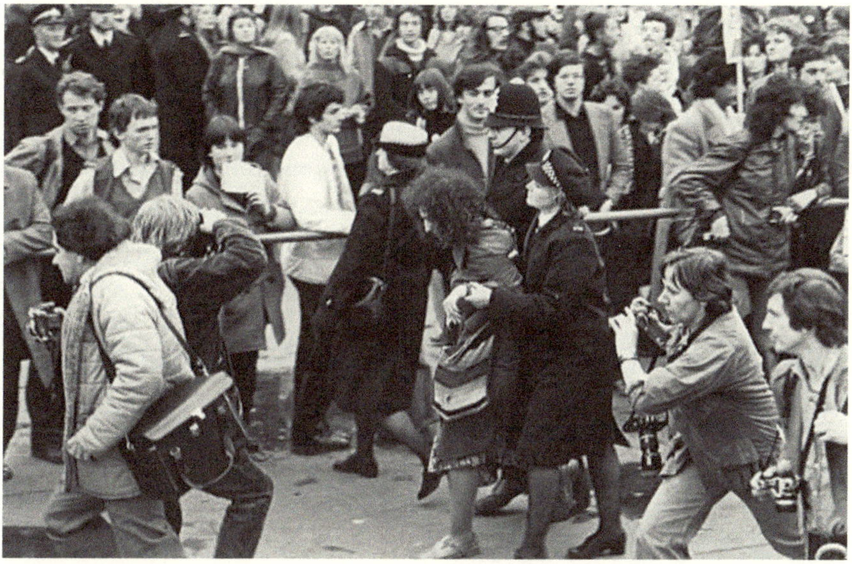

FIG. 10 Maggie Murray, photo from Val Wilmer and Maggie Murray, "Photography," *City Limits*, September 24–29, 1982, 48, courtesy of Maggie Murray.

among the founding members of Format Photography Agency in London, an all-female agency.[36] The idea of establishing this agency came to Wilmer and Murray following the launch of Network Photographers, which was then an all-male photojournalistic agency. This development motivated them to form an agency that followed a model similar to Network's but that advanced women's careers.[37] As mentioned earlier, although Format was a commercial agency like alternative photography agencies at the time, it also covered social and political issues.[38]

A theoretical feminist debate on the politics of space also began to emerge in the 1980s in Britain and the United States. This debate challenged the exclusion of feminism from contemporary urban discourses and from sociological and cultural literature on modernity.[39] Feminist writer Elizabeth Wilson, for instance, claimed that in literature on modernity, women on the street were often considered objects of sexual pleasure posing a moral and political threat.[40] Wilson also observed that feminist writing was often concerned with women's safety and comfort on city streets.[41] Nevertheless, she suggested that feminist writing about the street should emphasize women's right to seek pleasure and take risks in the urban sphere.[42] Drawing on Wilson, I will show that the Grunwick strike and Reclaim the Night marches manifested an element of risk and defiance of conventional beliefs associated with women's position in public space. Reclaim the Night, in particular, employed street strategies that had an element of humor and pleasure in order to challenge patriarchal social elements. Moreover, in light of the time's politicized view of photography, the photographic representations of Reclaim the Night and the Grunwick strike were designed to have a disruptive political role.

Photography Theory Challenging the Activist Camera

A theoretical engagement with photographic representation was absent from the Lewisham issue of *Camerawork*. As mentioned earlier, the mid-1970s saw the emergence of photography theory. Such theory mobilized psychoanalysis, feminism, Marxism, and Michel Foucault's notion of power to examine the processes involved in the production of photographic meaning. The advent of photography theory was spurred in part by the increased interest in and availability of translations into English of works by non-Anglo-Saxon intellectuals such as Louis Althusser, Roland Barthes, Foucault, and Walter Benjamin.[43] Photography theory, like various photography practices during that period, was considered radical and connected with a broader field of social activism that was not confined to academia.[44] It introduced new politicized perspectives into the field of photography and went against positivistic and humanist approaches to photography that had been predominant up to that time. In contrast to these approaches, photography theory sought to work against the grain and situate photography within a theoretical framework in relation to politics and the constraining relations of social power.[45] Some theorists, for instance, focused on challenging the assumed correlation between street photography, the "truth," and political action.

In a similar vein, John Tagg's essay "Power and Photography" challenged progressive notions of leftist documentary and street photography. Originally given as a talk at the Institute of Contemporary Arts in London in 1979,[46] it followed a lecture by Picton, who suggested that venturing into the street to photograph the "truth" of political events was a radical act that could disrupt ideological structures.[47] In contrast, Tagg argued that truth was not something that could be sought with a camera and found on the street but, rather, was sustained and produced by the institutional practices of power that emerged in the second half of the nineteenth century.[48] Therefore, unlike street photographers who asserted that the national news media were an oppressive structure that concealed the truth, Tagg maintained that power was an inescapable network of immanent relations rather than a particular force in the hands of a specific institution. Moreover, Tagg proposed that using photography to point to instances of "power" would not disrupt the systems and practices that produced them.[49] Such arguments were in opposition to the interventionist claims of the Lewisham issue of *Camerawork* concerning street photography and called into question photography's capacity to radically erode oppressive social structures. The conflicting positions of Tagg and Picton resembled those expressed by theorists and practitioners in parallel debates in the increasingly politicized field of photography. Although I acknowledge the presence of such conflicting positions during this time, I am predominantly interested in investigating the political expectations of street photography at this particular moment of social conflict. Therefore, the rest of the chapter will deal with the participatory and performative role of street photographers in political events and their contributions to debates about gender, sexual, racial, and class differences.

The Grunwick Strike

The Grunwick strike occurred between August 1976 and July 1978 at a film-processing lab in Willesden, North London, an industrialized residential area that since the 1950s had attracted large waves of immigrants from the West Indies and the Indian subcontinent.[50] Willesden was also well known for its tradition of left-wing trade union organizations.[51] The strike was led by Jayaben Desai and her primarily Asian immigrant women coworkers to protest unreasonable wages and management's refusal to recognize the women's right to unionize. The strikers were interested in joining the labor union Association for Professional, Executive, Clerical and Computer Staffs (APEX), which was also a source of support during the strike.[52]

Most of the workers at Grunwick came to Britain from East Africa. About half arrived from Uganda and the rest came from Kenya and Tanzania; both groups were originally subjects of the British empire who had been taken to East Africa by rulers of the British Empire when India was still a colony. As East African countries attained independence from Britain in the 1960s,

South Asian residents were forced to leave. In Kenya and Tanzania, South Asians were, for example, forced out gradually. In Uganda, however, South Asians were expelled forcefully in 1972 by President Idi Amin.[53] Unlike Indian, Pakistani, and West Indian immigrants,[54] who came to Britain in order to escape low living standards and unemployment, some East African Asians came from an educated middle-class background and often found themselves compelled to do unskilled or semiskilled work. Desai's husband, for instance, was a manager of a tire company before arriving in Britain. Unlike Asian immigrants who came in the 1950s, a period characterized by an expanding economy and high employment, East African Asians arrived at a time of rising unemployment and racism.[55] In addition, in Britain, the Grunwick workers experienced gender as well as racial discrimination. Approximately 50 percent of the weekly paid staff were women, as were 60 percent of the strikers. These women workers were subjected to particularly rigorous supervision within their workplaces. Moreover, their employment often conflicted with their patriarchally assigned domestic duties, such as fetching children from school and cooking meals.[56] Thus, the historical background of the striking immigrant workers' conditions, as well as the social ramifications of gender differences, sheds some light on the purpose of the strike and its feminist and political significance. The strike's eruption at a photo-processing business added another dimension to the dispute, as the strikers' refusal to develop photographs can be interpreted as an intervention in the sphere of representation and as calling attention to the dispute and its potential photographic representability.

Feminist Photography and the Grunwick Strike

The Grunwick strike was one of the most publicized and visually documented strikes of the 1970s.[57] It was also a significant politically mobilizing event, as it attracted massive secondary picketing support from various factions of the British Left and the women's movement. Some of the groups that showed solidarity on the picket line were the Gay Liberation Front, university students, the Communist Party, women organizations, the leadership of the National Union of Mineworkers, and several Labour members of Parliament.[58] Drawing on the work of Michael Warner and Judith Butler, I suggest that as in the Battle of Lewisham, the political alliances formed between these different political groups were integral in shaping the Grunwick strike as a political action.[59] According to Butler, crowds and bodies assembled on the street reconfigure the street's environment and render it a public space of political debate.[60] Butler's use of the term *public* evokes Hannah Arendt's understanding of the classical Greek polis and the Roman forum as spaces where political action was dependent on their constitution as "spaces of appearance." Furthermore, according to Arendt, the "true" space is located between the people, a claim that implies that action itself establishes a space as well as alliance.[61] That is to say, the exchanges between the divergent political bodies of the British Left, which came together and witnessed their mutual political mobilization around their shared experience of the event and discourse, became as politically significant as the strike itself.[62] Additionally, it can be argued that the presence of the street photographers' cameras and the political significance associated with their representational capacity added another dimension to the constitution of the strike as a "space of appearance."

The Grunwick strike attracted vast media attention and was featured in the national news and covered by live television and various feminist and alternative publications.[63] One of the earliest accounts of the strike to appear in a national newspaper was "Sari Power" by Graham Taylor, which appeared in the Communist Party of Great Britain's newspaper, *Morning Star* in October 1976. This newspaper had a relatively small circulation and was perhaps the only national daily that supported the Grunwick strikers throughout. The article dealt with one of the first Grunwick marches, that of October 1, 1976, which commenced in the plant's vicinity and terminated in a public meeting addressed by the strike committee and the trades council.[64] Taylor described the event as follows: "The High Road suddenly exploded into a blaze of colour. Down the road, banners flying, swept hundreds of demonstrators, led by Indian workers. In the vanguard, saris swirling, were Indian women. Not submissive housebound women but Grunwick strikers—fists raised in anger. Not the inarticulate immigrant women we are often told about. Hardly. For at every building they passed, they shouted their resounding slogan: 'Union! Union! We want Union!.'"[65]

Although supportive of the strike, the emphasis on the High Road exploding "into a blaze of color" refers to the use of banners but perhaps also to the saris and therefore seems to offer an orientalist spectacularization of the labor action and of the Asian women participating in it. Nevertheless, the mention of the Asian women's central position in the strike challenged the stereotype of Asian women as submissive.[66]

The publicity that the strike attracted resulted from alliances that the strike committee formed with established British political leaders, among them Jack Dromey, then secretary of the Brent Trades Council, who played an important role in the strike.[67] The extensive media coverage of the Grunwick strike began after June 13, 1977, the first day of action, when the strike committee called for support for a mass picket.[68] In the weeks that followed, the size of the picket line increased to twenty-five thousand people and violent confrontations between the police and the picketers occurred.[69]

The Grunwick strike was extensively covered by the national press, and its photographic representation often reflected a narrative that supported the official bodies of the state. Some of the arguments advanced through photographs in the national newspaper the *Times*[70] were that the police were victimized by the violent Grunwick crowd, that the strike's leaders were official British political figures, and that the Asian women strikers were only marginal participants. Implied support of these arguments was provided by photographs depicting an injured policeman lying on the ground and clasping his injured head; Arthur Scargill, the leader of the National Union of Mineworkers, marching with a crowd of white male trade union supporters who are chanting and holding up their fists on the picket line; and Home Secretary Merlyn Rees standing in the midst of policemen and white male picketers alongside Desai, who appears timid and concerned. Rees came to Grunwick during the weeks of action to mediate between the picketers and the police. In this particular image, Desai appears small and is towered over by Rees, the demonstrators, and the policemen (figure 11).

In contrast, various feminist and politically engaged street photographers set out to capture other images of the Grunwick strike. For example, Homer Sykes photographed four Asian women and a man holding picket signs outside the factory and surrounded by over twenty policemen (figure 12). Sykes mentioned that in this image, he tried to illustrate the power that the state authority had over the Asian strikers, who appear downcast. Furthermore, as will soon be discussed, the photographic representation of these women signaled the challenge they posed, not only to the factory management but also to the patriarchal codes and constraints of their communities regarding their presence in the public sphere.

According to Sykes, newspapers did not want to publish his photographs of the striking Asian women, claiming that such images would decrease their sales. Sykes also stated that since in the early days of the strike these women

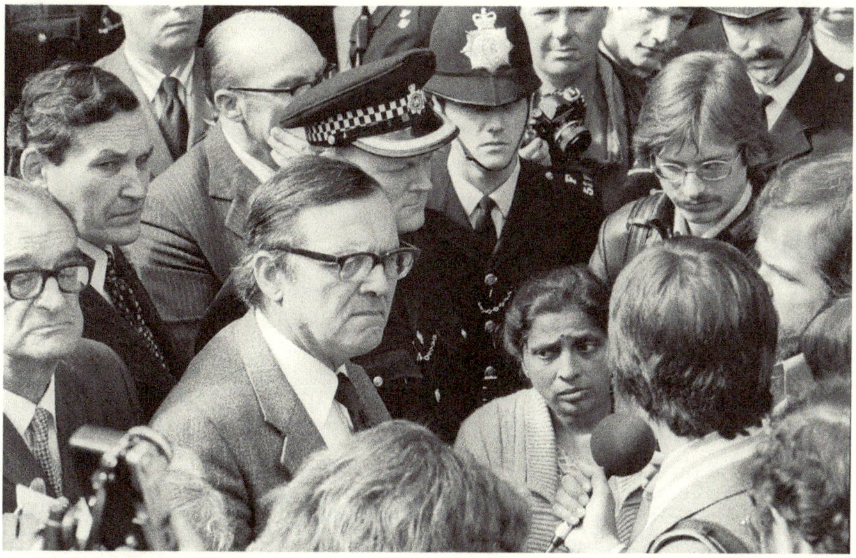

FIG. 11 Photographer unknown, "Mr Rees, home secretary, listening to the pickets outside Grunwick gates yesterday," from the *Times*, June 23, 1977, 2, courtesy of the *Times* Archive.

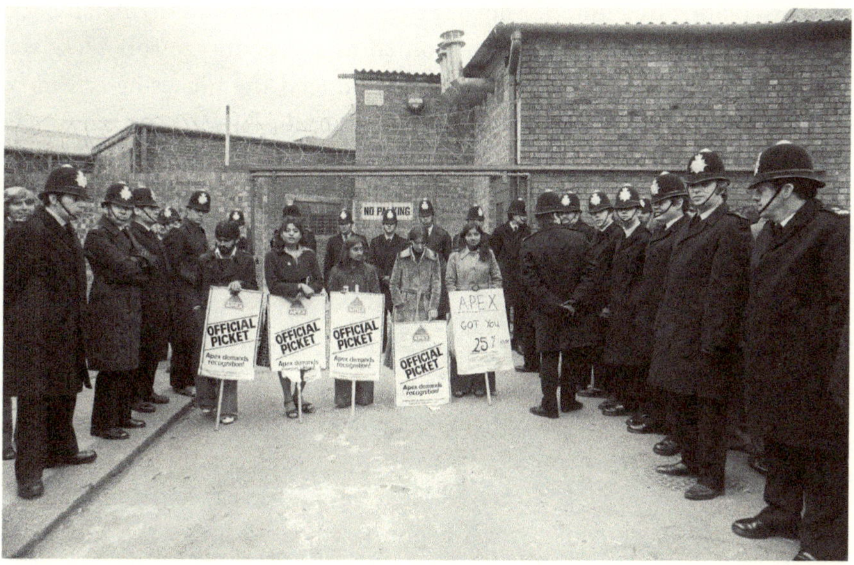

FIG. 12 Homer Sykes, "Pickets face police during the Grunwick strike, North London," 1977, courtesy of Homer Sykes.

were underrepresented in the national press, many people did not know that they were the leaders of the strike.[71]

In contrast, photographs that appeared in feminist and alternative publications often focused on Desai and her coworkers, depicting them in a heroic manner. For instance, the essay "Grunwick Women" in *Spare Rib* included a photograph by Caro Webb of Desai standing on the picket line with a clenched fist and a sign that reads "£28 for 40 hrs" (figure 13). Similarly, Wilmer's interview with Desai that was published in *Time Out* included a portrait by photographer Paul McNicholls of Desai on the picket line smiling confidently at the camera.

Although Desai was not a street photographer, she set out to control how the Grunwick strikers were represented by the media. For instance, she told the picketers not to communicate with reporters from right-wing publications such as the *Mail*, the *Telegraph*, or the *Express*. Thus, according to Dromey, from June onward, anguished reporters and photographers from these papers could be seen pleading with picketers for poses and comments, which were willingly given to the *Guardian* and the *Morning Star*.[72]

Many of the white workers who participated in the mass picket came to defend the trade union movement and viewed the strike as a struggle for the right to belong to a union. Many of these workers viewed the Asian background of most of the striking women as incidental.[73] This view was implied, for instance, when Scargill encouraged the picketing crowd by shouting, "Come on lads!" to which a large group of women's movement supporters responded by shouting, "And lasses!" Scargill then grabbed the megaphone and exclaimed, "There's no lasses down the pit!"[74] Nonetheless, the support of the trade unions had a significant impact on the Grunwick strike and was sought after by the strike committee from the outset.

The Grunwick strike was not the first labor dispute in 1970s Britain that was led by immigrant women workers, but it differed from other labor disputes in its political strategies and in the extent of its media exposure. The Imperial Typewriters strike, which took place in Leicester in the Midlands in 1974, was similarly organized by women workers, mostly from India but also from Uganda, who protested their economic exploitation by their employers. However, unlike the Grunwick strike, the Imperial Typewriters strike was not recognized by a union and was supported solely by strikers' community groups. The Grunwick strike, notably, did not initially set out to appeal to the wider black public but rather mobilized the support and influence of white British political groups to obtain union recognition.[75]

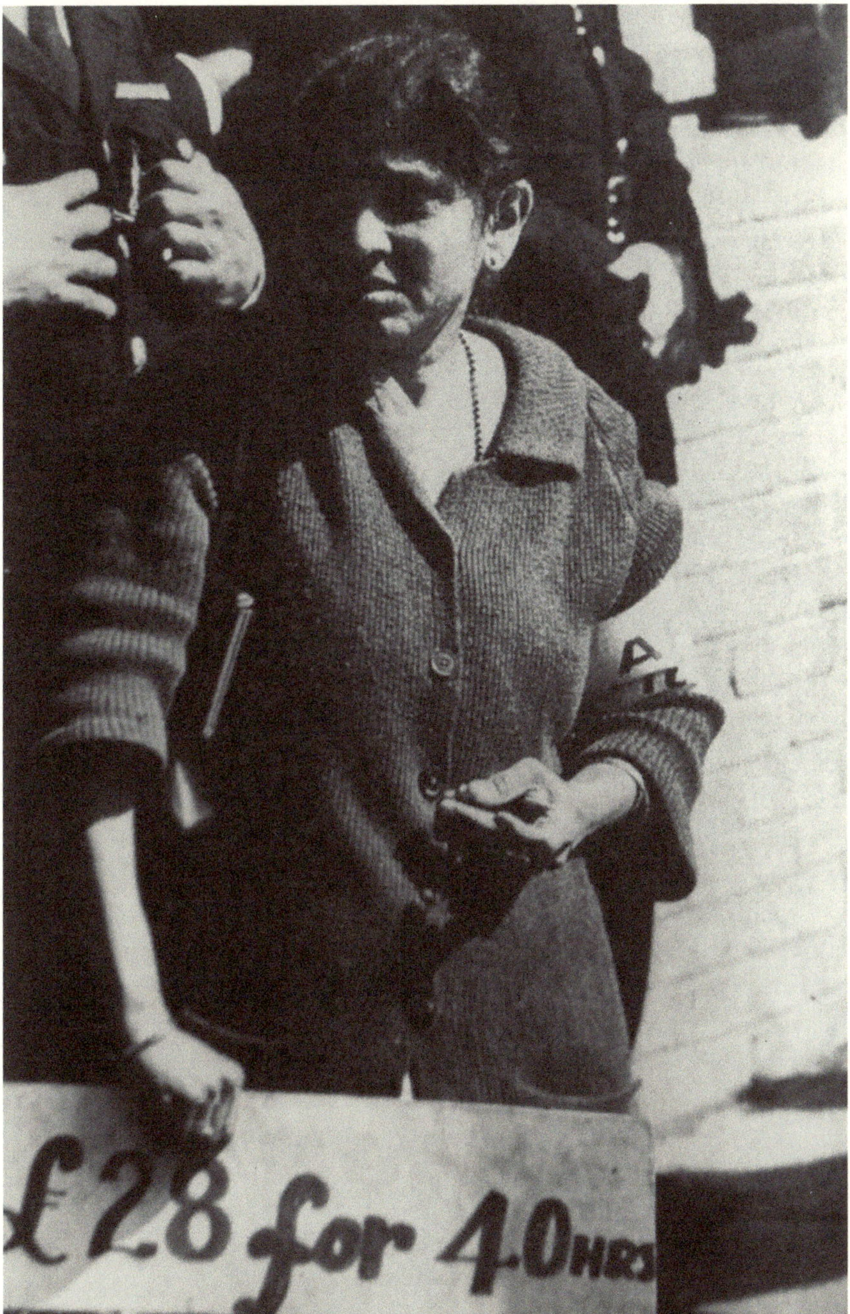

FIG. 13 Caro Webb, "Jayaben Desai," from Beatrix Campbell and Valerie Charlton, "Grunwick Women," *Spare Rib*, August 1977, 6.

Nevertheless, on November 21, 1976, several months into the strike, the strike committee and other Grunwick strikers came to support a demonstration against racism in London called by the Trades Union Congress (TUC) and the Labour Party. Furthermore, on the weekend of March 19–20, 1976, Desai and other strikers attended a conference against racism organized by Liberation at Friends House, Euston.[76]

As mentioned earlier, the Grunwick mass pickets attracted a range of leftist groups that were not associated with official political parties or unions. One such group was the Poster/Film Collective, which consisted mainly of artists, photographers, filmmakers, and former staff and students from various art schools in London.[77] This group, like various politically engaged photographers, viewed cultural production as a form of political intervention.[78] For example, it supported the strike by making picket posters, which were used by the strike committee (Desai, Vipin Magdani, Johnny Patel, and Yasu Patel) during their hunger strike, which began on November 22, 1977.[79]

Ultimately, following pressure from the Labour government, the TUC withdrew its support of the Grunwick strikers.[80] Additionally, APEX declared that the control over the dispute should remain in the hands of the APEX executive, and that any proposed trade unionist action should receive the official approval of the union rather than of the strike committee.[81] In response to the withdrawal of TUC support, members of the strike committee staged a hunger strike outside the headquarters of the Transport and General Workers Union,[82] an action that led to their immediate suspension from APEX.[83]

A photograph of the hunger strikers and some of the Poster/Film Collective's picket posters by Report photographer Andrew Ward appeared in an issue of *Spare Rib*.[84] The posters, which called for the unions to resume their support, incorporated photographic images of the strikers and political figures who were involved in the dispute and were captioned "Negotiation, Collaboration and Integration" and "TUC Collaboration." Ward's photo of the hunger strikers was captioned "Drowning in Sympathy but Starving for Action," suggesting that the strikers were desperate for the TUC to act against the factory.

The hunger strike drew on forms of resistance that were borrowed from Mahatma Gandhi's strategy against British colonialism in India.[85] When Desai was in school, she was active in the movement for Indian independence led by Gandhi, who was also Gujarati.[86] Furthermore, Desai's father, who was a landowner, had been politically involved with Gandhi.[87] Although an image of the hunger strike was published in *Spare Rib*, the historical use of this strategy in India was not alluded to. Parallels could also be drawn between the Grunwick hunger strike and an earlier moment in women's rights activism in Britain, when the suffragettes employed the tactic to protest the conditions of their imprisonment.[88] These facts position the strike primarily within a contemporary British political perspective.

From a different perspective, the support that the Grunwick strike received from various factions of the British Left can be understood in the context of other political alliances formed during this period between black and white political groups, in which the street played a significant part. One such alliance was the Rock against Racism movement (1976–1981) founded by a group of activists associated with the Anti-Nazi League, which was set up by the Socialist Workers Party. The formation of Rock against Racism is attributed to the publication of a letter by Rock photographer Red Saunders in the weekly music press. In this letter, Saunders opposed Eric Clapton's expression of support for Conservative member of Parliament Enoch Powell during a concert in Birmingham. Powell, in a famous speech also delivered in Birmingham in 1968, warned that if (nonwhite) immigration into Britain were not curtailed, he foresaw the "river foaming with . . . blood." As observed by Wendy Webster, Powell's speech rhetorically drew on 1950s British mainstream media imagery of the nation as a domestic sanctuary violated by immigrants.[89] Additionally, the assassination of Martin Luther King Jr. two weeks before the speech, the deadly five-day riot that took place in Detroit in 1967, and other eruptions of racial violence and unrest since that time in the United States were influential factors that shed light on Powell's underlying fear that a race war could erupt in Britain as it had in America.[90]

Another major catalyst of the Rock against Racism movement's formation was a refutation of the National Front and its incendiary street presence.[91] Thus, one of this movement's major street activities took place in 1978 in the form of a demonstration against racism and fascism in Trafalgar Square that was joined by multiple other political groups. The demonstration was followed by a march to Victoria Park in East London, where eighty thousand people attended a free concert featuring punk and reggae bands.[92]

Although the Grunwick strike ultimately failed in that the factory's management did not recognize the workers' right to join a union, it was influential in its mobilization of the British Left and the British women's

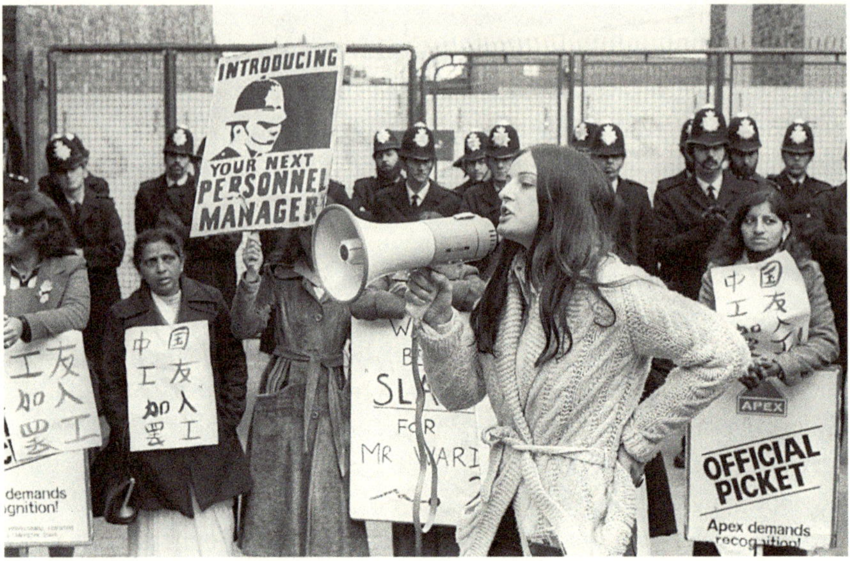

FIG. 14 Homer Sykes, "Feminist campaigner in support of the Asian Strikers. Mrs. Desai is the second from the left," North London, 1977, courtesy of Homer Sykes.

movement. A photograph taken by Sykes can be viewed as capturing the mobilization of white British feminists around the strike (figure 14). The photo depicts a white feminist demonstrator addressing the crowd on a megaphone while Desai and her coworkers behind her are surrounded by a group of policemen. The gazes of the crowd, policemen, and strikers behind the white demonstrator stand in for an imagined public gaze witnessing the women's movement as a player in this strike. Like Syke's previous image, this photograph was rejected by the newspapers.

As was discussed earlier, the Grunwick strike spoke to the politics of various political camps. For instance, for trade unionists, Grunwick was a struggle for the right to unionize and for union recognition. For antiracism groups, it was a struggle against racist discrimination, and for feminists it was an organized rebellion of oppressed female workers against management.[93] The Grunwick strike also succeeded in facilitating the recognition of immigrant workers as part of the British workforce and their desire for unionization. Until that time, the rights of immigrant workers of both sexes were not on the union's agenda, which was dominated by white males, and the Grunwick strike provided a venue for immigrant workers to penetrate the political structure of the trade unions.[94] At the same time, the strike redefined collective methods of industrial struggle, which were, to a certain extent, independent of trade union bureaucracy.[95]

The Night Cleaners' Campaign was another event in which the women's movement supported worker and immigrant rights and in which visual production was among the political strategies for advancing arguments. In the early 1970s the Pimlico branch of the London Women's Liberation Workshop was approached by May Hobbs, a night cleaner and activist in a night cleaner group that sought the support of the women's movement in their struggle for unionization. Earlier that year, the Berwick Street Film Collective was asked by the night cleaners' group to make a film about their campaign (1972–1975).[96] This film, entitled *Nightcleaners*, started out as a straightforward agit-prop film but was ultimately reedited as a theoretical film that employed Brechtian aesthetics and avant-garde notions of film construction. This campaign, although smaller in impact than the Grunwick strike, similarly challenged a set of exclusions within the organized Left, predominantly concerning the intersection of gender, class, and third-world politics. Furthermore, it broadened feminist politics to include working-class and immigrant women's experiences.[97]

Police Violence against Women

As in Lewisham, demonstrators at the Grunwick strike (and Reclaim the Night) were targets of police violence. Various feminist photographers and feminist publications drew particular attention to police attacks on women demonstrators. The magazine *Women's Report* also related the growing right-wing backlash in Britain to the excessive police control and violence against black communities and left-wing supporters.[98] Such police violence was addressed in the essay "Grunwick Women" by Beatrix Campbell and Valerie Charlton, published in *Spare Rib*. This essay described incidents that took place on June 13, 1977—the first day of the action in Grunwick, which attracted women supporters from such organizations as the London Communist Party, the Working Women's Charter, and other groups in the British women's movement.[99] The essay included a sequence of photographs by feminist photographer Michael Ann Mullen that portrays a white feminist demonstrator being pushed to the ground by the police and helped up by another woman (figure 15). Mullen's photos focus on the women's facial and bodily expressions, which seem anguished yet heroic. The captions for these

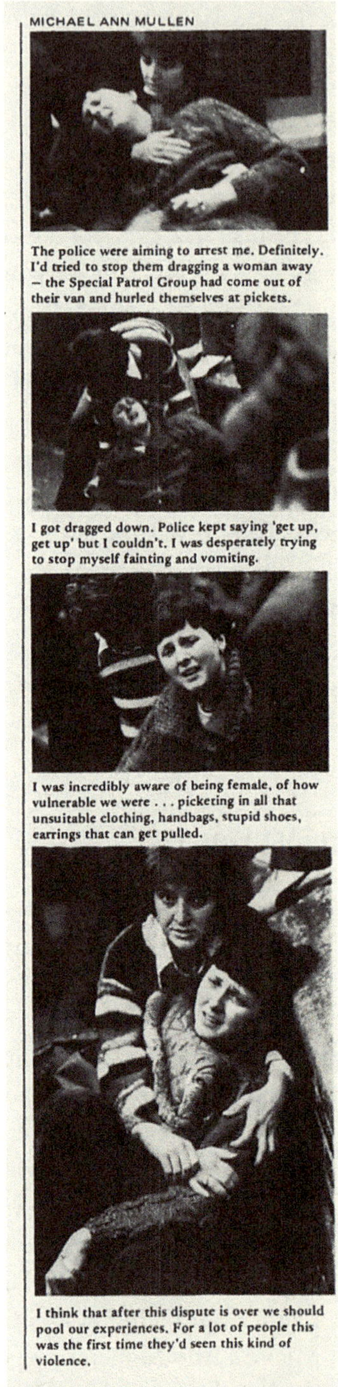

MICHAEL ANN MULLEN

The police were aiming to arrest me. Definitely. I'd tried to stop them dragging a woman away – the Special Patrol Group had come out of their van and hurled themselves at pickets.

I got dragged down. Police kept saying 'get up, get up' but I couldn't. I was desperately trying to stop myself fainting and vomiting.

I was incredibly aware of being female, of how vulnerable we were . . . picketing in all that unsuitable clothing, handbags, stupid shoes, earrings that can get pulled.

I think that after this dispute is over we should pool our experiences. For a lot of people this was the first time they'd seen this kind of violence.

FIG. 15 Michael Ann Mullen, photo sequence of police dispute, from Beatrix Campbell and Valerie Charlton, "Grunwick Women," *Spare Rib*, August 1977, 8, courtesy of Michael Ann Mullen.

photos were written in a personal tone, reflecting the feminist position that the personal is political and thus that it is necessary to mobilize individual affective experiences into collective action:

> The police were aiming to arrest me. Definitely. I tried to stop them dragging a woman away—the Special Patrol Group had come out of their van and hurled themselves at pickets.
>
> I got dragged down. Police kept saying "get up, get up" but I couldn't. I was desperately trying to stop myself fainting and vomiting.
>
> I was incredibly aware of being female, of how vulnerable we were . . . picketing in all that unsuitable clothing, handbags, stupid shoes, earrings that can get pulled.
>
> I think that after this dispute is over we should pool our experiences. For a lot of people this was the first time they'd seen this kind of violence.[100]

The poses and facial expressions of the photographed women appear somewhat staged and dramatic—for example, in the affected manner in which one demonstrator embraces the woman on the ground in the first photograph. This dramatization is also evident in the sequence's fourth image, in which the attacked woman stares, with a tormented expression, at a distant spot, and the woman embracing her looks back compassionately at the viewer, underscoring the suffering of the attacked woman and others like her. This image brings to mind tormented martyrs' portrayal in Christian art. Additionally, drawing on the work of Thomas Keenan, I argue that the feminist photographers' street presence, at demonstrations where other feminists participated, generated an affective exchange that rendered the photographers active participants who influenced the street action and shaped it politically. Thus, the enactment of the gestures in front of Mullen and her camera suggests an acknowledgment of the camera's and the feminist photographer's presence. The acknowledgment of this feminist presence arguably evoked a shared sense of identification and collectivity. Additionally, these gestures prompted the camera's witnessing and recording of the outcomes of the acts of police violence targeted at women. The women's gestures were also performed for an imagined viewer and for a public that would encounter the image in the future.[101]

Campbell and Charleton's *Spare Rib* essay also included personal accounts by various women's movement supporters who were present on that day. For example, Sarah Greeves described how she and her friends found themselves in the midst of a flying wedge and how she was arrested for assault after kicking a policeman to the ground. Feminist Maria Druggan mentioned that her leg was fractured because a police officer stomped on it. The essay also pointed out incidents, before the women's day demonstration, in which the Asian women participants were targeted by violence, including when Desai's foot was run over by a factory director's car and when two young Asian women were run over at the gate by a scab driver. The essay also reported that before the mass arrests began, Desai was arrested on the picket line.[102] Additionally, according to Dromey, one policeman dragged Desai by the hair across the road. Chris Wright, an official of the National Union of Bank Employees and a leading lay member of APEX, also recalled that he and several others saw Desai being repeatedly kicked by the police.[103]

The photographs and written accounts of such incidents not only recorded police violence against female demonstrators on the picket line but also represented the Grunwick strike as a mobilizing force generating a sense of solidarity and mutual support among British women's movement sympathizers.

The Grunwick Strike and Conflicting Approaches to Women's Rights

Although the Grunwick strike aroused concerns regarding women's rights and the women's movement was a significant source of support for the strike, Desai and her female coworkers' approach to feminist concerns differed from that of their British feminist supporters. Additionally, the white British feminists participating in the strike, depicted in Sykes's and Mullen's photographs, symbolically appear to occupy a separate physical space from the striking Asian women, as if signaling their separate political status. Drawing on feminist theorist Avtar Brah's notion of intersectionality, I argue that demographic and cultural differences between the immigrant women and the British-born feminists challenge the concept of "global sisterhood" implicit in the 1970s women's movement and the British feminists' support of the Grunwick struggle.[104] Within the Grunwick context, these differences stemmed from challenges originating from the immigrant women's cultures and the patriarchal structures of their communities. For example, in an interview with Val Wilmer, Desai mentioned that many of her coworkers had to overcome social restrictions imposed by their families, which viewed engagement in direct political action as an inappropriate activity for women. Although Desai claimed that she preferred to maintain the support of the family structure,[105] she acknowledged that many of the women participated in the strike against their parents' and husbands' will.[106] Indeed, young, unmarried women participated in the strike despite the fear of being ostracized by their communities. Relatedly, George Ward, the plant manager, who was of Anglo-Indian descent, threatened to spread rumors about Desai and other strikers being "loose women" in the hope that their families would force them off the picket line.[107] Although familiar with Indian culture, Ward, as an Anglo-Indian, presumably identified more readily with the British upper class. Moreover, Ward's departure from India in 1948 in the aftermath of Indian independence perhaps suggests the he aligned himself not with the nationalistic aspirations of Jawaharlal Nehru and Gandhi but rather with the politics of the departing British empire.[108] Nevertheless, as an Anglo-Indian, he likely faced prejudice in Britain.

When Desai was asked by a BBC journalist whether she was oppressed by men, she responded, "I don't think that way. We have a woman prime minister in India. We have had women warriors in India who fought with children on their backs."[109] In this response, Desai was referring to Prime Minister Indira Gandhi, who was in office from 1966 to 1977 (and 1980–1984), and perhaps to the iconographic image of the *virangana* (woman warrior), which was used by the nationalist movement in India as a symbol for overcoming British colonial domination. Such images drew on representations of the Hindu goddess Durga riding a lion and carrying a sword during battle, an icon whose attributes were ascribed to historical female figures. For example, Lakshmi Bai, queen of Jhansi, who led her troops against British rule in the 1857 revolt and later became a symbol of Indian nationalism, was often represented as holding a sword and riding a horse that corresponded to Durga's lion.[110] Thus, Desai evoked representations of female assertiveness that drew on this Indian mythology and history and associated Indian resistance to British oppression in India with that in Britain. Desai thus implied that she was operating not only within but also against these structures.

The Asian women's consistent presence on the street challenged cultural associations between women in the public sphere and sexual "looseness." The Grunwick strike was followed by the formation of various black feminist organizations, such as the Organization of Women of African and Asian Descent, founded in 1978, which operated as a national network for black women. The group addressed issues such as immigration legislation and the state harassment, health, and sexuality of black women.[111] Another group was Southall Black Sisters, which was founded in 1979 by Asian and Afro-Caribbean women following a mass protest in Southall against the National Front during which antifascism activist Blair Peach was killed by Special Patrol Group officers. The organization focused on combating racism but also challenged the patriarchy in its members' own communities by addressing issues such as domestic violence.[112] However, their activity often led to attacks by community leaders and an older generation of women, who warned that the group's actions might provoke a racist backlash that would encourage the press to represent Asian men as violent.[113] The preoccupation of groups such as Southall Black Sisters with issues of violence against women was consistent with the focus of the Reclaim the Night marches and groups such as Women against Violence against Women. Nonetheless, black feminist groups were challenged by the particular social structures of their own communities. For example, although Reclaim the Night organizers demanded increased police presence, which they believed would protect women in the public space, black feminists were wary of such a proposition, given the record of police violence against the black community.[114]

Feminism Photography and Reclaim the Night

As was mentioned earlier, the 1977 Reclaim the Night marches that took place simultaneously in a number of British cities (Leeds, London, Manchester, York, Newcastle, and Bristol) were initiated by Leeds feminists in response to the threat of the serial killer Peter Sutcliffe. The marches protested male violence against women and aimed to physically and symbolically claim the street as a space where women would be safe from male violence, pornography, and sexualized imagery.[115] The Leeds march took place in the public space of the City Square,[116] and the London march was led in the bohemian area Soho, which had a highly visible sex industry.[117]. Later, Reclaim the Night marches took place in Soho, London (1978), and Leeds City Centre (1980).

While the Grunwick strike was a massively supported and publicized strike, the Reclaim the Night marches attracted minimal attention despite appeals from the organizers to the national press and networks such as the BBC to cover these events.[118] The marches also differed from the Grunwick strike in that they were designated as women-only events. Notification about the first march circulated primarily in women's movement channels, such as WIRES, the *National Women's Liberation Newsletter*, originally based in Leeds, and in women's centers. Additionally, leaflets about the event were distributed in offices, factories, hospitals, shopping centers, and pubs.[119]

The first multicity Reclaim the Night march, which took place in 1977, was covered in a photo essay published in *Spare Rib*.[120] The cover of that issue featured a photograph by Angela Phillips depicting a group of women holding torches at the London march, accompanied by the headline, "We Will Walk without Fear: Reclaiming the Night, Leeds London Manchester York . . ." The *Spare Rib* photo essay included photographs from the Leeds and London marches, all of which were taken at close proximity, giving the viewer a sense of standing in the midst of the protesters and participating in the event. Included among the photographs was one by Phillips, captioned "London—plastering the windows" and depicting a woman pasting stickers that read, "This degrades women," on a Soho sex shop. Another photo, captioned "London—pornbrokers on the defensive," portrays two women confronting a man who looks angry and confused. Behind them is a poster plastered with a sticker that reads, "This degrades women" (figure 16).

The *Spare Rib* essay also included personal accounts by the marching women. A woman from Leeds wrote that before the march, she did not dare go out alone in the dark. She added that the spectacle of more than a hundred women marching with torches near the areas where women were attacked by Sutcliffe and other rapists made her realize that she was not alone.[121] Similarly, Pat Moan, who marched in London, expressed the exhilaration of moving freely in Soho and of not having to look down and appear as if she were going somewhere.[122]

The inclusion of these feminist accounts is consistent with the feminist strategy of politicizing the personal. Additionally, the photographic representations of the Reclaim the Night events in many ways claimed a space for women and for feminist resistance to violence directed at women, not only in the street but also in feminist media representations.

Moan also described the exuberance of walking through the streets of the sex industry area with other women, slapping stickers on windows, startling bystanders, and shouting slogans such as "sexist crap." She also mentioned confronting the manager of the Pussy Parlor, who angrily asked the women who pasted stickers on his shop window, "What does this mean?" to which

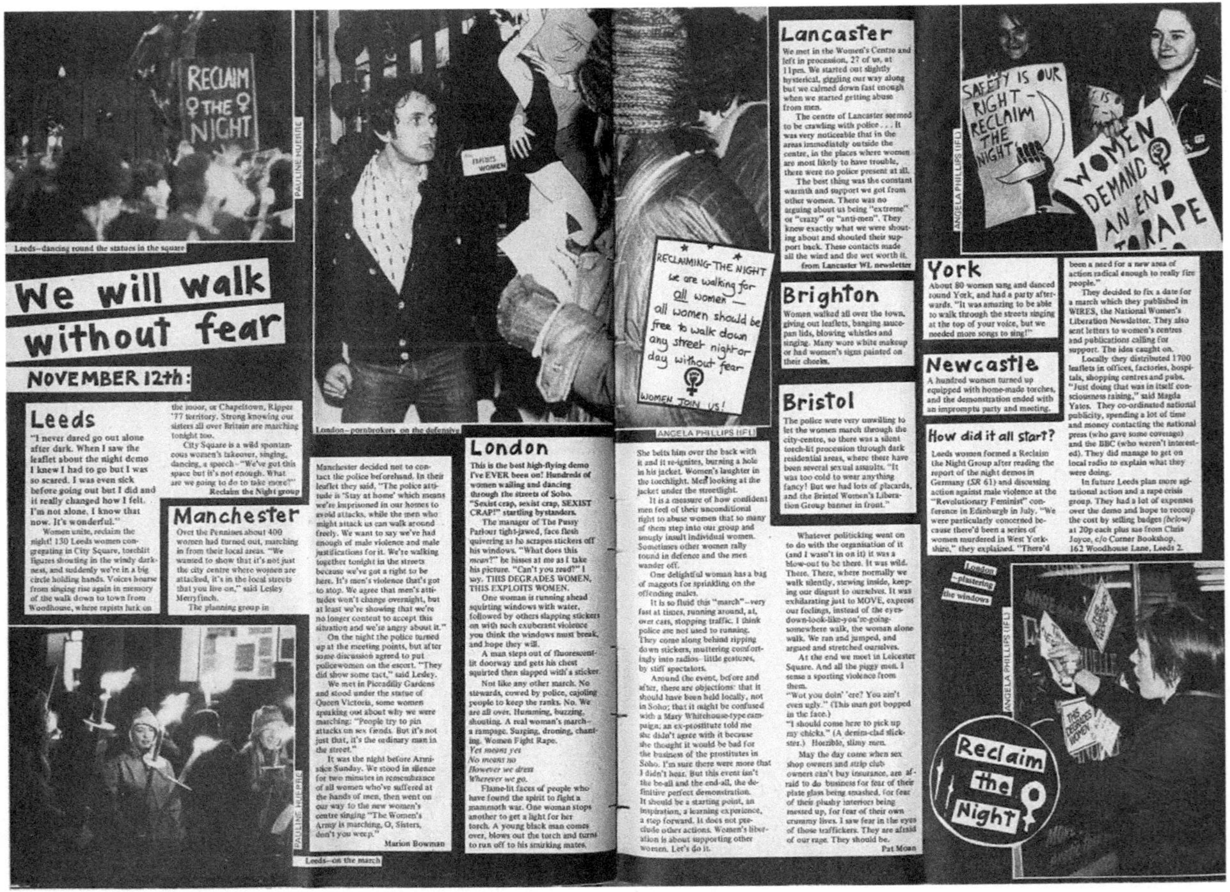
Leeds—dancing round the statues in the square

RECLAIM ♀ THE ♀ NIGHT

PAULINE HUERRE

We will walk without fear

NOVEMBER 12th:

Leeds

"I never dared go out alone after dark. When I saw the leaflet about the night demo I knew I had to go but I was so scared. I was even sick before going out but I did and it really changed how I felt. I'm not alone. I know that now. It's wonderful."

Women unite, reclaim the night! 130 Leeds women congregating in City Square, torchlit figures shouting in the windy darkness, and suddenly we're in a big circle holding hands. Voices hoarse from singing rise again in memory of the walk down to town from Woodhouse, where rapists lurk on the moor, or Chapeltown, Ripper '77 territory. Strong knowing our sisters all over Britain are marching tonight too.

City Square is a wild spontaneous women's takeover, singing, dancing, a speech—"We've got this space but it's not enough. What are we going to do to take more?"

Reclaim the Night group

Manchester

Over the Pennines about 400 women had turned out, marching in from their local areas. "We wanted to show that it's not just the city centre where women are attacked, it's in the local streets that you live on," said Lesley Merryfinch.

The planning group in Manchester decided not to contact the police beforehand. In their leaflet they said, "The police attitude is 'Stay at home' which means we're imprisoned in our homes to avoid attacks, while the men who might attack us can walk around freely. We want to say we've had enough of male violence and male justifications for it. We're walking together tonight in the streets because we've got a right to be here. It's men's violence that's got to stop. We agree that men's attitudes won't change overnight, but at least we're showing that we're no longer content to accept this situation and we're angry about it."

On the night the police turned up at the meeting points, but after some discussion agreed to put policewomen on the escort. "They did show some tact," said Lesley.

We met in Piccadilly Gardens and stood under the statue of Queen Victoria, some women speaking out about why we were marching: "People try to pin attacks on sex fiends. But it's not just that, it's the ordinary man in the street."

It was the night before Armistice Sunday. We stood in silence for two minutes in remembrance of all women who've suffered at the hands of men, then went on our way to the new women's centre singing "The Women's Army is marching, O, Sisters, don't you weep."

Marion Bowman

London—pornbrokers on the defensive

THIS DEGRADES WOMEN

London

This is the best high-flying demo I've EVER been on! Hundreds of women wailing and dancing through the streets of Soho. "Sexist crap, sexist crap, SEXIST CRAP!" startling bystanders.

The manager of The Pussy Parlour tight-jawed, face flesh quivering as he scrapes stickers off his windows. "What does this *mean*?" he hisses at me as I take his picture. "Can't you *read*?" I say. THIS DEGRADES WOMEN. THIS EXPLOITS WOMEN.

One woman is running ahead squirting windows with water, followed by others slapping stickers on with such exuberant violence you think the windows must break, and hope they will.

A man steps out of fluorescent-lit doorway and gets his chest squirted then slapped with a sticker.

Not like any other march. No stewards, cowed by police, cajoling people to keep the ranks. No. We are all over. Humming, buzzing, shouting. A real woman's march—a rampage. Surging, droning, chanting. Women Fight Rape.

Yes means yes
No means no
However we dress
Wherever we go.

Flame-lit faces of people who have found the spirit to fight a mammoth war. One woman stops another to get a light for her torch. A young black man comes over, blows out the torch and turns to run off to his smirking mates.

RECLAIMING THE NIGHT we are walking for all women— all women should be free to walk down any street night or day without fear ♀ WOMEN JOIN US!

ANGELA PHILLIPS (IFL)

She belts him over the back with it and it re-ignites, burning a hole in his jacket. Women's laughter in the torchlight. Men looking at the jacket under the streetlight.

It is a measure of how confident men feel of their unconditional right to abuse women that so many of them step into our group and smugly insult individual women. Sometimes other women rally round in defence and the men wander off.

One delightful woman has a bag of maggots for sprinkling on the offending males.

It is so fluid this "march"—very fast at times, running around, at, over cars, stopping traffic. I think police are not used to running. They come along behind ripping down stickers, muttering comfortingly into radios—little gestures, by stiff spectators.

Around the event, before and after, there are objections: that it should have been held locally, not in Soho; that it might be confused with a Mary Whitehouse-type campaign; an ex-prostitute told me she didn't agree with it because she thought it would be bad for the business of the prostitutes in Soho. I'm sure there were more that I didn't hear. But this event isn't the be-all and the end-all, the definitive perfect demonstration. It should be a starting point, an inspiration, a learning experience, a step forward. It does not preclude other actions. Women's liberation is about supporting other women. Let's do it.

Whatever politicking went on to do with the organisation of it (and I wasn't in on it) it was a blow-out to be there. It was wild. There. There, where normally we walk silently, stewing inside, keeping our disgust to ourselves. It was exhilarating just to MOVE, express our feelings, instead of the eyes-down-look-like-you're-going-somewhere walk, the woman alone walk. We ran and jumped, and argued and stretched ourselves.

At the end we meet in Leicester Square. And all the piggy men. I sense a sporting violence from them.

"Wot you doin' 'ere? You ain't even ugly." (This man got bopped in the face.)

"I should come here to pick up my chicks." (A denim-clad slickster.) Horrible, slimy men.

May the day come when sex shop owners and strip club owners can't buy insurance, are afraid to do business for fear of their plate glass being smashed, for fear of their plushy interiors being messed up, for fear of their own crummy lives. I saw fear in the eyes of those traffickers. They are afraid of our rage. They should be.

Pat Moan

Lancaster

We met in the Women's Centre and left in procession, 27 of us, at 11pm. We started out slightly hysterical, giggling our way along but we calmed down fast enough when we started getting abuse from men.

The centre of Lancaster seemed to be crawling with police . . . It was very noticeable that in the areas immediately outside the centre, in the places where women are most likely to have trouble, there were no police present at all.

The best thing was the constant warmth and support we got from other women. There was no arguing about us being "extreme" or "crazy" or "anti-men". They knew exactly what we were shouting about and shouted their support back. These contacts made all the wind and the wet worth it.

from Lancaster WL newsletter

Brighton

Women walked all over the town, giving out leaflets, banging saucepan lids, blowing whistles and singing. Many wore white makeup or had women's signs painted on their cheeks.

Bristol

The police were very unwilling to let the women march through the city-centre, so there was a silent torch-lit procession through dark residential areas, where there have been several sexual assaults. "It was too cold to wear anything fancy! But we had lots of placards, and the Bristol Women's Liberation Group banner in front."

SAFETY IS OUR RIGHT— RECLAIM THE NIGHT

WOMEN ♀ DEMAND AN END TO RAPE

ANGELA PHILLIPS (IFL)

York

About 80 women sang and danced round York, and had a party afterwards. "It was amazing to be able to walk through the streets singing at the top of your voice, but we needed more songs to sing!"

Newcastle

A hundred women turned up equipped with home-made torches, and the demonstration ended with an impromptu party and meeting.

How did it all start?

Leeds women formed a Reclaim the Night Group after reading the report of the night demos in Germany (*SR* 61) and discussing action against male violence at the "Revolutionary Feminist" conference in Edinburgh in July. "We were particularly concerned because there'd been a series of women murdered in West Yorkshire," they explained. "There'd been a need for a new area of action radical enough to really fire people."

They decided to fix a date for a march which they published in WIRES, the National Women's Liberation Newsletter. They also sent letters to women's centres and publications calling for support. The idea caught on.

Locally they distributed 1700 leaflets in offices, factories, hospitals, shopping centres and pubs. "Just doing that was in itself consciousness raising," said Magda Yates. They co-ordinated national publicity, spending a lot of time and money contacting the national press (who gave some coverage) and the BBC (who weren't interested). They did manage to get on local radio to explain what they were doing.

In future Leeds plan more agitational action and a rape crisis group. They had a lot of expenses over the demo and hope to recoup the cost by selling badges *(below)* at 20p each plus sae from Chris Joyce, c/o Corner Bookshop, 162 Woodhouse Lane, Leeds 2.

London—plastering the windows

ANGELA PHILLIPS (IFL)

Reclaim the Night ♀

Leeds—on the march

PAULINE HUERRE

FIG. 16 Angela Phillips (Report/IFL) and Pauline Huerre, Reclaim the Night photos, from "We Will Walk without Fear," *Spare Rib*, January 1978, 22–23, courtesy of Angela Phillips.

Moan responded, "Can't you read?" and took his photo.[123] Although Moan's photo was not included in the essay, the description of her personal account implied that photographing the man and thereby reducing him to an image was an act of defiance against what she viewed as his scrutinizing gaze toward women. A similar strategy of male objectification was used at a Reclaim the Night march in 1980 in Leeds City Centre, in which women "chatted up" passing men, pinched their bottoms, tweaked their cheeks, and told them they were "asking for trouble" for being out at night.[124]

As was mentioned in the previous chapter, the concept for Reclaim the Night was borrowed from similar marches that took place earlier in the United States and in a number of towns in West Germany.[125] The German march had a carnival-like atmosphere. In Berlin, the marching women painted themselves and used saucepans and pot lids to make noise. They used various strategies to chase away men who attacked the marching women, such as spraying them with flour, dye, and lemonade; handcuffing them; and chasing them away with firecrackers. They also spray-painted sex shops with women's symbols and ripped sexist posters off the city walls.[126] Like the Berlin march, the Reclaim the Night march in Britain used transgressive and playful strategies to highlight women's presence on the street and to defy the sexualized connotations associated with women on the street and in media representations. These defiant strategies and their social and cultural transgressions are implicit in the photographs Phillips took at Reclaim the Night, mentioned earlier. Such strategies also bring to mind Mikhail Bakhtin's notion of the carnival. According to Bakhtin, the medieval and Renaissance carnival allowed for a temporary suspension of social hierarchies. This suspension opened up a space for playful forms of communication liberated from otherwise imposed norms of etiquette predominant in everyday life.[127] Thus, during a carnival, the sacred becomes profane, authority is challenged and mocked, and all social groups join together in a saturnalia-like fusion.[128] Various feminist scholars employ ideas relating to Bakhtin's carnival in their feminist readings of cultural texts. Literature scholar Mary Russo, for example, uses the notion of the carnivalesque to analyze the subversive potential of the "misbehaving" female body.[129] Comparably, I argue that the feminist street strategies employed in Reclaim the Night, similar to Bakhtin's carnival, transformed the street into a site of spectacular disobedience. The marching women used humor, playful strategies, and "masculine" codes of behavior to challenge the official patriarchal culture and its codes of expected feminine comportment. Nonetheless, although the carnival offered transgressive freedom to break social hierarchies, it was not socially subversive. At the end of the carnival, a number of closing formalities took place that signified the return to the "normal," repressive rule. Thus, the carnival was a sanctioned form of political transgression, during which restrictions on public behavior were officially relaxed, only to be restored later.[130] In contrast, the discussed feminist street events employed transgressive strategies and reversed gender-assigned modes of behavior in order to disrupt and to generate an all-encompassing social transformation.

Punk Feminism and Defiance

The defiant attitude of "misbehavior" that women displayed in Reclaim the Night marches should be viewed in the context of the various cultural manifestations of the time. This defiant attitude seems to correspond with the punk, male-dominated subculture that gained force in the mid-1970s in Britain.[131] The aggressive masculinity of punk was also utilized by some female punks to transgress culture expectations of femininity. In his essay "Hiding in the Light," cultural theorist Dick Hebdige discussed women's position in the punk subculture, suggesting that while women in subcultures were often silenced or made in the image of men as their accessories, punk women often reshaped this approach by publicly parodying various iconographic images of "fallen womanhood," behaviors that Hebdige viewed as a refusal to submit to a dominating gaze.[132] Punk subculture was also gender defiant, since sexual ambiguity and androgyny were part of its visual esthetics. In addition, like Reclaim the Night, punk subculture had a political street presence, particularly within the Rock against Racism concerts.[133]

Punk zines were also a product of punk subculture. Such zines incorporated distinct aesthetic elements such as hand-drawn images, cut-and-pasted photographs, advertising slogans, newspaper headlines, and other printed media in order to form a countermessage.[134] A similar aesthetic was employed in publicity flyers for punk concerts.[135] Rock against Racism, a movement that produced a plethora of visual ephemera, also had its own punk zine, *Temporary Hoarding*, which employed these aesthetic strategies.[136] Moreover, a number of feminist punk zines were being published in the 1970s. Among them was *Jolt*, self-published in 1977 by Lucy Whitman (then Lucy Toothpaste). *Jolt* initially emerged from Whitman's interest in punk music and the possibilities it opened up for women; it also engaged in antifascism and antiracism politics. Like other punk zines, *Jolt* had a strong visual aspect and used collage as a predominant aesthetic strategy.[137] Whitman was also involved in the production of the zine *Drastic Measures* published by Rock against Sexism, which was a feminist alternative to Rock against Racism, and was a member of the *Spare Rib* collective.[138] The aesthetic developments in punk zines also infiltrated into the design of various feminist publications. The layout of the Reclaim the Night essay in *Spare Rib*, which consisted of photographs presented alongside strips of typed and handwritten text, was reflective of the cut-and-paste collage strategy of punk zines.

The punk attitude and visual language of punk zines can also be found in the collectively produced feminist publication *Shocking Pink* (1981–1982, 1987–1992).[139] The cover of *Shocking Pink*'s second issue consisted of an illustration that portrayed men and various symbols of femininity, such as a bridal dress, a women's magazine, and a high-heeled shoe, being pushed off a cliff. It also depicted a woman running Superman over with a bulldozer and a group of women triumphantly heading toward a mountain peak. Similar elements could be found in the comic strip *Penny Sillin* that was published in this issue. This comic strip focuses on Penny, a young feminist punk, who overhears men making racist and misogynistic remarks on the subway and squirts them with a water gun. She then emerges onto the street and is relieved to see two male punks like herself. However, when one of them describes a sexual encounter he has had with a girl, Penny accuses him of being "normal" and dumps a trashcan on him (figure 17).[140]

During this period, punk attitude also intersected with feminist art and musical performance. This can be viewed notably in the activity of feminist artist and musician Linder Sterling, who was also the lead singer of the Manchester punk band Ludus. Among Linder's activities was production of the art punk zine *The Secret Public* (1978) with music journalist Jon Savage. Linder also created a number of photomontages that depicted sexualized representations of women's bodies. Linder's images incorporated punk strategies of cut-and-paste, as well as Dada, the erotic imagery by British pop artists such as Richard Hamilton, media advertising, and pornography.[141] Linder's images developed alongside, and stood at odds with, the then radical and revolutionary feminist debates about pornography. While Linder claimed to have been deeply influenced by radical feminist texts by American

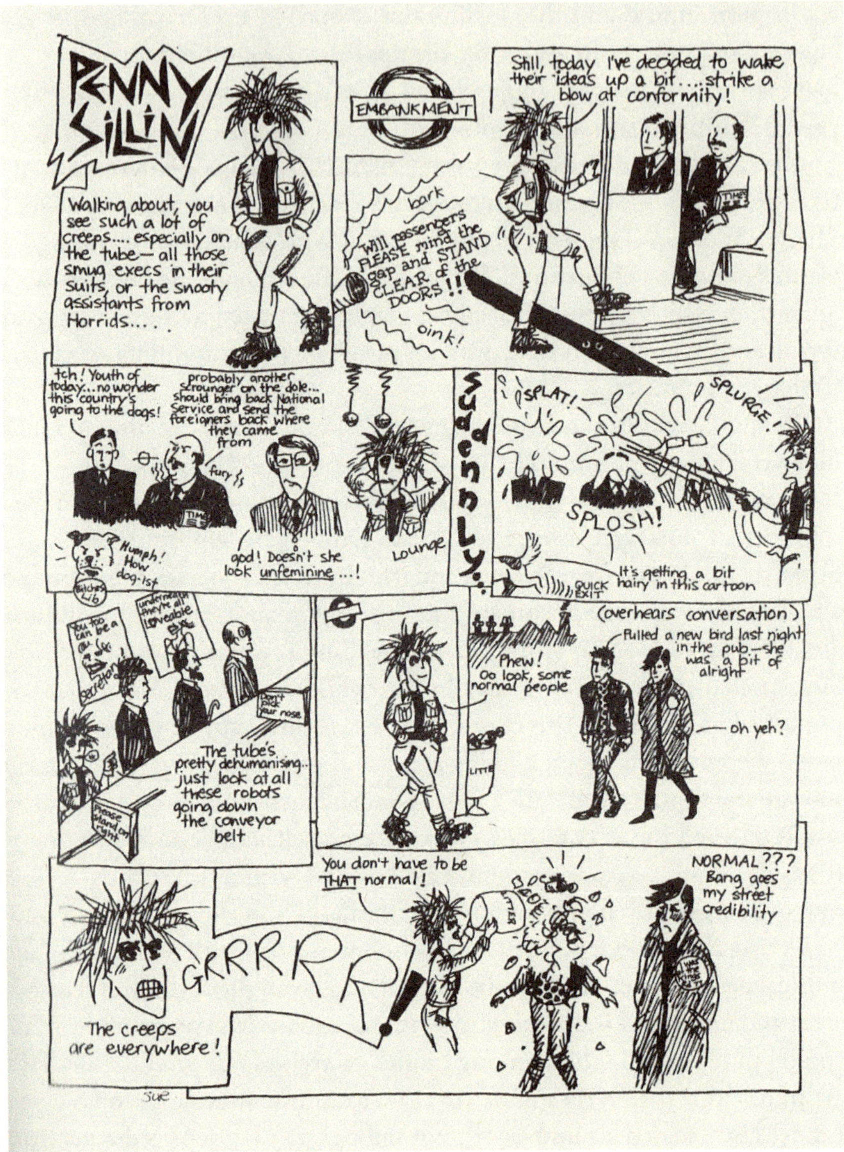

FIG. 17 Sue, *Penny Sillin*, from *Shocking Pink* 2 (1981): 4.

writers such as Betty Friedan and Kate Millett, who influenced feminist antipornography debates, she perceived her erotic images as a strategy for détourning female objectification.[142]

Linder's work was also part of the developments in feminist punk music that confronted gender boundaries and employed anger, aggression, and sexuality to explore female power.[143] She employed such feminist punk strategies in her music performances as a member of the band Ludus. For instance, in one of Ludus's shows in Manchester, which was performed for a predominantly male audience, Linder littered the floor with red-colored tampons and wore a black dildo. Her performance arguably also resembled the contemporary feminist performance art from the United States in which female artists employed their bodies to claim female subjectivity. In many ways, Linder's performance recalls Carolee Schneemann's performance *Interior Scroll* in 1975, in which the artist extracted a scroll from her vagina and read it to the audience, and Lynda Benglis's controversial "pinup" in *Artforum* in 1974, in which she posed wearing a dildo.[144]

Police Violence and Reclaim the Night

As in the Grunwick strike, police violence targeted women demonstrators during the third Reclaim the Night march. Photographs of such violent occurrences similarly appeared in feminist publications. The third Reclaim the Night march took place on Halloween night in 1978 in Soho, London, and it differed from earlier marches, in which the demonstrators marched fairly uninterrupted in the streets and the police generally served as onlookers aiming to prevent mischief.[145] In contrast, during this third march, as covered by the feminist magazine *Women's Report*, the police acted brutally. On the night of the march, approximately two hundred women carrying torches and dressed as witches participated.[146] When the march reached the porn theater New Swedish Cinema Club, a man came out of the theater and hit one of the marchers on the head with a chair. At that moment, police piled out of vans with truncheons and began to hit women viciously. In this attack, over thirty women were wounded, and three were taken to the hospital with severe head injuries. The police also arrested sixteen women on charges of obstruction of order and insulting behavior. *Women's Report* mentioned that the *Guardian* and the then-underground magazine *Time Out* were the only news outlets to cover these violent events. The *Guardian* criticized the police's unwillingness to conduct an internal inquiry and their statement to *Time Out* suggesting that the women's injuries consisted of fairly light blows to the head. *Women's Report* claimed that the police violence in Reclaim the Night showed that the women's movement was tolerated as long as it was invisible but was considered a threat once it became noticeable at a politicized site such as the street.[147] This observation seems to illustrate the transition of the Reclaim the Night events from what might have been taken as a passing episode to incidents that were perceived to be a threat to the social order.

The cover of the issue of *Women's Report* on this event featured a photograph by Diane Briley of a policeman grabbing a woman. The image was superimposed by two other ones: one depicted a woman looking startled, possibly after being attacked, and the other showing a policeman exuberantly attacking a demonstrator. These images were ironically accompanied by the headline, "Police Protection on Reclaim the Night" (figure 18).

This *Women's Report* issue asked readers who photographed incidents of police violence during the Reclaim the Night march to send their photographs to Eileen Meredith, who represented the sixteen arrested women.[148] This request by *Women's Report* could perhaps be understood in the context of the release of Ethel Findlay, who had photographed a policeman hitting her with a truncheon while she was on the ground. According to an article in *Spare Rib*, Findlay used the photograph in court to prove to the magistrate that the police had supplied false evidence. Consequently, one of the attacking policemen was forced to admit that he had crossed out a sentence in his notebook in which he described himself hitting a woman over the head. The magistrate dropped Findlay's case and released her.[149]

Thus, photographs capturing police violence against women demonstrators at Reclaim the Night were used by *Women's Report* to bring these incidents to the attention of the public and to counter their lack of media representation. In addition, these photographs proved useful in the sphere of law, thus further demonstrating their perceived feminist and political relevance.

Feminist Street Strategies and Challenging Representation

Reclaim the Night marches were also a public counterresponse to the media's and the police's recommendation that women stay off the streets after dark.[150] Other feminist marches responded to this issue, one of which was a militant protest organized by Women against Violence against Women in Leeds in November 1980. The protest was attended by approximately five hundred women, who marched with torches through town into the Odeon theater, which was showing the film *Dressed to Kill*.[151] This protest was

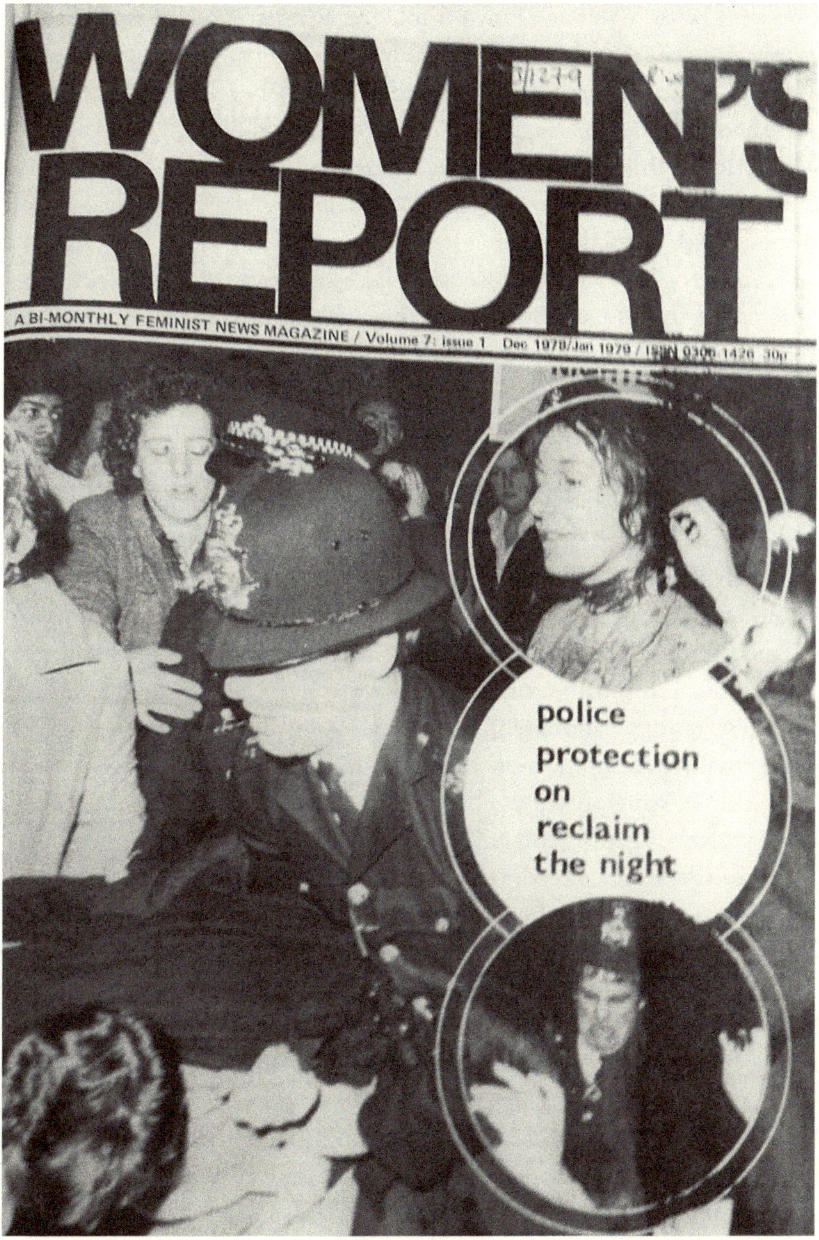

FIG. 18 Diane Briley, photo, Reclaim the Night, London, October 31, 1978, *Women's Report*, December 1978–January 1979, cover.

consistent with Women against Violence against Women's call in *Leeds Other Paper* that month for women to resist the curfew and impose a curfew on men.[152] Similarly, Eileen Fairweather's essay "Leeds: Curfew on Men," published in *Spare Rib*, suggested that men should be held responsible for their actions. This essay also implied that the Reclaim the Night marches responded to the media's and the police's spectacularization of Sutcliffe's attacks and their focus on the "virtue" of Sutcliffe's victims rather than on the severity of his crimes. Moreover, the essay criticized the *Daily Mirror* for referring to those of Sutcliffe's victims who worked in the sex industry as "good-time girls offering sex for sale" and for using headlines such as "Even Prostitutes Don't Deserve to Die like This."[153] Fairweather's essay also challenged the West Yorkshire police for suggesting that the murder of Josephine Whittaker, one of Sutcliffe's victims, was a mistake on his part since she was a "perfectly respectable girl."[154] It is worth noting that it was later revealed that the public was erroneously led to believe that Sutcliffe was solely a prostitute killer. By the end of 1980, Sutcliffe had already claimed thirteen murder victims, six of whom were "innocent" women.[155]

Thus, women activists viewed marching in the street—particularly in areas dominated by the sex industry—as a way to claim mobility and resist existing stereotypes about women's sexuality. In addition, the photographic and textual representation of the march in publications such as *Spare Rib* countered existing portrayals by the police and the mainstream media of sexual violence against women.

Feminist resistance to the coverage of sexual violence by the media was also manifested around this time in the United States. This can be viewed, for example, in Suzanne Lacy and Leslie Labowitz's media action performance piece *In Mourning and in Rage*, which they performed outside Los Angeles City Hall on December 13, 1977. This performance challenged the media representation of the crimes of Kenneth Bianchi, nicknamed the Hillside Strangler, who raped and murdered a number of young women in Los Angeles between 1977 and 1978. As did the British media in its coverage of Sutcliffe, the American press exploited the case for its sensationalist value and ignored its tragic effects on women's safety. In response, Lacy and Labowitz created a public forum of feminist collective action that contested this abuse of women. In the course of their performance, ten women wearing black stood outside Los Angeles City Hall. Two motorcycles and twenty cars driven by women escorted a hearse and circled the building. Each car was plastered with stickers that read "Funeral" and "Stop Violence against

Women." The motorcade occasionally stopped for the news and media representatives that Lacy and Labowitz had assembled before the event. The women dressed in black outside city hall walked up to a microphone and made statements such as, "I am here for the ten women who were strangled between October 11 and November 29!" while a chorus of additional women answered, "We fight back!"[156] In another work, which was part of a program of works from the project *Three Weeks in May*, Lacy collaborated with other women and stamped the word *rape* on a map on display near city hall to indicate where reported sexual assaults took place. Photographic documentation of this work was included in *Issue: Social Strategies by Women Artists*, a feminist art show at the Institute of Contemporary Arts that will be discussed in chapter 4.[157] Thus, in both Britain and the United States, the street was used as a space of spectacular performance to protest sexual violence against women and its media representation. However, while the British Reclaim the Night march hardly attracted the media's attention, *In Mourning and in Rage* was in many ways designed for the media and received wide coverage by local and statewide news. Moreover, the event held by American feminist artists was staged as a dramatic performance that resembled other forms of feminist performance art. Reclaim the Night was, in contrast, primarily a political march situated within the street politics of 1970s Britain. The photographic documentation of Reclaim the Night and its circulation were perceived as political and removed from art practice. Furthermore, the lack of media interest in Reclaim the Night sheds light on the significant political role of feminist street photographers, the small number of feminist publications that published their photographs, and these photographers' and publications' desire to counter mainstream media representations.

Conclusion

During the 1970s, the street in Britain was a highly political site at which various political advocates represented themselves, clashed, and formed alliances. Correspondingly, street photographers viewed themselves as active participants in demonstrations and as political activists. They also viewed their photographs as providing a "truthful" alternative to the photographic representations in the mainstream media and national press. The images that these photographers produced were often aimed at promoting particular social concerns. Moreover, the street presence of photographers in political demonstrations had a performative function. They did not simply convey what was happening on the street but also became part of the action. The photographs and articles in the Lewisham issue of *Camerawork* were aimed at criticizing the media's disregard of racism in its representations of the Battle of Lewisham. This issue challenged the portrayals of the police as brave victims as opposed to an oppressive force that turned against antiracism demonstrators and political photographers. Notably, the Lewisham issue of *Camerawork* mostly depicted violent encounters between men and disregarded the presence of women demonstrators and women photographers at the event. Furthermore, this *Camerawork* issue overlooked the existing intersections between feminism and antiracist views voiced in various feminist publications. Among these were publications such as *Jolt*, which engaged in antifascist and antiracist politics, as well as *Spare Rib* and *Women's Report*, which addressed issues such as the police violence that targeted women at the Grunwick strike and Reclaim the Night marches. Such publications also described police violence against women as not only a concern of the women's movement but also an indication of broader manifestations of extensive police control during that period. Feminist photographers Michael Ann Mullen and Diane Briley, whose works were published in feminist publications, documented police violence against women demonstrators but also asserted their own presence as women and as feminist photographers at street events. Furthermore, the street encounters between feminist photographers and feminist demonstrators opened up a space for feminist identification, the exchange of feminist arguments, and the cultivation of a shared sense of feminist collectivity. Thus, feminist photographers Val Wilmer, Maggie Murray, Angela Phillips, Mullen, and Briley challenged their marginalization as women photographers. Moreover, the dynamic produced between feminist photographers and women demonstrators opened up a space for ultimately challenging the marginalization of a feminist perspective in mainstream media, as well as in leftist publications. In a similar manner, photographers Homer Sykes, Caro Webb, Paul McNicholls, and Andrew Ward set out to portray Jayaben Desai and her immigrant coworkers as the main protagonists of the Grunwick strike, a depiction that was missing in the mainstream press in the early days of the strike. Phillips also captured and thus participated in the street strategies used by women during Reclaim the Night. Although the Asian women strikers apparently did not photograph the strike, they symbolically intervened in the sphere of representation by ceasing their work at the film-processing plant. Additionally, as mentioned earlier, Desai set out to influence how the Grunwick strikers were represented by the media by telling picketers with which publications they should avoid communicating.

The photographs of these events represented the street as a gendered site at which white and nonwhite femininity and masculinity were present in particular ways. This was manifested in the sexualized connotations of women in the street, as well as in the marginalized position of women street photographers. These gendered divisions paralleled a feminist discourse that was occurring around that time that challenged the arguments of the existing literature on urbanity and the street and criticized this literature's exclusion of women's experiences. Also challenged as well as appropriated was the gendered association of women's presence on the street with a "threat" to the social order. The Asian women in the Grunwick strike drew extra attention to their cause through their public appearance, and the women in Reclaim the Night employed transgressive behavior for the same purpose.

The Grunwick strike and the Reclaim the Night marches were political street events that differed in their impact and political concerns but were similar in that both promoted women's rights. Moreover, in both events, photography and visual production were among the tools employed to pose political arguments. The public assembly of demonstrators and photographers at such political street events in many ways formed a counterpublic for which the street served as a site for momentarily engaging in alternative politics. Within this counterpublic, different political groups formed alliances and shaped a shared political will that challenged state and police power.

Thus, despite its failure, the Grunwick strike became a significant political mobilizing force for the British Left and the women's movement. It also placed the issue of immigrant workers' rights on trade unions' agendas and motivated the emergence of black feminist organizations. In these organizations, the connections between racial differences and feminist concerns were rethought and negotiated and thus arguably became situated within the broader politics of British grassroots formations.

Reclaim the Night, although less publicized than the Grunwick strike, involved the use of street strategies to increase the awareness of feminist issues such as rape, violence against women, and pornography in the public sphere in a number of British cities. Resistance to these demonstrators by the police and various passersby was perhaps suggestive of the march's effective political force and perceived disruption of the social order.

Furthermore, in both the Grunwick strike and Reclaim the Night, gendered connotations of women in the public sphere were challenged. The striking Asian women from the Grunwick film factory defied their culture's patriarchal codes of female "respectability" by publicly participating in the picket line. Similarly, the marching women at Reclaim the Night playfully used masculine tropes of defiant confrontation that were reminiscent of the punk subculture in order to make themselves visible and heard.

Some street photographers maintained that their images were capable of radically transforming society and capturing the "truth" of political events that were otherwise misrepresented by the media institution and its ideological structures. However, the capacity and assumed transparency of street photography were questioned by the then emerging photography theory concerning the politics of representation, its effects, and how it operated.

Alternative and feminist publications such as *Camerawork*, *Spare Rib*, and *Women's Report*, which published many of the photographs discussed in this chapter, had a smaller circulation than national publications. The readership of these magazines was likely to already support the political arguments advanced by the photographs presented in these small publications. Therefore, such publications could hardly overpower pervasive mainstream messages. Nonetheless, the emergence of street photography and the platforms that were invested in publishing it is indicative of the political significance of the street and the photographic representations of it in the period under study.

Additionally, the political currency of the street and its photographic representations in the 1970s and early 1980s highlighted several central political issues in Britain, including racism, workers' rights, women's rights, immigration, police control, and violence against women. As a result, photography was viewed as a tool capable of promoting radical intervention. Furthermore, the photographs of these events became objects that supported arguments concerning these issues as well as the impact of photographic representation.

4

Entering the Museum

As seen in the previous chapters, feminist photographers in 1970s Britain often claimed a critical distance from the dominant museum culture and set themselves apart from it. Thus, they often exhibited in spaces such as community centers, alternative galleries, and feminist magazines. Similarly, politicized photography practices in the 1970s were featured mostly in venues such as political publications, libraries, community centers, pamphlets, and the streets.[1] Toward the end of the 1970s, however, there was a discernible change as feminist photographers, politicized photographers, and feminist artists began to exhibit their works in fine art museums and galleries. This shift in exhibition venues involved a strategy aimed at challenging the art museum as a culturally elitist place and transforming it into a forum for expressing political arguments to a wider public.[2] In this chapter I show that while some feminist photographers and artists viewed these changes as a necessary claim to a space of "their own," others perceived their work's entry into a mainstream cultural space as an act of "selling out."

Another development toward the end of the decade was an increased interest in creating a permanent feminist photography space that would advance the production, exhibition, and discursive development of feminist photography. These new tendencies were explored in early feminist photography shows, feminist art, and feminist photography exhibitions in major fine art institutions, as well as in the foundation of the first feminist photography space in Britain. Feminist photography's shift toward institutionalization marks a turning point in its approach to exhibition venues and was a precursor to the compromises and ruptures within feminist photography in the 1980s.

Historicizing the Fine Art Museum

The art museum emerged following the formation of the modern nation-state in late eighteenth-century Europe; as such, it was linked to the institutions and narratives that produced national mythologies.[3] The art museum thus developed into an institution that employed a set of disciplinary practices that constituted and defined cultural and social value. The emergence of the art museum led to the appearance and circulation of new discourses—including the discipline of art history—that played a role in sustaining the art museum's status and exercising its own practices of power.[4] One of the principal ideals of the art museum—frequently reconfigured and at times challenged—was aesthetic value. Furthermore, the practice of viewing and contemplating the museum's objects made possible various transformative experiences of eminent pleasure, moral enlightenment, and spiritual revelation.[5] Previously, the production of art objects displayed in museums had often been and generally continues to be framed as an elevated activity disconnected from social function. Networks of various interested economic and cultural agents—including patrons, dealers, critics, publishers, collectors, and gallery owners—sustained and articulated the material and symbolic value of the museum and its objects, and they continue to do so today.[6] The modern museum also employs a set of conventions including the picture frame, the pedestal, and the gallery wall as disciplinary structures to mark museum objects with value and designate them as "art." In addition, the museum structure itself operates as a frame that encloses, displays, and cuts itself off from the world as a pure interiority saturated with worth. Thus, the museum's delineation—like that produced by the frame, the pedestal, and the gallery wall—is effaced by the visibility of the artworks that it contains, further marking the division between "inside" and "outside" the museum with unquestioned authority. Consequently, the museum as "frame" grants its objects the status of art by separating them from all the heterogeneous objects it excludes, which it simultaneously reduces to nonart.[7]

The Diversity of Photography and Its Meaning

Since its introduction in the nineteenth century, photography has not been perceived as a unified medium but rather has been defined in multiple ways by the different institutions and discursive fields within which it has operated (commerce, law, art, etc.).[8] Not exclusively framed as art objects, photographs have been featured in museums with different agendas, such as anthropological, historical, or scientific ones. Furthermore, within such museums, photographs have had diverse functions, such as providing evidence for other objects on view, acting as supporting documents, illustrating events, and demanding aesthetic consideration as artifacts themselves.[9]

Photography's undisputed place in the fine art museum and its contemporary fine art status was in many ways advanced by the Museum of Modern Art (MoMA) in New York, which opened in 1929. Early on, this museum incorporated photography into its exhibition space. This was notably manifested in *Photography 1839–1937* (1937), an exhibition curated by Beaumont Newhall, then the museum's librarian. This show comprised over eight hundred photography works grouped according to technical processes (daguerreotype, calotype, wet plate, and dry plate) and their present-day applications (press photography, infrared and x-ray photography, astronomical photography, and "creative" photography).[10] The advancement of photography as a fine art practice was distinctly championed by John Szarkowski, the director of MoMA's Department of Photography between 1962 and 1991. Szarkowski wrote extensively about photography and curated a number of influential photography exhibitions that set out to redefine photography as a medium possessing a legitimate autonomous aesthetic nature.[11] Among the exhibitions that he curated was *New Documents* (1967), which featured previously unknown photographers Diane Arbus, Lee Friedlander, and Garry Winogrand. These photographers were advocated as marking a shift in American documentary photography toward individual expression and stylization.[12]

MoMA's promotion of photography as fine art had a major impact outside the United States. The Arts Council of Great Britain's attitude toward photography was in many ways influenced by MoMA's attitude, which prompted the Arts Council to recognize photography's potential. The shift in the Arts Council's attitude was notably embodied by the formation of its Photography Committee in 1973.[13] This committee was headed by photography officer Barry Lane (in office from 1973 to 1995), who was a key figure in photography's development in 1970s Britain. Lane asserted that unlike art, photography had its own techniques, social and aesthetic concerns, and public outlets that deserved further attention. He recognized that photography was an undersupported medium in Britain, hardly exhibited in art galleries and museums, and rarely addressed by art publications. When Lane worked at the Arts Council, he received an £800 scholarship from Kodak to travel to New York to meet with Szarkowski and spend time at MoMA's photography department. Lane attests that this visit further influenced his thinking about photography's potential. He claims that he was impressed that the U.S. National Endowment of Arts supported art and photography equally. These findings motivated him to continue to improve the Arts Council of Great Britain's attitude toward photography and to develop further ways to support it.[14] Thus, under his leadership, the Photography Committee encouraged the production of photography by funding a number of regional photography galleries, offering grants to a variety of photography projects, and supporting several photography-related publications—such as *Camerawork*, *Ten.8*, and *Creative Camera*—and photography exhibition catalogs.[15]

MoMA and the Arts Council of Great Britain engaged in several early collaborations. For instance, in 1969 Szarkowski curated an exhibition of British photographer Bill Brandt's works for MoMA; this work was also curated in the following year for the Arts Council's Hayward Gallery in London.[16] It should be noted that while Szarkowski's activity at MoMA advocated photography as a distinct fine art practice, the Arts Council was chiefly interested in encouraging photographic activity. The Photography Committee did not insist on a certain standard of image quality or reject politically engaged projects.[17]

The Arts Council supported photography produced within the context of conceptual art shows featured in fine arts venues. Yet photography's inclusion in conceptual art shows was often intended to mark a distance from art values.[18] The biggest conceptual art show that took place in 1970s Britain was *The New Art* (1972), an exhibition curated by Anne Seymour for the Hayward Gallery, a main Arts Council contemporary art gallery at the time. Some of the artists included were Victor Burgin, Gilbert & George, Keith Arnatt, John Stezaker, and Art & Language. Seymour described their work as expanding beyond the aestheticism of modern art and repudiating an aesthetic discussion of art.[19]

Feminist, Politicized Photography, and the Museum

During the 1970s feminist and women artists were notably excluded from the fine art museum and from other fine art networks, institutions, and discourses. The marginalization experienced by women artists became a feminist issue that was addressed early on by feminist art collectives such as the Women's Workshop of the Artists Union. This body was a subgroup of the Artists Union that, like the Artists's Union, desired to defend artists' rights, challenge the myth of individual creativity and the exploitation of artists, as well as to promote collective creative production. The Women's Workshop, however, also tackled issues pertaining to women artists. These issues included breaking women artists' isolation in order to advance feminist collaboration, protesting against the discrimination of women within art education institutions, and challenging the lack of public acknowledgment of women artists.[20] The Women's Workshop members were informed by the politics of the women's movement, as well as its egalitarian and collaborative strategies. The group members met regularly to discuss each other's works and plan group projects.[21] Among the Women's Workshop projects was *Women and Work* (1975), a documentary exhibition at the South London Art Gallery. This show was organized by Mary Kelly, Margaret Harrison, and Kay Hunt; focused on women workers in a Metal Box Company factory in Southwark; and included photography, film, and installations.[22]

The Women's Workshop members familiarized themselves with feminist artwork and debates related to feminist art from elsewhere in the world, particularly the United States.[23] A distinctly influential feminist art project was *Womanhouse* (1971–1972), which was initiated by Judy Chicago, Miriam Schapiro, and their students from the feminist art program at the California Institute of the Arts in Los Angeles. Over the course of this project, they collectively converted an old mansion into a feminist art space in which they exhibited their art works and performance pieces that addressed issues such as domestic labor, menstruation, sexuality, and childhood.[24] Consciousness raising, a distinct women's movement strategy for politicizing women's personal experiences, was one of the techniques used to develop this project.[25] *Womanhouse* served as a model for various British feminist art projects. For example, in the early 1970s, the Women's Workshop, inspired by *Womanhouse*, planned to take over a derelict house, decorate it with art expressive of women's lives, and use it as a studio and meeting place.[26]

The Women's Art Alliance, established by New York feminists, was another feminist art collective active in 1970s Britain that set out to develop various forms of feminist art production. This group facilitated a makeshift space for feminist art production and exhibition. The Women's Art Alliance was led by American artist Kay Sterling, who later left the alliance, and was operated in a rundown building in London's Regent Park. Their meeting place had a bookshop and a space for classes in drawing, theater, and drumming, as well as an exhibition location. The collective's first show, *Off the Fence*, featured various feminist works, including photographs by Alexis Hunter.[27]

Thus, feminist art and feminist photography were not always produced or exhibited separately. Moreover, as discussed earlier, both feminist artists and feminist photographers were informed by the politics and collective strategies of the women's movement and utilized them to challenge their marginalization. Despite these overlaps, I will show that feminist photography had distinct attributes situated within the developments in the field of photography in 1970s Britain, its prevalent politicization at the time, and marginalization within the fine art museum.

Early Feminist Photography Shows

Among the few photography exhibitions that were held in the early 1970s, a small number were dedicated to feminist concerns. *Women* (1974) and *Men* (1976), exhibited at the Half Moon Gallery in London, were among the earliest photography exhibitions pertaining to feminist issues.[28] While *Women* and *Men* were small shows overlooked by feminist art history, I argue that they are significant, as some of their themes, arguments, and strategies would reappear in feminist shows exhibited in art museums at the end of the decade.

The Half Moon Gallery was situated in the hallway of the Half Moon Theatre, a community left-wing theater considered at the time to be more prominent than its gallery.[29] The Half Moon Theatre was also home to the feminist theater company the Women's Theatre Group, whose activity set out to challenge the limited availability of roles for theater actresses and to contest the mainstream theater's demand that actresses be stereotypically attractive.[30] *Women* and *Men* were organized by Julia Meadows, who volunteered at the Half Moon Gallery and was a member of the Women's

Theatre Group.[31] She planned *Women* and *Men* collectively with a group of women photographers assembled by word of mouth because there were only a few visible women photographers at that time.[32] The participants included Angela Phillips, Val Wilmer, Maggie Murray, Sally Greenhill, Claire Schwob, Diane Orson, and Jessie Ann Matthew.[33] This group, like other woman-centered formations during the same period, deliberately consisted of both professional and less experienced photographers. This strategy was viewed as a means to foster an egalitarian climate for women who were otherwise marginalized in social and cultural spheres.

The preparation for *Women* began in 1972 and the exhibition was in 1974; soon after this, the group began to plan *Men*. The organizing principle behind *Women* was to exhibit photographs taken of women by women, whereas that of *Men* was to show photographs of men taken by women.[34] Both shows' ideas and selection processes were developed collectively by the group.[35] Consciousness raising was the primary method used to conceptualize these exhibitions and discuss the photographs and the experience of taking them.[36] Meadows recalled that the questions that the group addressed in their discussions included the following: How do women look at women? How do women look at men? Do women take pictures differently from men? How does the power imbalance between men and women affect photographic representation? Is there anything inherently different between a photograph taken by a man and one taken by a woman?[37]

Thus, although *Women* and *Men* were not publicized as feminist photography shows, their production was informed by collective forms of organization associated with the women's movement and with the feminist strategy of consciousness raising. The photographers participating in both these shows engaged in finding ways of employing photography to articulate feminist arguments and define a woman-based identity and outlook. Several women photographers who attended the planning meeting drifted away because they were reluctant to be identified with a show of "women photographers,"[38] which suggested that the show had feminist connotations and was regarded with caution by some.

One of the photographs by Schwob that was included in the *Women* show and on its publicity poster features a housewife in her disorganized kitchen happily embracing her children (figure 19). Although this photo does not appear particularly radical, Meadows stated that it was one of several that showed women in a variety of social roles, including as mothers, workers, and writers. She indicated that this image might have been read as a "positive"

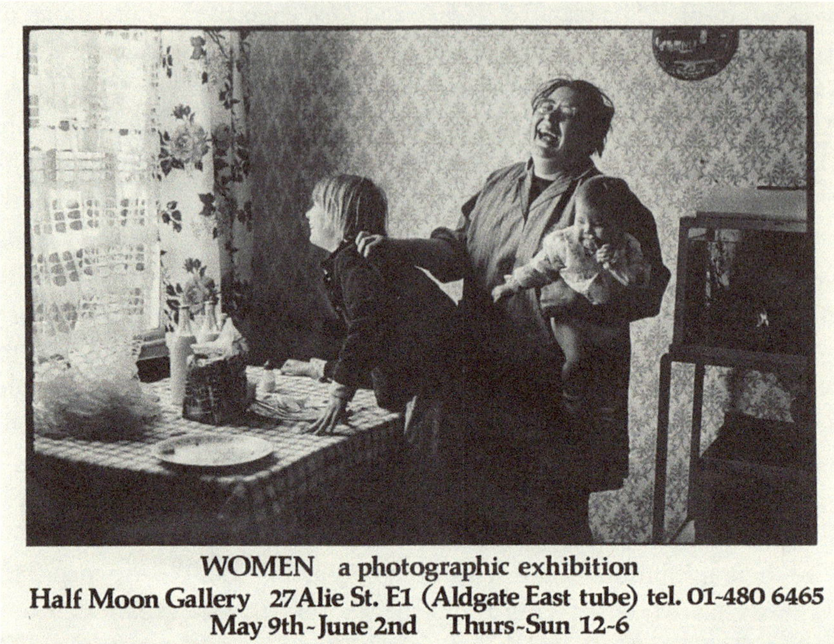

FIG. 19 Exhibition poster for *Women*, Half Moon Gallery, London, 1974, photograph by Claire Schwob, courtesy of Julia Meadows.

representation of a woman managing to make "a go of things" at home.[39] This view was consistent with the feminist discussion at the time regarding positive and negative images of women and with feminist debates that politicized housework. For example, this debate was at the center of the art project called *Portrait of the Artist as Housewife* (1974–1976), which was organized by the Bristol-based women's artist group Feministo. This project began as a long-distance consciousness-raising activity in the form of mail exchanges among women artists living in distant regions. The women sent one another small-scale works made from domestic objects that addressed their experiences in the domestic sphere, motherhood, and their sense of isolation. One of the projects in the show featured a place setting that consisted of a salad plate on top of which a papier-mâché reclining female nude was placed, as if ready to be consumed.[40] Feminist interpretations of domestic labor were also included in local publications in Leeds, such as Lee Comer's book *Wedlocked Women* (1974) and the collection of articles *Conditions of Illusion* (1974), both of which analyzed the social and economic subordination of housewives.[41] These were arguably influenced by the Wages for Housework campaign that was led in 1972 by the feminists Selma James and Mariarosa Dalla Costa, who argued that housework was a productive activity and should therefore receive compensation.[42] Thus, the image of the housewife in *Women*, although not overtly critical, was related to other feminist interpretations of art practice and debates of the time.

Women brought many people into the gallery and went on a tour of various community centers.[43] Meadows recalled that *Women* received favorable reviews from feminists and the national mainstream press, though Meadows attributed its support to the show's lack of explicit or controversial feminist statements.[44] However, *Women* was innovative in other ways. It was the first photography show in Britain to exhibit photographs taken exclusively by women that represented other women. Additionally, its collective strategies of organization challenged traditional forms of fine art exhibition. This show also challenged fine art's emphasis on aesthetic value, its uncritical positioning of women as objects of representation, and its traditional division between artist and curator. Several of the photographers involved in this exhibition would form other feminist photography collaborations. Jo Spence, for instance, attended a number of planning meetings and befriended Maggie Murray, and these associations led to the formation of the Hackney Flashers.[45] Additionally, several participating photographers became involved in the *Spare Rib* visual group, which developed an ongoing critique of how photographs should be used in the magazine; notably, a decade later, Wilmer and Murray would form Format.[46]

Following the success of *Women*, the *Men* exhibition made more overt feminist political statements. Nonetheless, *Men* attracted a smaller audience than *Women*.[47] According to Meadows, most of the photographs in *Men* depicted men in the company of other men and emphasized how they regarded women.[48] For example, Diane Orson's photograph, which appeared on the exhibition poster, depicts a couple of men playing rugby in a public park, posing in a somewhat flirtatious and amused manner and looking directly into the camera (figure 20).[49] Another photograph shows a group of men watching a soccer game with their backs to the camera and a woman with a baby stroller who is standing behind the men in the picture's foreground and glancing distractedly over her shoulder, as if she were conscious of her exclusion from the main event.[50] These images—and perhaps the consciousness-raising discussions that they evoked—set out to investigate the power dynamics at play when a woman holds a camera and represents men.

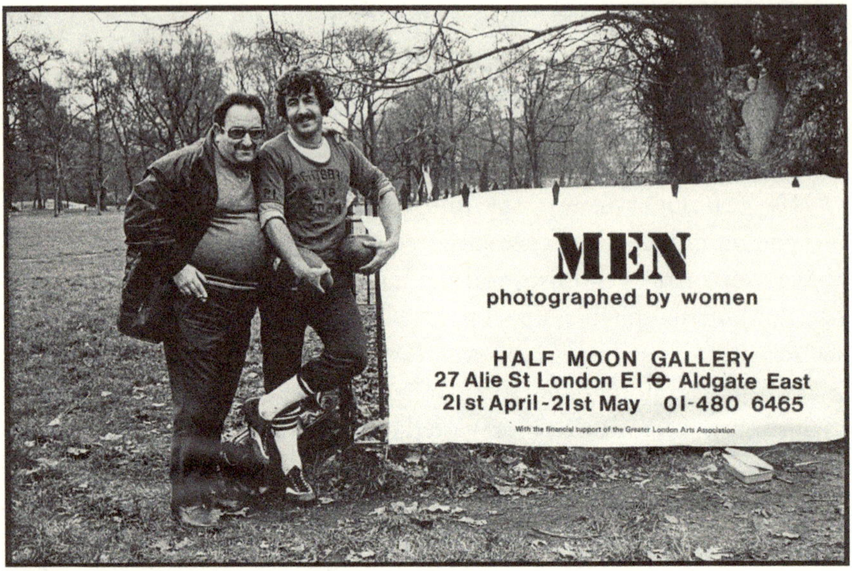

FIG. 20 Exhibition poster for *Men*, Half Moon Gallery, London, 1976, photograph by Diane Orson, courtesy of Julia Meadows.

Similar questions appeared in other feminist practices, such as in Laura Mulvey's "Visual Pleasure and Narrative Cinema" (1975), discussed earlier. The exploration of the reversal of the gender roles of photographing subject and photographed object also appeared in Hunter's photograph project called *Sexual Rapport Series* (1972–1976).[51] This series documented working-class men on the streets of Hoxton in London and Little Italy in New York.[52] Hunter's project might have been offering a feminist response to street photography and particularly to the Garry Winogrand project called *Women Are Beautiful* (1975) that featured photographs of women on the streets of New York whom the photographer found sexually attractive.[53] One of Hunter's photographs shows a group of male workers having their lunch on the pavement; some of the men are in their undershirts and smiling with amusement, looking flirtatiously at the camera (figure 21). Hunter indicated that in the course of her project, she deliberately wore a miniskirt or tight jeans and aimed to document her subjects' responses, their particular forms of sexual expression, the clothes they wore, and their "street presence." She recalled that her subjects tended to assume that she was not a professional photographer because she was a woman; however, this supposition tended to make them more cooperative.[54]

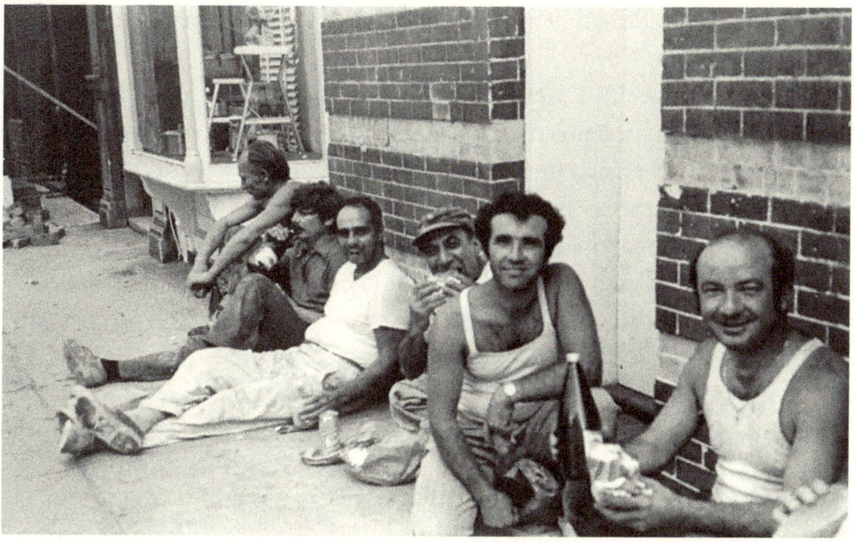

FIG. 21 Alexis Hunter, image from *Sexual Rapport Series*, 1972–1976, Hoxton, London, and Little Italy, New York, courtesy of Richard Saltoun Gallery.

Questions of Feminist Art

Questions regarding gender roles and their representation were at the center of *Women* and *Men*. These issues were also the focus of *Women's Images of Men*, a feminist art exhibition curated by members of the Women's Art Alliance feminist collective: the photographer Joyce Agee and the artists Catherine Elwes, Jacqueline Morreau, and Pat Whiteread. *Women's Images of Men* was exhibited at the London Institute of Contemporary Arts (ICA) in 1980 and was among the first feminist shows to be held in a fine arts institution. This show exhibited photography, as well as sculpture, drawing, and painting. Like *Men*, *Women's Images of Men* included artworks made by women representing men. The planning for the show began in 1978 and was motivated by a number of factors, including the desire of the Women's Art Alliance to create a space where women could exhibit their work and that would attract a wide audience. Additionally, the Women's Art Alliance viewed the show as a protest against Alan Jones's show *Alan Jones: Graphic Works 1958–1978*, which was exhibited at the ICA in 1978. That exhibition featured life-size sexualized sculptures of women positioned as furniture supports. The collective believed that exhibiting a feminist art show at the ICA that represented women's attitudes toward men would challenge Jones's work and other forms of sexism in the visual media.[55]

As with *Women* and *Men*, *Women's Images of Men* included both established and less experienced artists.[56] It was an open-submission show for which an ad was placed in *Time Out* asking women to send in works that depicted how they saw men. According to Morreau, the organizing group received approximately one thousand slide submissions. The selection process was undertaken by the exhibition organizers; Sandy Nairne, the ICA's new exhibitions director; and Lisa Tickner, an art history lecturer at Middlesex Polytechnic.[57] Forty women artists were chosen to participate. The organizers deliberately chose figurative works that they believed would present the most accessible arguments.[58] Because the number of submissions was overwhelming, some pieces were exhibited as part of a slide show that was projected during the show.[59]

Women's Images of Men attracted thousands of visitors and extensive coverage in the press[60] and went on tour in various regional galleries.[61] Some of the works included Philippa Beale's *Rough and Smooth* (1979), which dealt with female desire, the eroticization of men, and class in a manner similar to that of Hunter's project. Beale explained that the work's name derived from clichés used by women to classify men: a "rough" was a man whose appeal was in his scruffy physical appearance, and a "smooth" was a man whose attractiveness was in his witty conversations, fine clothes, and fine grooming. Beale also wanted to suggest that women "categorize" men in a way that resembles men's classifications of women.[62]

One of the photographic pieces included in the show was *Bold* (1979) by Lill-Ann Chepstow-Lusty, which criticizes representations of women in the media (figure 22). The photograph shows a nude man holding a box of laundry detergent against his pelvis next to a laundry machine. Chepstow-Lusty explained that her work was a feminist response to a London underground ad featuring two women in T-shirts with diagrams of the London underground system across their chests that was captioned, "A Lovely Pair from London Transport."[63] Chepstow-Lusty's playful gender reversal brings to mind the illustration with the tagline "Hunky, Chunky, Big & Crunchy, Stuart's Nutz Are Best" that was published in *Spare Rib* and discussed earlier, which similarly challenged the gender roles found in advertisements. However, whereas that illustration circulated in a feminist magazine, *Bold* brought its argument into the art museum and to a wider public.

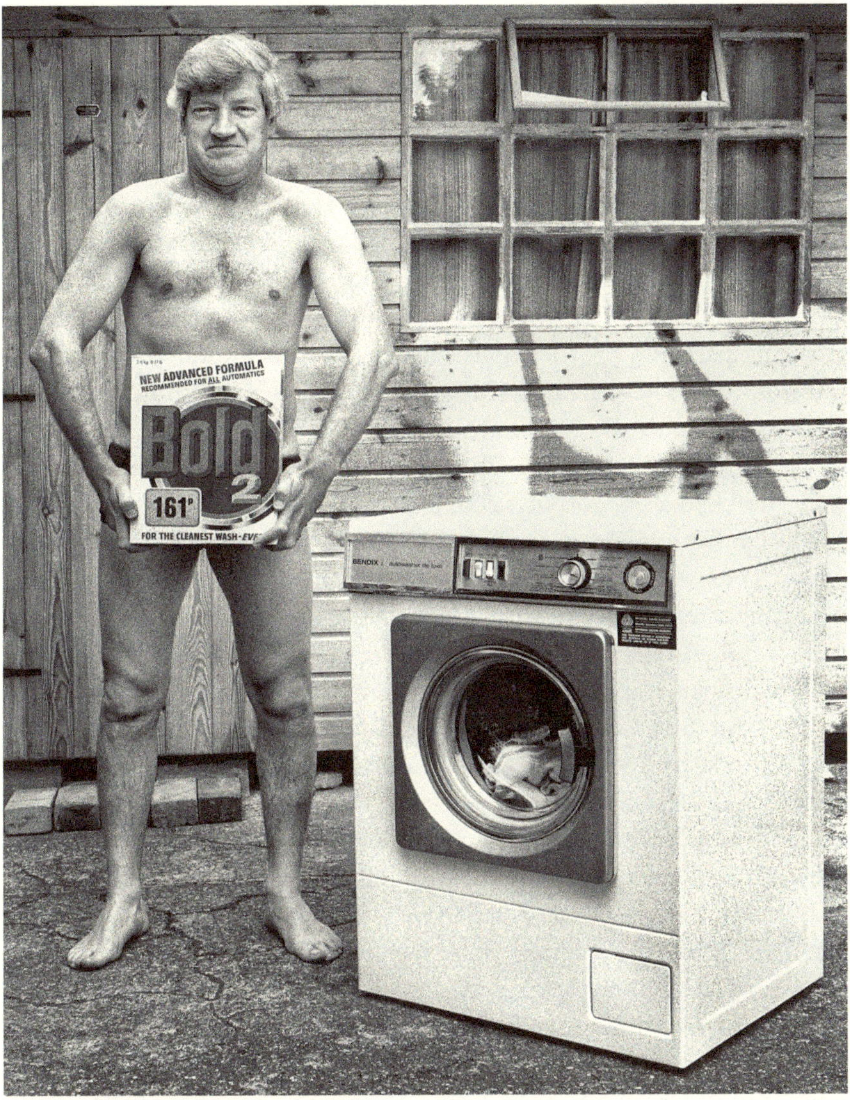

FIG. 22 Lill-Ann Chepstow-Lusty, *Bold*, 1979, courtesy of Lill-Ann Chepstow-Lusty.

Women's Images of Men was followed by two other feminist shows that exhibited at the ICA in 1980. The first was *About Time: Video, Performance and Installation by 21 Women Artists*, which included some of the works initially submitted to *Women's Images of Men*. As the number of submissions to *Women's Images of Men* was overwhelming, Elwes and the artists Rose Garrard and Sandy Nairne decided to form a separate show that would focus on video art, performance, and mixed media. As with *Women's Images of Men*, the works were selected through an open submission process and included ones by women that set out to articulate women's perspectives on experiences of patriarchy and to extend beyond the traditional boundaries delineated by painting and sculpture.[64]

The third feminist show, *Issue: Social Strategies by Women Artists*, was curated by American artist and critic Lucy Lippard. Unlike the earlier feminist shows, *Issue* moved away from women-centered politics. Instead, it promoted the position that feminist artistic strategies must be acknowledged as taking part in a broader political struggle and should be invested in transforming society at large. The artists included in the show came from different parts of the world. They included Alexis Hunter from New Zealand[65]; Mary Kelly from Britain; Leslie Labowitz and Suzanne Lacy from the United States; Nil Yalter, born in Cairo and of Turkish descent; Nicole Croiset from France; and Miriam Sharon from Israel. The inclusion of artists of several nationalities was intended to offer a global, cross-cultural dialog about feminism and social issues, such as imperialism, racism, migrant work, rape, and health care. Thus, this show attempted to frame feminist art as a growing transnational phenomenon.

The exhibits in *Issue* included photography, painting, conceptual art, and performance art.[66] Among the works included in the show were Hunter's photo sequence *A Young Polynesian Considers Cultural Imperialism* (1980), which depicts a young Polynesian girl putting a white European woman's necklace around her neck and then breaking it angrily. Hunter suggested that her work commented on Polynesian women's double subordination to and rebellion against the dominant European culture and their own patriarchal culture.[67] Also included was a section from Kelly's *Post-partum Document*.[68] In this work Kelly used photographs, feeding charts, diapers, diary imprints, and notes to record her relationship with her infant son. This work also mobilized Lacanian psychoanalytic and linguistic theories to address the gradual process of her son's formation as an independent subject and this process's impact.[69] Also included were documents of Lacy and Labowitz's performance work from their project *Three Weeks in May*, which addressed rape and sexual violence against women and was produced collectively in Los Angeles during three weeks in May 1977. In addition, the show included photographer Loraine Leeson's political poster campaign called *East London Health Project* (1978), which was produced in collaboration with the East London Trades Councils and health workers' unions, the Women's Health

Information Centre Collective, and Radical Statistics (figure 23). This project contested the cutbacks in health care and documented their impact on women.[70]

The three feminist ICA exhibitions differed in their dispositions toward skill, gallery reputation, and forms of organization. *Women's Images of Men* and *About Time* were open-submission shows that included works of varying degrees of professionalism, and the process of organizing the show was performed collectively. *Issue* was perhaps politically sophisticated in its articulation of a social-theoretical framework that went "beyond" focusing on images produced by women. Nevertheless, it complied with certain traditions of exhibition, such as having a single curator execute the selection process. Additionally, several of the artists chosen, such as Hunter, Margaret Harrison, Kelly, and Adrian Piper, were developing into visible gallery artists, a fact that conferred a certain status on the exhibition.[71]

A two-day conference at the ICA, "Questions on Women's Art," followed the opening of *Issue* and hosted participants from the three feminist ICA exhibitions and from the *Eight Artists: Women* (1980) exhibition, which was an all-female abstract painting and sculpture show presented at the Acme Gallery. During this conference, clashes erupted between the participants regarding the use and goals of feminist art strategies. Some artists criticized works that used art in an overtly propagandistic manner or used text heavily, while others criticized works that set out to maintain a certain degree of alignment with art as beauty and truth. Furthermore, the *Issue* artists were criticized either for not being radical enough or for focusing on politics rather than art.[72] The *Issue* artists, however, claimed that figurative painting, female imagery, and female self-expression were strategies that were out of date. Lippard criticized feminist art shows that emphasized overcoming women's discrimination in privileged exhibition spaces and suggested that feminist art exhibitions must focus on wider social concerns.[73] Another major source of conflict was the feminist strategy of framing the personal as political; several of the feminist artists called attention to the danger of its lapsing into conventional notions of expressive individuality.[74]

These arguments are illustrative of some of the splits among the different networks of feminist artists and feminist photographers and the exacerbation of these tensions by the end of the decade. This conference posed these polarizations against one another in a powerful way, and at the same time exposed the diversity of debates and strategies that developed in the growing field of feminist cultural production at the time.[75]

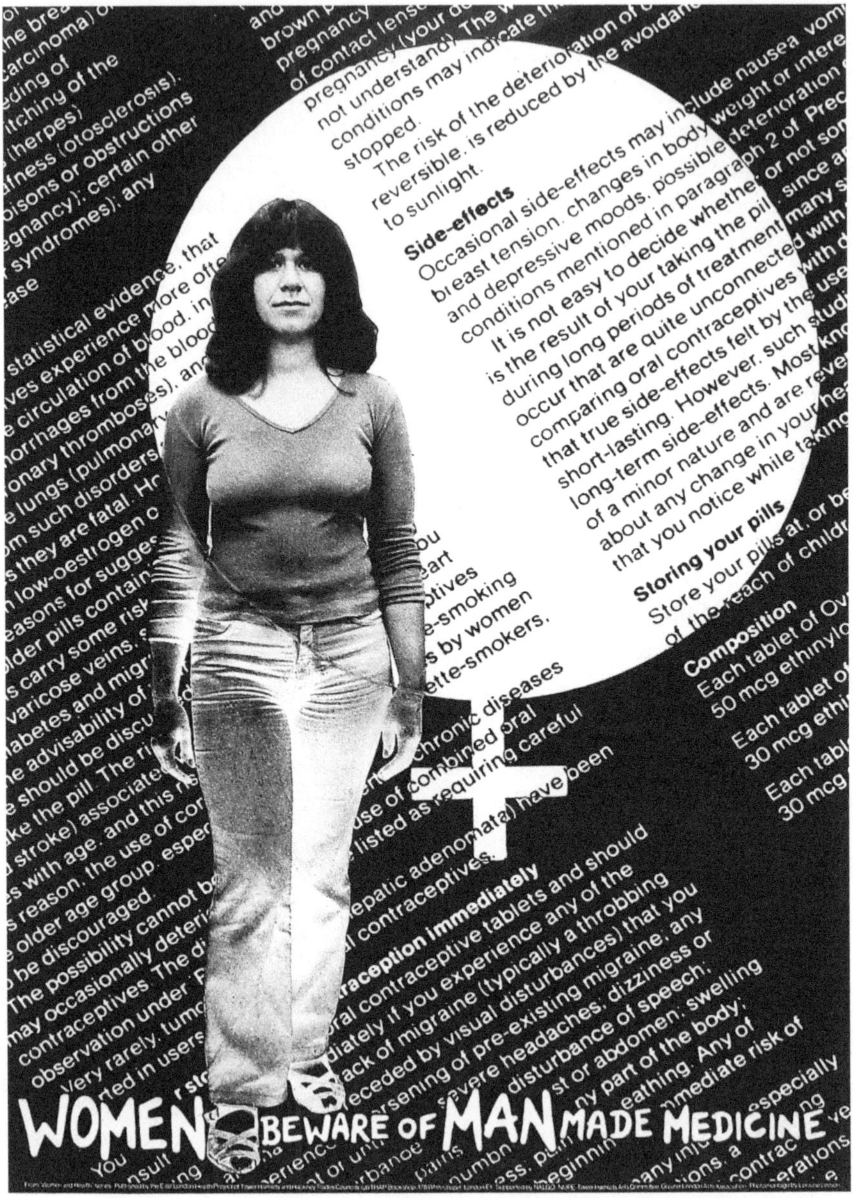

FIG. 23 Loraine Leeson, *Women Beware of Manmade Medicine*, 1980, East London Health Project, produced and distributed in conjunction with East London Trades Councils and health workers' unions, A2 poster, © Loraine Leeson.

Reception of the Feminist ICA Shows

The feminist ICA shows and other feminist art and photography exhibitions attracted a lot of public attention and curiosity. Yet the political goals of these exhibitions were often met with indifference or hostility. For example, a review of *Women's Images of Men* in the *British Journal of Photography* suggested that there was nothing unusual about the exhibition other than its title. The review added that if the sex of the artists and subjects of representation were reversed, the result would have been the same and, therefore, there was no need to define it as a women's show.[76] The review blatantly overlooked the show's feminist arguments and focused on its visual aspects. Similarly, according to an article in *Spare Rib*, several male visitors at Feministo's postal event at the ICA claimed that they did not see what the fuss surrounding this show was about and that its artists were "miserable bitter, and twisted." The article noted that a female visitor accused the artists of wanting to make viewers as unhappy as the artists. Moreover, the North West Arts Association, which housed Feministo's first show, announced that it was "unsuitable for children."[77]

Likewise, a press review of Kelly's *Post-partum Document* exhibition at the second Hayward Annual in 1978 claimed that the piece did not belong in an art gallery. The review of Kelly's work suggested that it was fit for the foyer of a maternity hospital, the shop Mothercare, or a women's magazine.[78]

The organizational politics of *Women's Images of Men* and *Portrait of the Artist as Housewife* were women-centered, while Kelly's work belonged to the feminist theory camp. Nonetheless, the reception of these exhibitions and of Kelly's work was equally dismissive, and the exhibitions were accused of lacking aesthetic value.

The dismissal of Kelly's work was arguably an underhanded critique of the second Hayward Annual's selection process, which was carried out, for the first time, by only female selectors. In 1975 the Women's Workshop of the Artists Union protested outside the Hayward Gallery against its exclusion of women artists.[79] The group also handed out a petition to the London Arts Council offices demanding parity for women in exhibition and funding. Following this protest, five women artists, Gillian Wise Ciobotaru, Rita Donagh, Tess Jaray, Liliane Lijn, and Kim Lim, were invited to choose the works for the second Hayward Annual exhibition. These artists selected twenty-three artists, out of whom seven were men. Nonetheless, while works by Kelly, Hunter, and Susan Hiller addressed feminist art debates, the rest of the works by women artists in the show did not.[80] Moreover, the political aspects of the few included feminist works were undermined by the show's primary emphasis on visual aesthetics and pleasure.[81] Thus, although this was hardly a feminist exhibition, patronizing journalists labeled the show as "ladies' night" and as a "girls' annual."[82] Such responses to the second Hayward Annual are reflective of the marginalization experienced by women in the art world. Thus, these critiques mark the feminist significance of the second Hayward Annual' selection process.

Photography and *Three Perspectives on Photography: Recent British Photography*

In the feminist ICA shows, photography was exhibited alongside painting, sculpture, performance art, and installation. Thus, photography was positioned among the mediums categorized as "feminist art." Nonetheless, feminist photography was situated within the unique developments in photographic activity in 1970s Britain, and it was influenced by photography's distinct theoretical underpinnings and politicization. As discussed earlier, photography's presence in the museum was perceived as unusual. The inclusion of photography in the feminist ICA exhibitions and their recognition by the Arts Council arguably laid the groundwork for another photography show in which feminist photography had a prominent place. This show was *Three Perspectives on Photography: Recent British Photography* (1979), which was the first and perhaps only exhibition aimed at displaying the diversity of British photography that developed in the 1970s.[83] This exhibition was initially intended to be the first in a series called the British Biennial of Photography, which was to be regularly funded by the Arts Council of Great Britain.[84] It was also intended to be exhibited in photography galleries and museums abroad.[85]

The idea for *Three Perspectives* was put forward by Victor Burgin, who was then a member of the Arts Council's Photography Advisory Committee and photography lecturer at the Polytechnic of Central London. As show selectors, Burgin recommended Paul Hill, a photographer and lecturer in photography at Trent Polytechnic in Nottingham; John Tagg, then lecturer in photography theory at the Polytechnic of Central London; and feminist photographer Angela Kelly. Each was responsible for a section that reflected a different perspective on photography.[86] Hill's section, "Photographic Truth, Metaphor and Individual Expression," dealt with formulism and photography as fine art. Kelly's section, "Feminism and Photography," dealt with the diversity of feminist photography's contributions. Lastly, Tagg's section, "A Socialist Perspective on Photographic Practice," presented photographic practices engaged in social and feminist issues.[87] Most of the selections in both Kelly's and Tagg's sections had previously circulated in other venues, such as the alternative press, community centers, community handouts, libraries, church halls, conferences, and the streets.[88] Conversely, Hill wished to exhibit photography that embodied the qualities of fine art and to pose it as a counterpractice to photography in the world of advertisements and commercial magazines.[89]

Up until the *Three Perspectives* show, the Hayward Gallery had exhibited a mix of modern and contemporary art shows. Among these were artist retrospectives and themed surveys such as *Matisse: A Retrospective Exhibition at the Hayward Gallery* (1968) and *French Symbolist Painters: Moreau, Puvis de Chavannes, Redon and Their Followers* (1972).

In retrospect, *Three Perspectives* was a significant event that is often regarded as an influential moment in establishing the status of British photography. In 2009 the photography publication *Portfolio* dedicated its fiftieth issue to this show and considered it to be the occasion that marked the arrival of contemporary British photography in the art world.[90] However, at the moment of the show's inception, it posed a challenge to the values governing art museums' practices of selection and exclusion, thus reflecting the aim of the feminist ICA exhibitions.[91]

Kelly indicated that one of her political roles as a feminist selector was to provide women photographers the opportunity to display their work in an art institution.[92] This statement echoed the motivations of the feminist ICA shows' organizers, as well as of the Women's Workshop of the Artists Union and the second Hayward Annual selectors: to challenge the exclusion of women artists from fine art networks. Kelly also aimed to exhibit the range of feminist photographic practices that had developed during the 1970s and the diversity of their feminist arguments. Some of the issues presented in her section were the role of the media in women's socialization, the political significance of women's "personal experience," feminist uses of documentary, and feminist critiques of the transparency of photographic representation and of the stability of the category "woman."[93] She was also

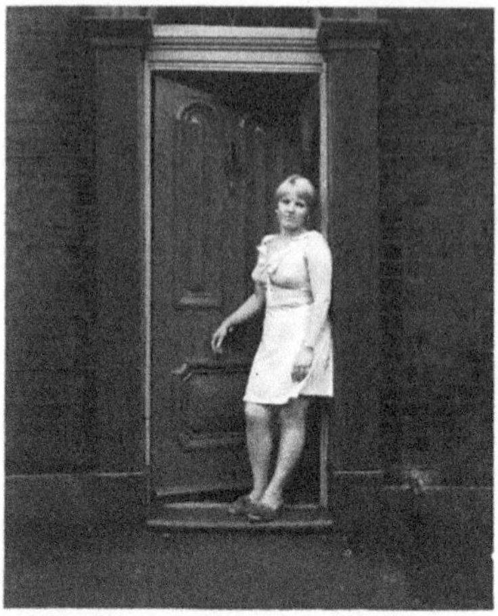

Marie 1

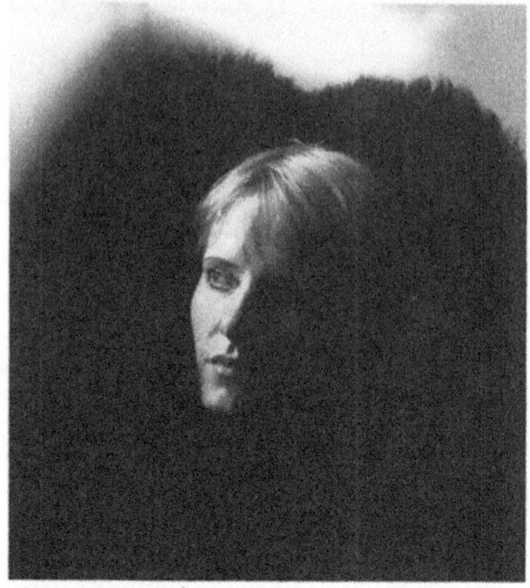

Marie 2

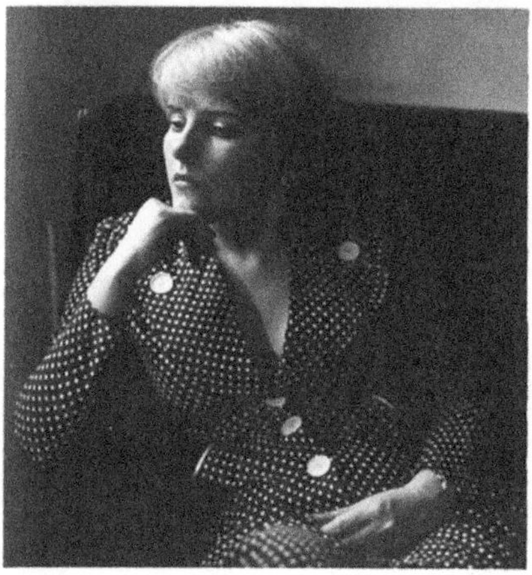

Marie 3

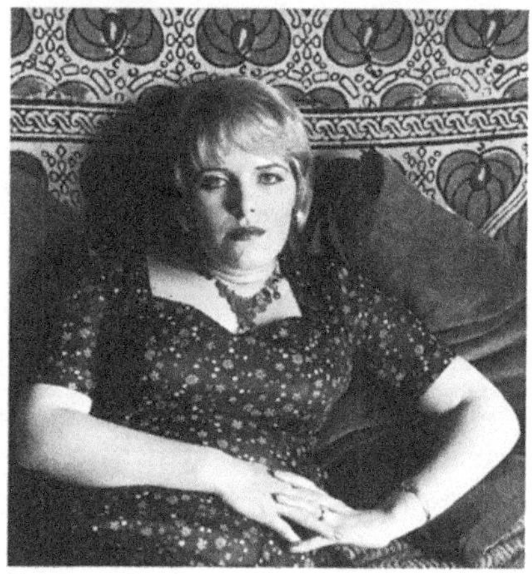

Marie 4

FIG. 24 Aileen Ferriday, *Marie 1–4*, 1976, courtesy of Arts Council Collection, Southbank Centre, London, © Aileen Ferriday.

interested in portraying the plurality of the sites in which feminist photography emerged, which included community centers, consciousness-raising groups, women's conferences, and film and literary theory journals.[94] Among the works in Kelly's section was Aileen Ferriday's portrait series, which engaged in feminist media politics and used photography as a consciousness-raising tool. Ferriday depicted her working-class friends in a manner reminiscent of late 1950s Hollywood glamour images (figure 24). She indicated that she presented her subjects with the photographs and that together they discussed their reactions to the variations in their appearances.[95] Also exhibited was Christine Voge's (formerly Hobbeheydar) social documentary photo series *Chriswick Women's Aid* (1978), which contained images taken at a refuge center for abused women and children. One of her photographs features a young girl standing in the center's hall, timidly covering her face with her hand, thus evoking empathy and identification in the viewer (figure 25).

Other works in Kelly's section were concerned with the language of photographic representation. An example is Yve Lomax's conceptual work, which was exhibited in book form and included a photo sequence of a woman driving a car (figure 26).[96] The sequence was accompanied by a text informed by feminist psychoanalytic and linguistic theories that deconstructed the category "woman" and its assumed stability. The image series, which offers a fragmented depiction of the woman, similarly resists being added up into a coherent representation; in this way, the work challenges the capacity of photographic representation to access the "real" experience of women, as well as the coherence of the category "woman," positions that photographers such as Voge might have resisted.[97]

Similarly, Jo Spence's work *Beyond the Family Album: Private Images, Public Conventions* investigates the language of photographic representation by addressing the family album as a set of conventions and exclusions. One of her images consists of two photographs of Spence lying on her stomach in the nude, one as a baby, and the other as a fully grown, middle-aged woman. These images are captioned, "Me at 8 1/2 months" and "Me at 44 years 9 months" (figure 27).[98] Thus, Spence humorously shed light on the family album's constraints, conventions, and modes of representation.

The *Three Perspectives* selectors aimed to challenge not only the art museum's selections but also its conventions of exhibition and display.[99] This position was manifested in the presentation of Report/IFL's work *A Statistical Survey of Lost Working Days in 1978*, which was included in Tagg's section; it consisted of hundreds of black-and-white photographs placed on extensive wall panels alongside unemployment statistics. Similarly, Hunter's piece in the same section, *Domestic Warfare/the Wedding Anniversary*, which criticized the institution of marriage, was projected as a slide show behind a sheet of gauze.[100] Also, as mentioned earlier, Lomax's work was exhibited in book form, a format considered unusual for photography at the time.[101] Furthermore, most of the photographs in Hill's section were framed in a 31.5 × 21.5 cm format, perhaps with the intention of giving them the appearance of traditional objects of fine art.[102]

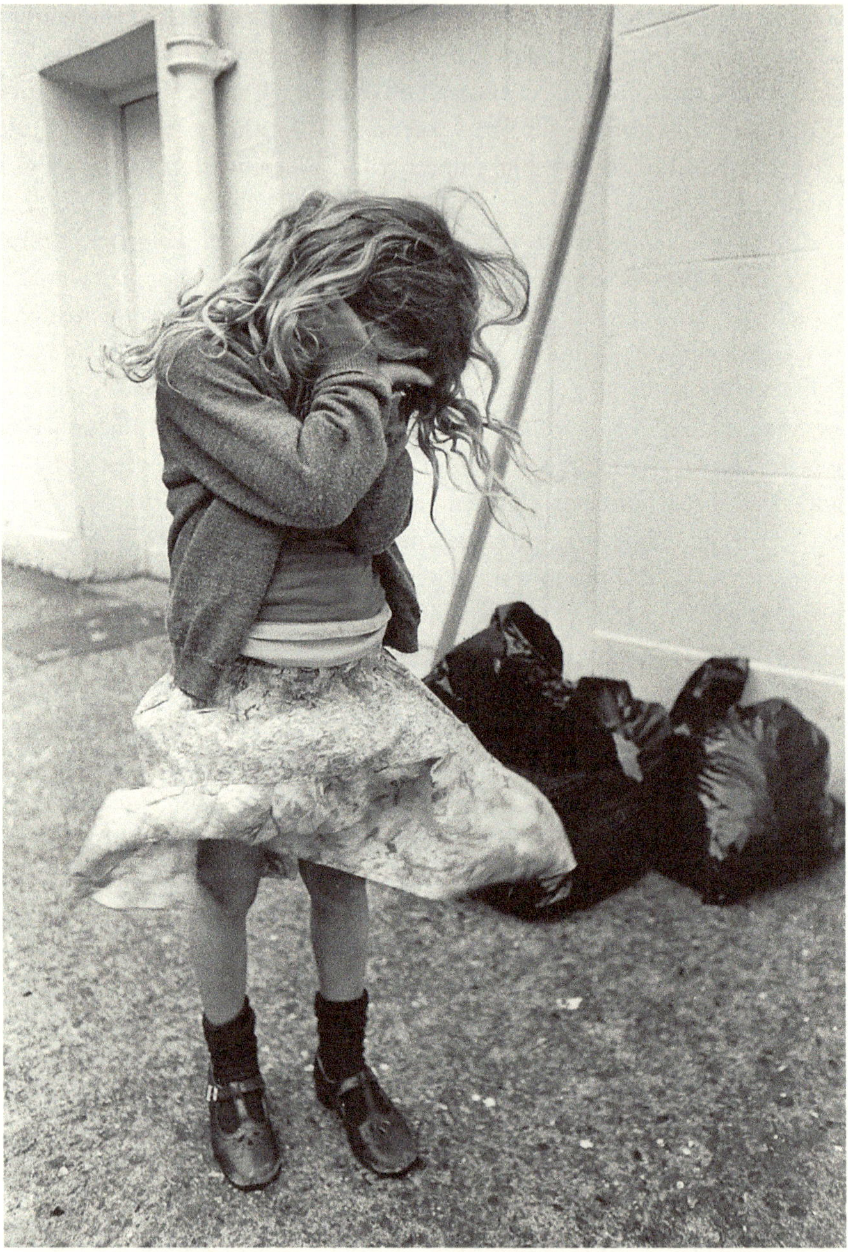

FIG. 25 Christine Voge, *Crying Child*, item from Chiswick Women's Aid, a refuge for battered and emotionally tormented women and children, 1978, from Paul Hill, Angela Kelly, and John Tagg, *Three Perspectives on Photography: Recent British Photography*, exhibition catalog (London: Hayward Gallery, 1979), 50.

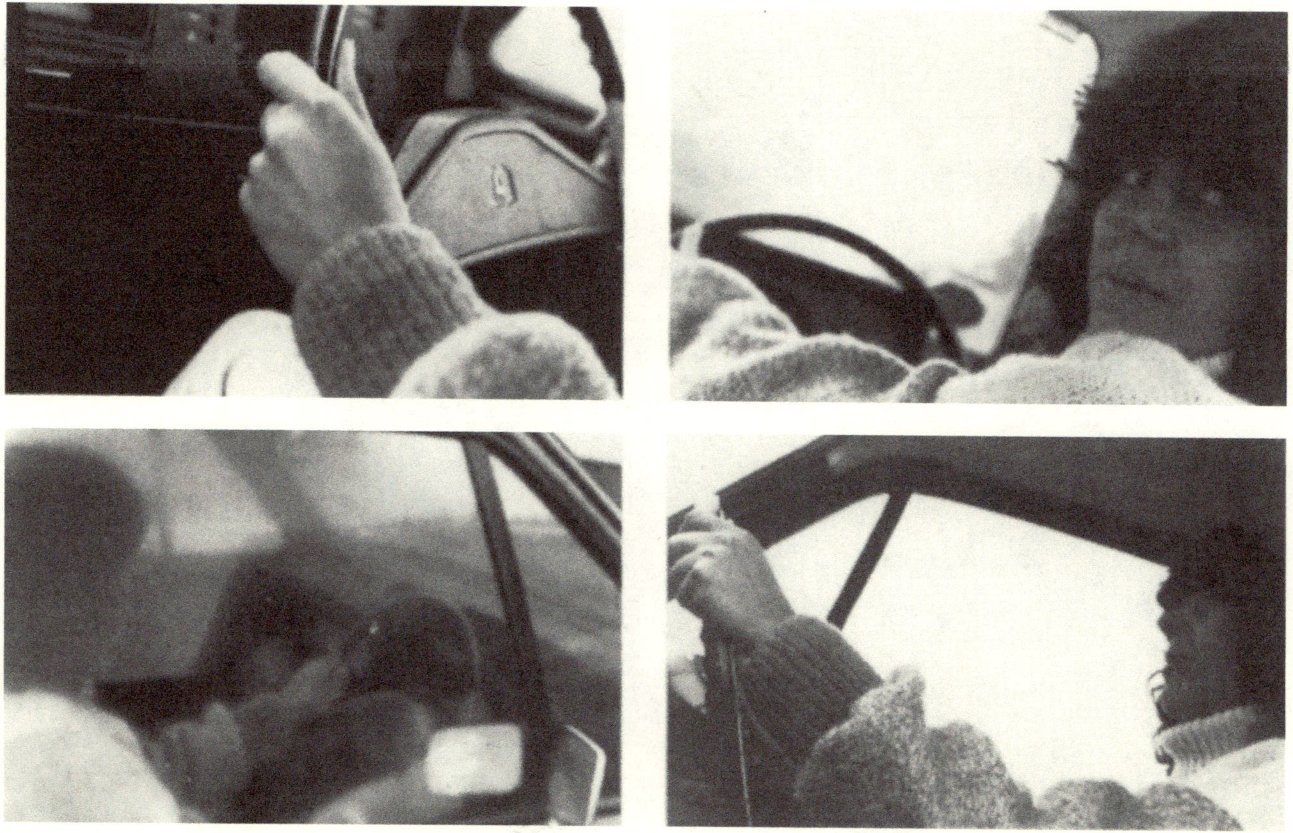

FIG. 26 Yve Lomax, *Recto/Verso and Selection of Photographs Works towards a Book*, ca. 1978, from Paul Hill, Angela Kelly, and John Tagg, *Three Perspectives on Photography: Recent British Photography*, exhibition catalog (London: Hayward Gallery, 1979), 52–53, courtesy of Yve Lomax.

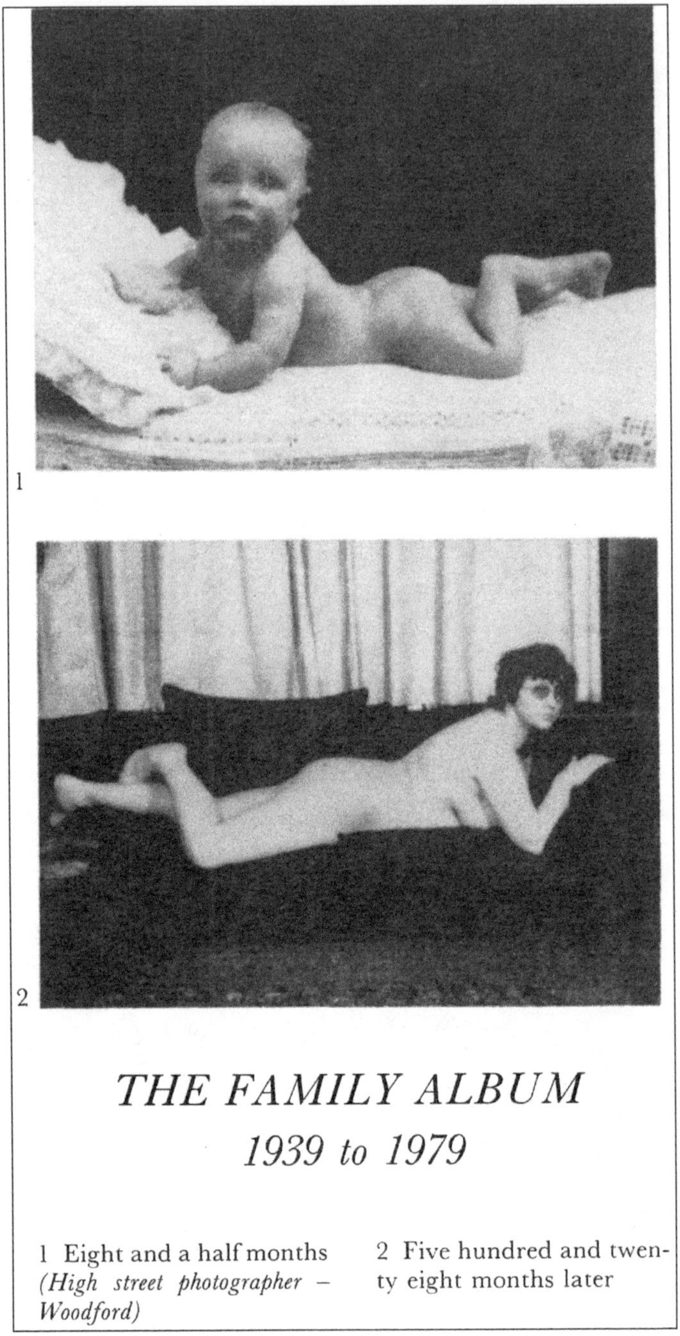

FIG. 27 Jo Spence, item from *Beyond the Family Album*, 1979, copyright the Estate of the Artist, courtesy Richard Saltoun, London.

Despite *Three Perspectives*' success in attracting a large viewing audience, as was the case for the feminist exhibitions discussed earlier, some of its exhibits and strategies were met with hostility. The works in Kelly's and Tagg's sections were criticized for prioritizing political content over photography's aesthetic quality.[103] Additionally, a review in the *Evening Standard* attacked two Hackney Flashers projects exhibited in Tagg's section, *Women and Work* and *Who's Holding the Baby*, for being something that an earnest schoolmistress might pin on a notice board in a church hall.[104] A review in *Art and Artists* by Richard Erlich criticized the photographers in the feminist and socialist sections for using the camera to make a polemical argument rather than displaying an interest in photography's special qualities.[105] Similarly, Ian Jeffery suggested in *Artscribe* that the exhibits in these two sections consisted of loose ends that required further work, and that the general attitude guiding their selection was that "anything goes as long as we cover the walls."[106] However, both Erlich and Jeffery praised the works in Hill's section for their aesthetic quality. They admired Ferriday's portraits for their aesthetic value but ignored their feminist underpinnings.[107] Interestingly, a review in the *Guardian*, a major liberal newspaper, denounced the Hackney Flashers' work and claimed that the group's "amateurism was refreshing as it was deceptive" and that it was "incorporating slogans written in the style popularized by the high street supermarket proclaiming its special offers . . . and in a cunning attempt to ingratiate themselves with the housewife."[108] A review in *Spare Rib* by Laura Margolis, however, exemplified a positive attitude toward *Three Perspectives* and particularly toward Tagg's and Kelly's sections, claiming that the show marked a growing recognition of the importance of feminist and socialist work.[109]

In addition to the *Three Perspectives* exhibits, several events organized at the Hayward further intervened in the conventional fine art museum practices and exclusions. Some of these events were dedicated to photography, such as the open Slide Evening for Women Photographers and a talk titled "Race, Class, Sexuality—Representation and Stereotyping" that was chaired by Angela Kelly and included Spence, Burgin, and Rasheed Araeen as panelists. This was one in a series of talks that consisted of open conversations with the audience regarding current photography debates; all were well attended. In addition, the Hackney Flashers organized events that challenged the Hayward Gallery in more direct and explicit ways; their activities highlighted the divide between the group's political strategies and what the Hayward was willing to contain. As a group, the Hackney Flashers were primarily focused on using photography for posing political arguments, for educational purposes, and for working collectively.[110] When they were approached to participate in *Three Perspectives*, they were divided regarding whether exhibiting their political work in a "high art" institution was an act of selling out. However, they ultimately decided that participating in the show would be an opportunity to challenge high art and to show that photography could be used politically. They agreed to participate on the condition that they could host events related to nursery care instead of hosting a typical gallery artist talk.[111] Members of Report/IFL were similarly uncertain as to whether their work should be put up in a gallery, and like the Hackney Flashers, they were persuaded that their participation might provide an opportunity to intervene in an institutional space.[112] The Hackney Flashers' talk about nursery care was chaired by Maggie Murray, who brought her one-year-old son to the panel as a means of emphasizing her arguments. Some of the questions raised at this talk were why prams were not allowed inside the Hayward, and why the gallery did not provide facilities for young children who accompanied adults to its exhibitions.[113] In addition, Tagg organized a major childcare event at the Hayward with Nicki Roads and Linda Smith, both active in childcare campaigns in the boroughs of Wandsworth, Lambeth, and Southwark. The childcare event included speakers Tessa Woodcraft, under-fives officer of the National Association of Local Government, who addressed issues related to children under five, and Linda Smith from the Southwark Trade Council.[114] A nursery and children's entertainment were supplied at the aforementioned events.[115] The Hackney Flashers' biggest event was arguably a demonstration outside the Hayward that demanded free childcare and state recognition of the needs of children under five. According to Hackney Flashers member Michael Ann Mullen, people were brought down from a nursery to join in the demonstration with placards.[116] The demonstration was followed by a party inside the gallery, which included clowns to entertain the children and a rock music performance by the all-female theater group Cunning Stunts.[117]

Ultimately, the Hayward Gallery considered the Hackney Flashers events vulgar and intrusive. Tagg recalled that the Arts Council and the Hayward found various elements of the shows to be too disruptive and removed from what they initially expected. Moreover, the Arts Council conducted a long investigation of the Photography Advisory Committee's role and status;[118] soon after, the committee was abolished. This decision was certainly affected by the cuts in public spending following the election of Margaret Thatcher that year.[119] Nevertheless, Lane continued to support photography as the Arts Council's photography officer until 1995.

Three Perspectives did not travel abroad, and it was the last initiative of its type. A number of the Hackney Flashers' members left the group as a result of differences that deepened among the group members following the show, making *Three Perspectives* their final major project.[120] The politically engaged photography practices and events were not readily contained by the Hayward Gallery or the Arts Council. Nonetheless, the photography practices that aimed at attaining the status of art were more easily accepted because they were already aligned with the values of the art museum and had set out to be incorporated within it.[121] I will soon show that in the following decade, feminist photographic practices that emphasized aesthetic value were more inclined to be integrated into the art museum. In contrast, practices that emphasized political content and challenged fine art traditions and values continued to be criticized.

The Leeds Pavilion: A Feminist Photography Center

The *Three Perspectives* exhibition at the Hayward and the feminist art shows at the ICA brought a variety of feminist practices into the art museum, a venue in which they had not been exhibited before. However, within these venues, their presence was temporary. Although during the 1970s and early 1980s there were several regional photography galleries, none was committed to supporting feminist photographic activity.[122]

As the organizers of *Women's Images of Men* implied, the desire to exhibit in the art museum was coupled with a desire to establish a feminist exhibition space. In 1983 this desire materialized in the foundation of the first British feminist photography gallery in Leeds, the Pavilion Feminist Photography Centre. Although the Pavilion faced a number of transitions and continues to operate today, I will discuss its first phase, which includes its planning in 1981, its opening in May 1983, and its temporary closure in April 1984.

The plan for the Pavilion was formulated by Dinah Clark, Carolyn Taylor, and Shirley Moreno, as well as Griselda Pollock and John Tagg, their former tutors from the Leeds University Fine Art Department.[123] Their idea was to establish a permanent feminist exhibition space that would focus on photography, pose an alternative to mainstream museum culture, and be accessible to the general public.[124]

Certain strategies and underlying assumptions employed by some of the feminist art and photography initiatives discussed earlier were also incorporated into the Pavilion. For example, the Pavilion was managed collectively, its exhibits were mainly produced by women, its shows were dedicated to themes rather than to particular artists, and it refrained from exhibiting works that emphasized style and image quality.[125]

Before the Pavilion's foundation, Clark, Taylor, and Moreno were involved in local feminist art activism that led to the plan for the Pavilion. For instance, they organized the Leeds Women's Arts Program, which held adult educational courses on the history of women artists, and ran a women's art group that operated collectively. In many ways, the women's art group was informed by Judy Chicago's feminist art program in Fresno, California (1970–1971), which combined art history courses with art practice.[126]

The Leeds Women's Art Program produced the show *Anonymous: Notes towards a Show on Self-Image*, which it exhibited in Leeds at the St. Paul Art Gallery in 1982. The show addressed topics such as women's self-representation and incorporated "women's" skills such as knitting and mixed media into its works.[127] One of the works, for example, consisted of a sequence of photographs of a woman's face whose appearance was altered by various cutouts of hairstyles, lips, and accessories taken from posters and magazines.[128] Thus, the piece arguably participated in the prevalent feminist debate of the time regarding the media's role in shaping gender stereotypes.

The Leeds Women's Art Program, like many other feminist art collectives in Britain at that time, did not have its own exhibition space. Clark, Taylor, and Moreno set out to procure one. Because a mixed-media center required a great deal of funding, they decided to concentrate on photography. This decision was influenced by additional factors, including that photography was an accessible form of representation that was easy to learn, and that a feminist engagement in photography presented an opportunity to challenge its image as a masculine activity. Additionally, according to Moreno, the threat of Peter Sutcliffe in Leeds reinforced feminist debates about the effects of sexualized images on women's lives. Thus, producing feminist photographs was a potentially counteractive strategy, which a feminist photography center could facilitate.[129]

The idea for the Pavilion was negotiated with Leeds City Council, which designated for the purpose an old pavilion in Hyde Park not far from Leeds University. The Pavilion was renovated in 1982–1983 with the assistance of a grant from Leeds City Council's inner-city urban aid fund. It opened on May 1, 1983, and operated as a volunteer-based collective.[130] The Pavilion had an advisory board whose members were mostly associated with the photography department at the Polytechnic of Central London. Local councilors were also involved in the Pavilion's management.[131] The central funding bodies that sustained this project included the Arts Council of Great Britain and the Yorkshire Arts Association (YAA).[132] Additionally, Tagg, who was active in the YAA at the time, had a crucial role in securing funding for this project.[133] The physical appearance of the Pavilion and its facilities was designed to be different from that of a typical fine arts gallery. Thus, its walls were painted nursery-pink, green, blue, and yellow instead of an austere white.[134] Like the Half Moon Photography Workshop gallery, it had a darkroom dedicated to teaching women photography skills.[135] It also had a space for a nursery, which—in a way—answered the need for childcare posed by the Hackney Flashers at *Three Perspectives*. Additionally, the Pavilion had a dedicated exhibition space for talks, a workshop area, a kitchen, a handicap-accessible bathroom, and a ramp for wheelchair access, which was unusual at the time.[136]

The Pavilion's opening photography exhibition, *Collective Works* (May 1983), produced by the Pavilion collective, addressed themes related to working collectively and setting up a feminist center like the Pavilion. The collective noted its attempt to use photography in unusual ways, such as setting it on expansive panels alongside other mixed media. The collective deliberately avoided exhibiting its photographs in small, neat frames because it did not want them to appear to have an aura of precious objects.

The show was divided into a number of sections; one section addressed the town in which the project was located and depicted it as a map consisting of feminist networks. Another section addressed problems of funding, and the largest section documented the process of the Pavilion's renovation.

One of the exhibited works was a large-scale image of a cloudy sky superimposed with a number of images of women holding cameras. Another panel in the show addressed the political significance of working in a collective and the different roles that might be assumed by a member in a single day, which might range from being a janitor to being the managing director (figure 28).[137] Another work, titled *The Collective's View of Itself*, depicted a group of women, each holding a camera.[138]

Other photography exhibitions held in the Pavilion that year were the Hackney Flashers' project *Who's Holding the Baby* and Spence's project

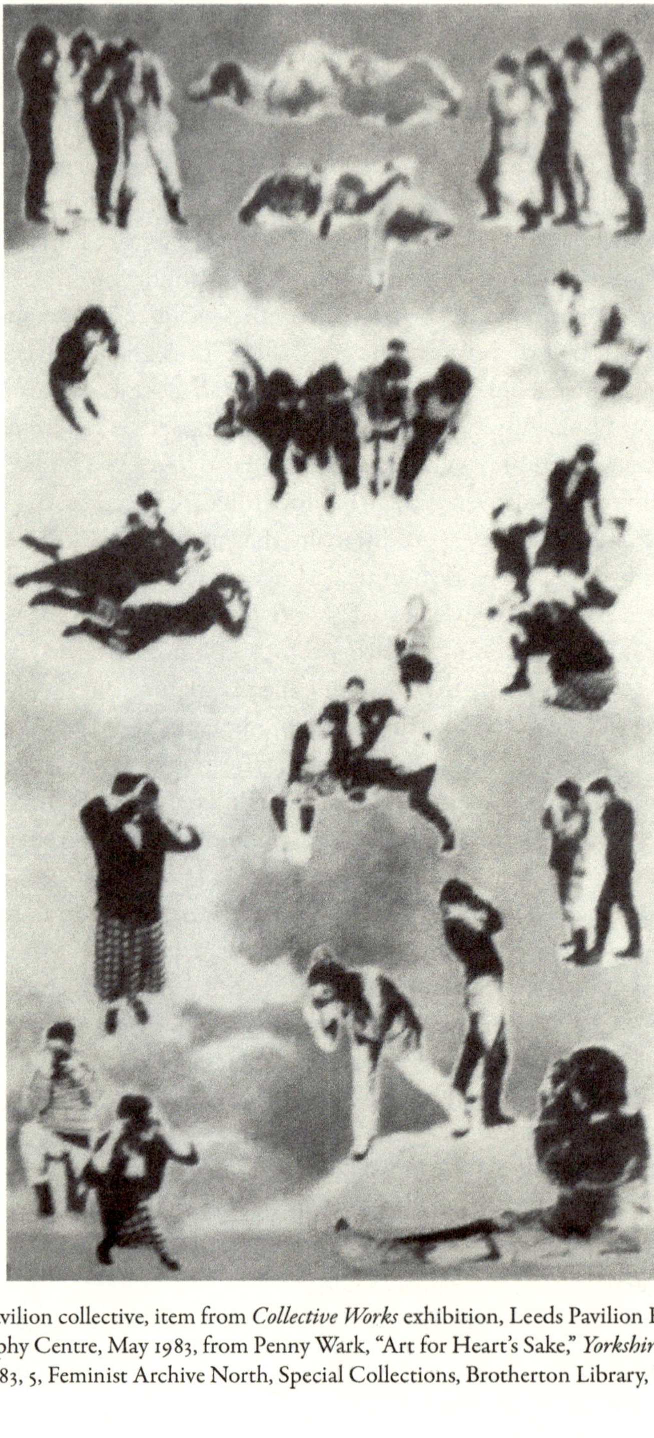

FIG. 28 Pavilion collective, item from *Collective Works* exhibition, Leeds Pavilion Feminist Photography Centre, May 1983, from Penny Wark, "Art for Heart's Sake," *Yorkshire Post*, May 4, 1983, 5, Feminist Archive North, Special Collections, Brotherton Library, University of Leeds.

Beyond the Family Album, both of which were earlier exhibited at *Three Perspectives*. Additionally, the Pavilion exhibited a show about and by disabled people titled *No Access*, an exhibition on the uses of community photography, and an open-submission show.[139]

The Pavilion closed within a year of its opening because the YAA withdrew its funding. The YAA explained its decision by claiming that the works produced and displayed in the Pavilion by then had insufficient aesthetic value. This statement resembled previous dismissive responses to feminist art and photography works exhibited in an art museum context. Thus, although the Pavilion was a later project that derived from feminist photography practices and debates that had begun in the previous decade, feminist photography was still regarded as an unworthy activity.

The YAA also claimed that the Pavilion operated as a separatist organization, an orientation that went against the YAA's policy to fund art designated for viewing by the general public. *Separatism* was a particularly loaded term in the early 1980s in Leeds, when revolutionary feminist groups such as Angry Women were taking direct action against sex shops and cinemas. Indeed, although the Pavilion was not initially planned to function as a separatist space,[140] in the course of the first year of its opening, under the influence of Angry Women and Women against Violence against Women, groups that increasingly became involved in the Pavilion's activity and advocated for a separatist space, the Pavilion moved toward separatism. It hosted a number of women-only shows and events; one exhibition, *Visible Women* (February 1984), was open to men for two weeks only.[141]

Taylor recalled that a number of women from the Pavilion collective objected to the separatist idea and argued that a feminist gallery should be a place for developing a feminist politics that could be shared with men. These conflicts ultimately caused a rupture in the Pavilion collective that shifted its underlying values and its management structure. Consequently, both groups of women—those who strove for a separatist space and those who wished to maintain an alliance with men—left the group. Ultimately, the members who stayed wanted to transform the Pavilion from a feminist photography gallery informed by feminist art history and theory into a space for local Leeds women.

The difficulties faced by the Pavilion were also affected by the 1983 political debates in Britain that had moved far to the right, and by an economic recession that had badly distressed Leeds and put a strain on its public funding. Additionally, the Left, which was focused on survival, became less engaged with new forms of cultural activity.[142] The Pavilion's location in peripheral Leeds, away from the cultural center of London, arguably put further strain on its struggle for survival.

The Pavilion reopened in 1985 with the help of a grant from the West Yorkshire Metropolitan County Council (a body that was abolished in the course of that year). Hoping to rely on local Leeds connections, the newly established collective dismissed the Pavilion's advisory board.[143] The Pavilion's new focus was on rendering photography as a social service, providing photographic resources, and running educational projects for girls, women, and youth workers in Leeds.[144] In the late 1980s, its emphasis shifted to photography by people of color and ethnic minorities.[145]

The institutionalization of feminist photography and art practices, which earlier had developed in marginal spaces, granted them visibility to a wider public and marked their presence. Nonetheless, as was manifested in *Three Perspectives* and in the Leeds Pavilion, this shift caused ruptures in some of the feminist groups involved in these endeavors, due either to conflicts surrounding institutionalization or to issues of separatism. Although several of these practices entered established art spaces, a number were excluded again soon after for lacking artistic value and were deemed unworthy of support from official funding bodies.

The Institutionalization of Photography as Fine Art

Beginning in the late 1970s, photography was radically reevaluated by fine art institutions, situated within the traditional visual art mediums, and framed with a particular set of "fine art" expectations.[146] Consequently, out of the diverse set of feminist photography practices and forms of organization that developed in the 1970s, those that adhered to fine art values would prevail in the art museum in the following decade.[147] This development paralleled the entry of photography into academia and the establishment of new degree programs in photography following the incorporation of art schools into the university sector. Such photography programs approached photography semiotically and psychoanalytically and were often critical of traditional art history but maintained some of its values. Thus, the artists employing the feminist photography practices that came out of such programs were predominantly encouraged to be theoretically engaged but also oriented toward individual artistic production.[148] This development in many ways set such feminist photography practices apart from some earlier feminist photography practices that were removed from "artistic" considerations and "high theory" and oriented toward self-designed forms of organization. This shift can be observed in the works of German-born photographer Karen Knorr and Iranian-born photographer Mitra Tabrizian,[149] both of whom studied photography at the Polytechnic of Central London in the late 1970s and early 1980s.[150] Knorr related that she encountered two conflicting arguments during her studies: the first criticized students who developed fine-grain, quality photographs for prioritizing form over content, and the second encouraged students to practice photography for art's sake. Knorr claimed that she distanced her practice from these polarities by combining political statements and feminist questions with visual allure in her images.[151] This disposition is demonstrated in Knorr's photo-text series *Gentlemen* (1981–1983), which criticizes the gendered and racial exclusionary connotations associated with British gentlemen's clubs. Her work, like other theoretically engaged photo-texts of the time, employed advertising rhetoric, text, and visual conventions to make critical statements. At the same time, her photographs were of fine-grain quality.[152] One of her images features a black waiter at a gentlemen's club whose gaze confronts the viewer (figure 29). It is captioned, "Men are interested in Power. Women are more interested in Service." Thus, this work situates the black man in a feminine service position at a men's institution that had traditionally excluded nonwhite members and women. Furthermore, the gentlemen's clubs that were founded under British colonial rule in places such as India prohibited the entry of locals.[153] Thus, Knorr's work sheds light on the power relations that are enacted by racial and gender differences and criticizes the associated social roles inscribed by these differences.

Similarly, Tabrizian treated her images artistically and addressed intersections of gendered and racialized power relations. This approach can be viewed in her photo-text series *The Blues* (1986–1987), produced with Andy Golding. This series consists of lavishly colored photographs that enact fabricated scenes reminiscent of film noir.[154] One of her images depicts a black man in a white mask being interrogated by a white woman (figure 30). The image is captioned, "He played right into her hands. But her world was still out of his reach." In many ways Tabrizian's work also relates to the then developing feminist film theory, its semiotic and psychoanalytic analysis of the

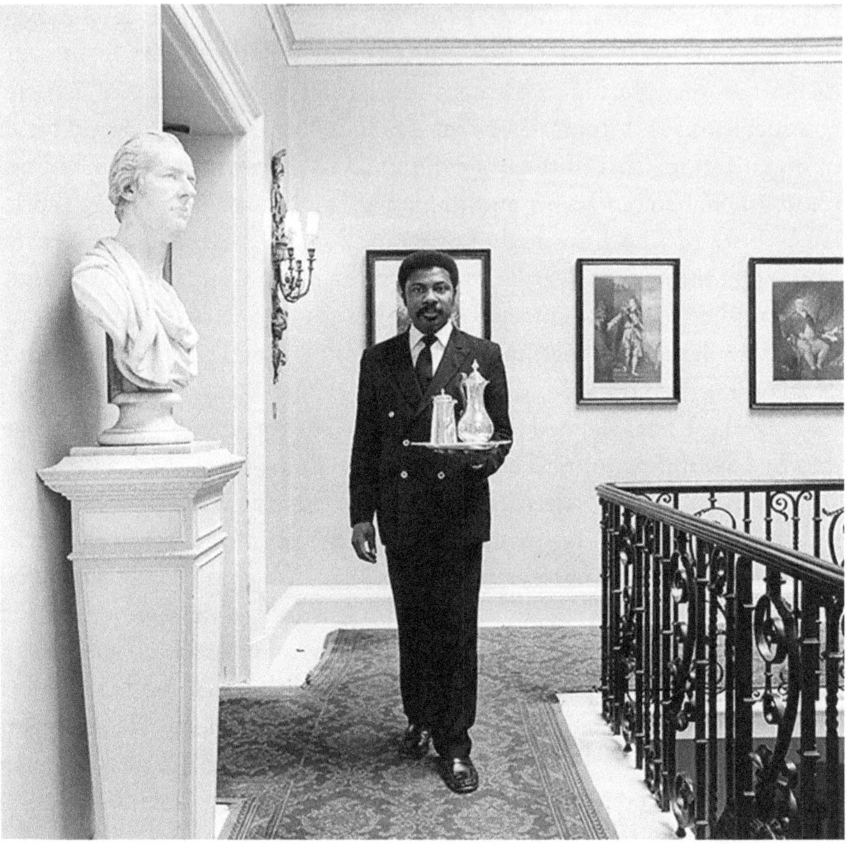

FIG. 29 Karen Knorr, image from *Gentlemen* photo-text series, 1981–1983, courtesy of Karen Knorr.

figure of the femme fatale, and its articulation of a female gaze.[155] Additionally, Tabrizian's work, like Knorr's, signals the feminist preoccupation with racial difference that was taken up toward the end of the decade.

After *Three Perspectives*, several contemporary British photography exhibitions took place that framed photography as a fine art practice. One of these was *Through the Looking Glass: Photographic Art in Britain, 1945–1989*, curated by Gerry Badger and John Benton-Harris and held at the London Barbican Art Gallery in 1989. This show included works by Knorr and Tabrizian, in addition to documentary photography, photojournalism, and color photography. Commenting on the exhibition, the critic Peter Turner called the included works "independent photography," which he explained to be a form of image making in which the photographer's "personal

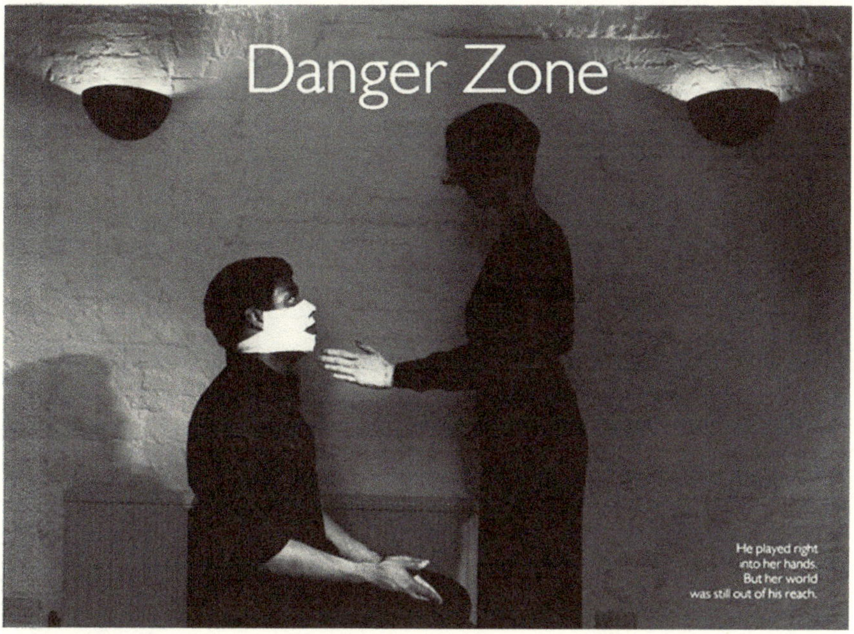

FIG. 30 Mitra Tabrizian and Andy Golding, item from *The Blues*, 1986–1987, courtesy of Mitra Tabrizian.

stance"—and not the external constraints of cultural conditioning—guides the work's appearance.[156] This assessment positioned the photographers in the show as self-expressive artists removed from social engagement. This disposition is clearly in contrast with the 1970s notion of the photographer as political activist. Similarly, Susan Kismaric, who curated *British Photography from the Thatcher Years*, which was exhibited at MoMA in 1990, emphasized the social detachment among contemporary British documentary photographers included in her show. Kismaric claimed that earlier documentary photographers wanted to use their images to influence social order, whereas the works in the current show were concerned mainly with personal expression.[157] It should be noted that all the photographers included in her show were men and that feminism was an absent topic.[158]

The foregoing discussion addresses the shift in the photography toward fine art status, and the incorporation of fine art values into some feminist photography practices. David Bate comments that this development resulted mainly from accelerated cuts made to the public sector in the 1980s—and the increased role of the art market as a central source of support for photography. Bate's explanation seems to correspond with my observation that photography's initial public support had a major impact on the plurality and diversity of its content and forms. In any event, this new development compelled photographers such as Knorr and Tabrizian to compete with and operate according to art market values and demands. The Arts Council continued to fund a number of politically engaged photography projects, such as Autograph ABP (Association of Black Photographer), founded in London in 1988, which aimed at promoting ethnic diversity in visual arts.[159] But in the 1980s, the Arts Council also began preferring photography projects that would have a market.[160]

Today, there is an increasing interest in a broad, transnational range of feminist photography and feminist art practices produced in the 1970s and early 1980s. Moreover, as suggested by art historian Ruth Iskin, feminist art and art made by women is now being facilitated by museums in ways that were not possible during the 1970s. For instance, women and feminist curators presently hold significant museum positions, and affluent women such Elizabeth A. Sackler, founder of the Elizabeth A. Sackler Center for Feminist Art at the Brooklyn Museum, and Sarah Peter, founder of Modern Women's Fund at MoMA, have donated money specifically to increase the visibility of women artists in museums. Since the 1970s, feminism has also had a significant cultural impact on the mind-set of audiences, artists, and curators, which has contributed to its acceptability and popularity in the field of art.[161] Such developments were reflected in the United States particularly by the *Wack! Art and the Feminist Revolution* exhibition curated by Cornelia H. Butler for the Geffen Contemporary at the Museum of Contemporary Art in Los Angeles in 2007. This show offered an extensive international survey of a broad range of feminist art practices produced around the 1970s. While some of the participating artists, such as Judy Chicago and Marina Abramovic, had by then established positions in contemporary art history, others, such as the black women's artist group Where We At and the Native American–based group Spiderwoman Theater, were less known and were thus offered an institutional platform and recognition of their work.[162] Another significant event that marked an institutional interest in feminist art was "The Feminist Future: Theory and Practice in the Visual Arts," a conference that took place in 2007 at MoMA. It should be noted that this was the first feminist art conference that took place at this museum. Among the participants were key feminist scholars and artists who were active in the 1970s and 1980s, such as Lucy Lippard, Martha

Rosler, Linda Nochlin, and Griselda Pollock. Furthermore, in 2007 the Brooklyn Museum established a center for feminist art and selected Judy Chicago's work *The Dinner Party* (1974–1979) as its permanent installation.[163]

In 2010, about four decades after the disintegration of the Hackney Flashers, twenty-three panels from the *Who's Holding the Baby* project were acquired by the National Museum Reina Sofia Center of Art in Madrid for the "Feminist Revolution" section of its From Revolt to Postmodernity (1962–1982) collection.[164] One of the goals of this collection is to exhibit works shaped in the context of various political, social, and cultural events of that time, such as the uprisings of 1968, the Cuban Revolution, the rise of feminist movements, the economic crisis, and the increased influence of popular culture. Moreover, this collection is intended to display works that challenged traditional art conventions and their aesthetic value, as well as traditional forms of artistic production.[165] Some of the feminist works exhibited alongside the Hackney Flashers' work are photographs from the Spanish feminist artist Esther Ferrer's performance piece *Intimate and Personal* (1977), in which she measured parts of her nude body as a means to criticize the fetishization of women, as well as the video *Boy Meets Girl* (1978) by the feminist Spanish filmmaker Eugènia Balcells, which challenges images of romantic couples in Hollywood cinema.[166] An interest in politically engaged photography was also manifested in David Alan Mellor's *No Such Thing as Society: Photography in Britain, 1967–1987*, exhibited in 2008 at the Hayward Gallery. This show offered an aestheticized social realist account of British photography and its take on issues such as racial tension, communities in crisis, and youth alienation. The show included thirty-three photographers, including women photographers Tish Murtha and Marketa Luskacova. Works addressing domestic violence by feminist photographers Hunter and Voge were also included in the show. However, this show did not exhibit the diversity of feminist photography practices, and the majority of the photographers in the show were men.[167]

The fine art museum's recent interest in feminist art produced in the 1970s is paralleled by a growing academic pursuit found, for instance, in Siona Wilson's and Kathy Battista's writings, which "uncover" British feminist art practices and situate them within narratives of feminist artistic activity.[168]

The contemporary interest in earlier cultural political strategies produced in a moment of social upheaval arguably arises in part from the present social and economic crisis and the corresponding global surges of cultural political activity. Related contemporary developments include demonstrations by the Occupy movement, feminist activities by groups such as *Pussy Riot* in Russia, the Me Too movement, transnational SlutWalk marches, and the circulation of political content and images in social networks.

Ultimately, the exhibition of feminist photography and artworks from the 1970s in fine art institutions has framed them as historical art objects and detached them from their initial sites of circulation, their forms of display, and the challenges they posed to fine art practices. Nonetheless, this development grants their work a visibility that calls for further investigation of the intersections between politics and cultural production, inventive forms of organization, and their interventionist potential.

Conclusion

At the end of the 1970s, feminist photography and feminist art practices that had initially developed outside the art museum sought to secure a space within it, as well as to challenge the art museum's modes of operation, values, and exclusions. The feminist ICA shows and *Three Perspectives* brought feminist works—and the diversity of their arguments—into the art museum; these shows featured an emphasis on political content, a challenge to aesthetic values, theoretical engagements with feminism, collective forms of organization, and works produced by women. Feminist photography and feminist artworks were at times exhibited alongside each other and shared some feminist arguments and forms of organization. However, feminist photography was situated within the developments of photographic activity and debates that were taking shape during the 1970s independent of established institutions such as the art museum, art schools, and academia. Additionally, feminist photography, like other forms of politicized photography, frequently responded to photographic depictions in the mainstream media and advertising and addressed the role of photographic representation in the social sphere.

The feminist ICA shows and *Three Perspectives* were successful in attracting attention, curiosity, and audiences. However, their politicized feminist arguments and the challenges they posed to aesthetic quality were mostly met with suspicion or hostility from art critics and funding bodies. Works such as the Hackney Flashers' projects were considered disruptive and removed from the art museum. Similarly, the Leeds Pavilion—initially designated to be a feminist exhibition space that offered an alternative to the art museum—was criticized by its funding body for its lack of works of aesthetic quality and its separatist direction, which then led to the Pavilion's closure. In addition, the process of institutionalizing feminist photography caused breaches among the Hackney Flashers and the Pavilion collective and led to their disintegration.

Although its presence in the art museum was earlier considered unusual, photography continued to gain the status of a fine art practice over the course of the 1980s. It also entered academia as new degree programs in photography were being established. At the same time, works by several feminist photographers posed critical and theoretically engaged questions while emphasizing aesthetic value. This trend corresponded with several contemporary British photography exhibitions that were framed as fine art shows. Consequently, the initial desire to claim a space for feminist photography in the art museum resulted in the incorporation of fine art values and accommodation of them in the established museum space. Thus, the process of institutionalizing feminist photography eventually altered some of the features that characterized it when it operated on the margins. This route dulled its confrontationally critical edge, narrowed the plurality of the sites where it circulated, and spurred a departure from self-designed forms of organization.

Nonetheless, there is a current institutional and academic interest in the arguments, visual strategies, and organizational structure of feminist art and photography practices produced in the 1970s that were initially viewed as controversial. The recent economic crisis, social unrest, and technological developments in image production and circulation have arguably propelled a desire to reexamine the interventionist potential of photographic and cultural activity produced in an earlier moment of upheaval.

Ultimately, feminist photography and feminist art have advanced from their initial process of institutionalization at the end of the 1970s and their incorporation into the art museum. This process enabled their infiltration into other institutional structures and discourses, including the university and the field of art history. In this way, articulating a perspective on British feminism and photography in the 1970s and early 1980s has become an accessible and viable project. I believe that a further investigation of the diverse arguments, conflicts, and production processes of these practices might offer a way of critically thinking about the political potential of feminist photography and other forms of cultural practices in the present time.

5

Conclusion and Afterthoughts

This book centers on feminist photography that developed in Britain during the 1970s—a time of profound social and economic instability but also a time of increasingly politicized cultural activity. It shows how feminist photography flourished as a unique countercultural practice whose concerns intertwined with politicized developments in the field of photography, the growing social impact of the British women's movement, and the emergence of diverse feminist cultural initiatives. Particularly emphasized is the intersection between feminist photography and the interventionist potential attributed at the time to the broader field of photography. This is historicized and explained in light of photography's predominant development outside the institutional spaces of the museum and academia, which positioned it as politically unrestricted and as capable of meeting a set of social expectations. Photography was independent from the art market's demands, and it received support from official state bodies that were focused on encouraging its diversity and dissemination rather than on its content or aesthetic qualities. Consequently, a range of feminist and politicized photographers did not aspire to have their work attain fine art status but rather viewed it as a political and feminist tool.

Feminist Photography and Representation

This book has argued that the concept of representation was central to the developing fields of photography and photography theory. This concept was present in debates on the politics of representation, and in their competing photography arguments associated with street photography that advocated the political significance of capturing the "true" representation of events sidelined by the media. Nevertheless, this book argues that both of these positions had an underlying "objective" approach to analyzing photographic meaning and aimed to offer an alternative to the then prevalent models of photography analysis rooted in personal reflections and photographers' biographies.[1]

This book had also situated debates about photographic representation and its political potential in relation to shifting debates within the British Left during the 1970s, which moved away from economic determinism toward an interest in the impact of ideology and the production of ideological representations on the social field. This shift politicized cultural activities, such as photography, and made room for new forms of political struggle, such as feminism and antiracism, that had previously been marginalized within the official political structures of the Left.[2]

My discussion has accentuated how the concept of representation and its perceived social and political ramifications were central to feminist photography. Feminist photographers intervened in the sphere of representation by theoretically engaging with this concept, by subverting mainstream representations of gender stereotypes, and by capturing underrepresented street events pertaining to women's rights. This book emphasizes that some feminist photography practices were informed by certain arguments that had developed within the women's movement, such as the notion that the personal is political. I have demonstrated that photographers such as Jo Spence,[3] Liz Heron, Jini Rawlings, and the initiators of the *Women* and *Men* shows used photography as a consciousness-raising tool to enable personal reflection on media images, articulating women's overlooked experiences and expressing a collective feminist argument. Such feminist explorations of subjective experiences through photography stood out from the time's other politicized photography practices, photography theory, and burgeoning discourses of cultural analysis that advocated an "objective" approach avoiding interpretations rooted in "feelings."[4]

Feminist Photography's Distinct Contributions

Intervening in the sphere of representation was undoubtedly an integral strategy for feminist photography and for other politicized photography practices in 1970s Britain. Nonetheless, my discussion illustrates that feminist photography's contributions and subversive underpinnings were not limited to its representational content. Feminist photography also employed original strategies of collective organization that corresponded with the nonhierarchical modes of operation that characterized the women's movement. Additionally, feminist uses of photography were marked by politicized desires to democratize photography skills and challenged the perceived masculinity associated with photographic technology and production. As shown, this ungendering of photography skills was manifested in feminist photographers' individual practice and in the establishment of photography workshops for women by feminist collectives, such as the Hackney Flashers and the Leeds Pavilion.

Feminist photography also reflects some of the period's distinct feminist cultural strategies. An examination of the broad range of feminist countercultural practices of 1970s Britain reveals that, in contrast to a long-standing misconception that feminists lacked a sense of humor, many of them mobilized it as a political strategy, using a successful joke to ally the spectator with the joke's initiators rather than the joke's object. Examples of such playfulness include the media spectacle surrounding the feminist interruption of the 1970 Miss World competition using whistles and flour bombs, as well as the Reclaim the Night marchers' humorous objectification of male onlookers. The use of humor is also evident in feminist photography—for example, in the Hackney Flashers' photomontages addressing the media's lack of representations of working-class women's personal experience, the biting wit employed in feminist billboard graffiti, and the whimsical gender reversals by photographers such as Lill-Ann Chepstow-Lusty that commented on the limited representations of gender roles in advertising. Such humorous strategies could variously jolt the public or draw its attention to feminist arguments. As Jo Anna Isaak has argued, such uses of humor can be viewed as participating in a rebellious strategy available for those who do not have access to power and as a skill often used to avoid violence from aggressors by making them laugh.[5] Furthermore, the use of wit, which was employed most prominently in feminist billboard graffiti, can be perceived as asserting that women can outsmart men and advertisers at their own "cerebral masculine" game.[6]

Along similar lines, David Green and Joanna Lowry have argued that feminist photography had an indexical value that traced the unique feminist photographic act of producing it, the distinct employment of feminist strategies, and the subversive feminist claim to represent the "real."[7]

Finally, I argue that the repetition of feminist photographic acts, the circulation of feminist photographs in various feminist arenas, and the act of viewing such photographs had significant affective qualities that narrated a set of socially shared feelings with which feminists could identify and that could potentially generate a sense of feminist collectivity that would prompt further political mobilization.[8]

Main Themes and Present-Day Relevance

This book suggests that feminist photography posed arguments that corresponded with the distinct ideologies of the period's feminist subgroupings, such as socialist, radical, black, and revolutionary feminism, and with contemporaneous developments in feminist theory. Given the broad range of feminist expressions manifested in feminist photography, I have avoided looking through the limited lens of any particular feminist camp. Instead, I have observed feminist photography through the frame of the cross-cutting campaigns and concerns with which it engaged. With this methodological approach, I have portrayed feminist photography as having yielded a broad thematic scope that went beyond the politics and circumstances of any particular feminist faction. This approach helps to flesh out several predominant themes pertaining to feminism and photography: the feminist critique of media images, feminist street photography, and the relationship between feminist photography and the museum. However, despite the historical lens this book brings to those themes, those same themes are also germane to present-day feminist photography, as I shall discuss presently.

Media Images as a Continuing Site of Feminist Dispute

Although the various factions within the women's movement in 1970s Britain were in conflict on many points, they were nevertheless in agreement that media images were a necessary target of feminist politics due to their central place in the socialization of women. A variety of feminist photography practices responded to media representations and posed photographic alternatives to mainstream media images of women. For example, these practices utilized advertising strategies to call attention to the need for state-funded childcare and documented feminist graffiti that resisted sexualized representations of women on billboard advertisings.

The feminist debates of the 1970s notably contested sexualized media representations of women and suggested that they perpetuated stereotypes about women and limited women's social roles. I have underlined how radical and revolutionary feminist debates furthermore suggested that sexual and pornographic images were actually acts of violence against women and that sexual lust was therefore implicitly associated with male oppression of women. Consequently, the topics of female sexuality and desire were censored from radical and revolutionary feminist debates and related visual practices. Many radical and revolutionary feminists identified as lesbians or as "political lesbians" and therefore distinguished themselves as sexual "others." However, instead of discursively linking their sexual orientation to questions of desire and female sexuality, they characterized it as stemming from political separatism from men.[9] Nonetheless, as I have noted, the late 1970s and early 1980s saw the emergence of American and British feminist pro-pleasure debates, which set out to develop a feminist discourse on sexuality and on varied sexual practices and identities. Such pro-pleasure debates, followed by postfeminist ideas of sexual self-empowerment and the queer theory that emerged during the early 1990s, foregrounded a cultural shift that reconceptualized sexuality as political.[10] Such deliberations, although not fully explored in this book, had influenced changes in feminist photography practice.[11] Despite such discursive shifts, feminist approaches toward sexualized media images of women today remain an integral, yet ambivalent, feminist concern. Some feminists, such as the social psychology scholar Rosalind Gill, criticize the increasing popularization of hypersexualized images in mainstream media and situate this phenomenon within manifestations of what Gill calls the "pornofication of everyday life." Thus, feminists such as Gill are skeptical of feminist views that perceive "female sexual empowerment" as potentially subversive.[12] The feminist philosopher Nina Power likewise challenges the commodification of feminism and its representations of female empowerment by neoliberal and conservative forces that previously opposed feminism. Power suggests that such viewpoints reduce feminism to a form of consumerism that dulls feminism's political edge.[13] At the same time, contending feminist voices view self-expressions of female sexuality as an empowering representational strategy for condemning slut shaming and rape culture and breaking racial stereotypes associated with nonwhite female sexuality.[14]

Today, just as in the 1970s, feminist countermedia photography practices continue to exist. While some of these practices carry on some aspects developed in 1970s feminist media debates, others challenge and reframe them. One such example is the "sexy selfie" media phenomenon, which manifests a contemporary feminist attitude toward representations of self-expressive female sexuality. Sexy selfies are mostly taken by young girls who pose in a conventionally seductive manner for their camera phones. Such images are often posted by the young girls themselves through free media apps such Instagram and other social media platforms. Girls whose Instagram accounts attain popularity often attract advertising companies who pay for product endorsements. This phenomenon—its potential monetary gain and the supposed consenting self-agency performed by the girls—surely complicates the boundaries between sexual empowerment and self-commodification.[15]

On the other hand, current feminist debates trouble the mainstream media's standards of female beauty. For instance, a prevalent feminist critique targets the media's promotion of unrealistic beauty standards and its use of unhealthily skinny models. This critique recalls 1970s feminist objections to the feminine beauty standards advocated by the media, but it also reflects the fact that the images produced by the media are now perceived not only as socially oppressive but also as a potential health threat.

Feminist billboard graffiti writers, both in the 1970s and today, have defaced misogynist advertisements; today, images of these defaced ads are easily shared on social media. One particular billboard ad (ca. 2015) that attracted feminist opposition was an advertisement for Protein World weight-loss products. This ad was positioned in a number of subway stations in Britain and depicted a slender yet curvy, light-skinned female model in a yellow bathing suit against a yellow background. This ad featured the tagline, "Are You Beach Body Ready?" and stated that "substituting two meals of an energy restricted diet with a meal replacement contributes to weight loss." This ad was defaced by numerous feminist commuters. Among the feminist responses written on the ad were "everyone is beach body ready" and "stop encouraging women to starve themselves."[16] In May 2015, this advertisement also spurred a protest march in Hyde Park, London, where protesters wore bathing suits showing off their diversely shaped and colored bodies.[17] The protesters ultimately prevailed, as this ad was eventually banned by the British Advertising Standards Authority in April 2015 for misleading health claims.[18]

The defacement of the Protein World ad resembles feminist billboard graffiti practices of the 1970s in many ways. Most crucially, the products of both practices were photographed and circulated on feminist platforms. However, whereas the feminist billboard graffiti of the 1970s was photographed using analog technology and its images were processed slowly and redistributed in small-circulation feminist publications, nowadays, the billboard defacements (like the sexy selfies) are captured by digital cameras that allow for instant processing and posting on feminist social media platforms. Thus, unlike in the earlier uses of feminist photography, in present-day uses, the immediacy of photo processing and photo sharing expands the potential local and international audience for such defacements, the exposure to their feminist arguments, and perhaps their impact on further political mobilization.

Feminist Street Photography and Political Mobilization

During the 1970s in Britain, there were no laws requiring police permission for public assembly or marches. Thus, the street functioned as a highly political site in which political forces advocated for themselves, clashed, and formed alliances. Feminists, like other politicized photographers, turned to the street to represent and circulate political proceedings. As mentioned in chapter 3, photographic representation of street events such as the Battle of Lewisham, Reclaim the Night, and the Grunwick strike was perceived as a political activity that captured the "truth" of the events that was overlooked by the mainstream media. At the same time, this was also a moment in which the nascent photography theory rethought the relationship between political action, photographic representation, and "truth."

My analyses emphasizes that the street photographer's camera had political ramifications beyond its representational capacities and that the street photographer's presence and activity became part of the street action. Drawing on the writings of Judith Butler and Michael Warner, I have argued that the crowd consisting of photographers and demonstrators assembled in the space of the street becomes a force that confronted power structures, shaped a shared political will, and reconfigured the space of politics as located in the space of the street.[19] Furthermore, given the perceived political potential attributed to photographic representation of the street and its capacity to convey political arguments to imagined viewers, the presence of photographers and their street cameras had a performative power. This power was implicit in the exchange between the camera and those photographed, thus influencing the events taking place in front of it.[20] Additionally, the camera's street presence drew the public's attention toward the event taking place and to its potential political underpinnings. The performative exchange between the camera and the street proceedings occurred regardless of whether an actual photograph was taken, thus transcending the photograph's representational value.[21] Nevertheless, some of the street dynamics captured by the photographers were shaped as evidence that conveyed a "truthful" form of knowledge.[22]

Pertinent to this topic is the correlation between feminist and antiracism concerns, photographic representation, and the street's political status. The street was characterized by gendered and racialized power relations that influenced politicized street photography. The close examination of the Grunwick strike and the Reclaim the Night marches in chapter 3 emphasized the way both events challenged gendered implications associated with the public sphere and the way in which photography became part of the political protest. This aspect is common to both events, despite the divergent political agendas advocated in each case. The striking Asian women from the Grunwick factory defied their culture's patriarchal codes of female "respectability" by publicly participating in the picket line. The strike, which erupted in a film-processing lab, disrupted its workers' production of photographic representations and thus symbolically drew attention to the Asian working women's revolt and its own need for photographic representation. It should be noted that the photographs of the Grunwick strike examined in this book were taken by British-born photographers. Unfortunately, photographs of the strike taken by the Asian strikers have not surfaced and are thus missing from my analysis. This lacuna deserves further exploration that could potentially shed additional light on the power structures implicit in the relationship between race, photographic representation, and the sites of its circulation and conservation.

Similar to the striking Asian women of the Grunwick strike, the marching women at Reclaim the Night used "masculine" tropes of defiant confrontation to make themselves heard. This style of confrontation was reminiscent of the punk subculture. I view the presence of women street photographers during these events as having challenged the gendering within the field of photography and street photography in particular. The presence of feminist photographers prompted particular performative interactions between feminist protesters and the camera, thus generating a shared sense of feminist community.

Thus, the Grunwick strike and Reclaim the Night both became sites of spectacular feminist street disobedience. Contemporary feminist scholars such as Mary Russo have drawn on Mikhail Bakhtin's understanding of the socially liberating potential of the medieval and Renaissance carnival in order to analyze the prospects of subversive feminist behavior.[23] My analysis similarly employs the notion of the carnivalesque to suggest that the Grunwick strike and Reclaim the Night were both sites of cultural transgression that challenged gendered cultural hierarchies. The women's street presence at the Grunwick strike and Reclaim the Night playfully mocked patriarchal culture and oppression. Yet Bakhtin's carnival was a sanctioned form of political transgression, whereas the discussed women demonstrators aimed to generate social transformation.

Issues of photographic representation and circulation are equally germane to feminist street events of the 1970s and those of today. Some similarities can be found between Reclaim the Night and the contemporary SlutWalk movement. This latter movement emerged in 2011 in Toronto following a safety presentation delivered by a police officer at the law school of York University. The officer advised women that, in order to prevent being raped and sexually harassed, they should avoid dressing like "sluts."[24] This remark prompted students Sonya Barnett and Heather Jarvis to post their outrage on Facebook and to organize a response. With the help of three other local women, SlutWalk Toronto was held on April 3, 2011, with an estimated crowd of three thousand to four thousand participants. The organizers proclaimed in their statement of purpose that they were tired of being oppressed by slut shaming and judged for their sexuality, since no one should equate enjoying sex with attracting sexual assault.[25]

Both SlutWalk and Reclaim the Night reclaimed public space, contested sexual violence against women, and demanded that the street become a safe place for women. However, while Reclaim the Night identified any sexualization of women's bodies as patriarchal and oppressive, SlutWalk participants performed so-called male-defined female sexualities by wearing "sexy" uniforms and lingerie as a strategy to resignify the derogative term *slut*.[26]

Reclaim the Night organizers were interested in attracting mainstream media attention to their cause, although they were only moderately successful in this regard. Media coverage was likewise recognized as an integral part of the Toronto SlutWalk, which drew considerable global media attention, as well as extensive coverage on the internet.[27] In contrast to Reclaim the Night, which was discussed primarily in women's movement channels, SlutWalk has enjoyed significant local and international visibility due to the availability of social media. Following the first Toronto march, the idea of a SlutWalk as a form of protest went viral throughout the world. Within six months, feminist groups had planned marches in more than fifty cities and regions in Canada and the United States, as well as in thirty-three cities in Europe, New Zealand, South America, India, and the Middle East.[28] The Toronto SlutWalk organizers also created a web of Facebook pages dedicated to various SlutWalks with links to numerous feminist blogs and websites, thus creating a transnational network of activists and organizations around the globe.[29] Consequently, unlike the Reclaim the Night marches, which attracted hundreds of women, SlutWalk involved thousands of local participants and formed a broad, international feminist community.

Nonetheless, despite SlutWalk's global impact, it turned into a target of feminist criticism and a manifestation of racial power relations within the Western feminist community. Some feminists contested SlutWalk's focus on the expression of female sexuality, arguing that reclaiming the term *slut* sent the wrong message to young girls and therefore did not solve the real issue that the movement targeted. Additionally, black feminist organizations, such as Black Women's Blueprint and Black Women for Reproductive Justice, proclaimed that given the history of slavery and the manner in which it constructed black female sexuality, *slut* was a privileged term that did not reflect black women's historical and lived experience.[30]

During the 1970s, the political power associated with democratizing photography skills and with photographs taken by feminists participating in street events was often exalted by politicized photographers. Not only are these ideas still in circulation today but, given the technological deskilling of image processing, the immediacy of photo circulation in social media, and the wide, transnational viewing audience for which these platforms are available, they have become astonishingly amplified. The current significance of participant photography and its related technological ramifications is no doubt situated within broader shifts in the news coverage of political street events. A prominent recent example is the Arab Spring of 2010. During this uprising, documentation in the form of mobile-phone snapshots and videos captured by citizens and participants was sought after by the mainstream media rather than framed as offering an alternative to the media.[31] Although differing from the Arab Spring in their political goals and circumstances, SlutWalks events were similarly documented by feminist participants' cell phones. The photographs and videos produced from SlutWalks were immediately posted on a variety of social media sites, including both personal Facebook pages and Facebook event pages for SlutWalks, and some of these images were incorporated into mainstream media.[32] Thus, whereas feminist photographs and accounts of Reclaim the Night countered the mainstream media's disregard of this event, the multiple photographs and texts posted by SlutWalks' participants shaped the movement's local and international representation on the web and in the mainstream press.[33]

The extensive impact of the SlutWalk movement and its visual documentation can also be viewed as reflecting changes in the political goals of feminist street events. SlutWalk was a spectacular street protest whose main goals were reclaiming the term *slut*, challenging sexual violence, and occupying public and social media space. Reclaim the Night and the Grunwick strike were similarly spectacular street protests, but they differed in their demands for broader structural and social changes whose attainment was far more complicated.[34]

SlutWalk might be perceived as echoing Reclaim the Night's resistance against violence and sexual violence, feminist occupation of public space, and reclamation of photographic representation. However, shifts in feminist debates about female sexuality, technological advancements in image processing and circulation, and contemporary manifestations of feminist street photography have reshaped the feminist capturing of political street events. Nonetheless, the tensions between the street, gender, racial difference, and physical safety continue to be unresolved issues that deserve rethinking and further political action.

Feminist Photography and the Museum

At the end of the 1970s, feminist photography (as well as other forms of feminist art) that initially did not aim to be exhibited in the art museum had brought its arguments and strategies of organization into this space and to challenge its values and exclusions. Chapter 4 shows how photography, and especially feminist photography, not only changed its exhibition venue but was gradually becoming accepted by fine art institutions. Despite these shifts, I am wary of implying a teleological narrative of feminist photography's progression from a noninstitutional practice to its final, "evolved" destination within the fine art museum.

Although British photography had ultimately attained local and international fine art status, feminist photography was often marginalized within it. This was manifested in exhibitions dedicated to British photography such as *British Photography from the Thatcher Years* (1990) and *No Such Thing as Society* (2008), which were exhibited at the prominent fine art spaces of the Museum of Modern Art and the Hayward Gallery, respectively, but included few, if any, women photographers and disregarded the diversity of feminist photography. Moreover, feminist photography's initial entry into the museum was not without conflict. Two cases in point are the reception of Mary Kelly's *Post-partum Document* at the second Hayward Annual in 1978 as "fit for a foyer in a maternal hospital" and the critical reception of the feminist and politicized photography works exhibited at the Hayward's *Three Perspectives on Photography: Recent British Photography*, which were frequently met with suspicion and criticized as lacking aesthetic quality, though *Three Perspectives* was successful in attracting a large audience. Additionally, the feminist photography collective the Hackney Flashers, whose work was included in the *Three Perspectives* exhibition, were considered disruptive for the adjacent events that they organized, as well as for their work, which was judged as lacking in aesthetic quality. Thus, this collective, which was received with hostility, was ultimately expelled from the art museum. Furthermore, the shift toward institutionalization caused ruptures among existing feminist photography collectives and contributed to their disintegration, as was the case with the Hackney Flashers and the Leeds Pavilion.

The entry of feminist photographic practices into the museum was an important intervention in fine art spaces due to the political arguments and strategies they employed. Indeed, by the 1980s, some photographers—including feminist photographers—who sought recognition for their work as fine art were increasingly successful in achieving it. For example, works by feminist photographers Karen Knorr and Mitra Tabrizian, who gave their photographs artistic treatment, entered fine art spaces. Whereas the process of the institutionalization of feminist photography had initially aimed to disrupt the art museum's values and mode of operation, by the 1980s it had compromised on this goal in order to enter the fine art museum. I have situated these shifts in photographic strategies and status within the social and political changes that took place in Britain at the end of the 1970s. Among such social changes were accelerated cuts made to the public sector, which limited public funding for photographic activity and strengthened the position of the art market as a patron. Such developments likely drove certain feminist photographers to operate according to a new set of values and demands.

Nevertheless, despite cuts to public spending, some feminist countercultural practices that began in the 1970s continued to exist well into the 1990s. For example, the Leeds Pavilion, in its first instantiation, operated until the mid-1980s. The feminist photography agency Format likewise remained active until 2003, and the feminist magazine *Spare Rib* operated until 1993. Additionally, feminist photographer Jo Spence continued to create politicized photography works until her death in 1992.[35] Moreover, since the 1980s, photography engaging with issues of race has increasingly gained visibility. This is evident, for example, in Autograph ABP (Association of Black Photographers) and Judy Harrison's Mount Pleasant Photography Workshop in Southampton (1977–2013), which encouraged photographic self-representation among local black and Asian communities.[36] The Mount Pleasant Workshop also had feminist underpinnings, such as an all-girl photography group held in the 1980s that made photography technology available to black and Asian girls who then used the camera to express themselves.[37]

The institutionalization of feminism and photography transformed these spheres. This processes led to the ultimate expansion of feminism's and photography's discourses and activity. For instance, during the 1980s, a number of events foregrounded the contributions of women photographers to the field of photography as culturally significant. Among these were the publication of Val Williams's *Women Photographers: The Other Observers, 1900 to the Present* (1986), which traced the history of women photographers, and Spectrum Women's Photography Festival, which was launched in 1988 and whose works were disseminated in a published catalog later the same year.[38] Those aspects of feminist photography that were transformed by its institutionalization during the 1980s eventually paved the way for the recent revival and growing institutional interest in the earlier dismissed feminist photography and its visual language and inventive forms of production. An example of this shift is the recent acquisition of panels from the Hackney Flashers' project *Who's Holding the Baby* by the National Museum Reina Sofía Center of Art in Madrid for its permanent "Feminist Revolution" section. This is *Who's Holding the Baby*'s first museum exhibition since *Three Perspectives on Photography*.[39] Furthermore, the Photographers' Gallery in London exhibited *Feminist Avant-Garde of the 1970s* from October 2016 to January 2017, a show that included approximately two hundred works by forty-eight women artists from twenty countries, among which were photographs by Cindy Sherman, Penny Slinger, and Birgit Jürgenssen.[40] Additionally, Homer Sykes's photographs of the Grunwick strike (discussed in chapter 3) appeared in *Good Bye to London: Radical Art and Politics in the 70's* at the Neue Gesellschaft für bildende Kunst in Berlin in 2010. Also included in that exhibition were photographs by Jo Spence, posters by the Hackney Flashers, feminist artworks by Margaret Harrison, and images from the Berwick Street Collective's film *Nightcleaners*.[41]

The revived interest in women photographers and early feminist photography practices is perhaps influenced by the social turn in art, which, as suggested by Claire Bishop, began in the 1990s and is manifested by an interest in collectivity, models of collaboration, and direct engagement with social issues.[42] At the same time, the critical self-evaluation of fine art institutions is currently shifting. Museums are increasingly becoming interested not only in challenging gender-based marginalization but also in advocating the inclusion of artists based outside western Europe and North America and examining the relationship between Western and non-Western art traditions.[43]

The exhibition of works by feminist photographers such as the Hackney Flashers in fine art institutions framed them as historical art objects and detached them from their initial sites of circulation and forms of display, as well as from the challenges they posed to fine art practices. Similarly, the Photographer's Gallery show framed the feminist works it featured within the elitist art-historical tradition of the avant-garde. Nonetheless, despite these ramifications, the fine art museum's and academia's recent interest in feminist cultural production granted such works a visibility that calls for further investigation of the intersections between feminism, photography, and its interventionist potential.

In many ways, the premises of this book stem from the discursive shifts that have taken place in academia since its institutionalization of fields such as photography, feminism, gender studies, cultural studies, and visual culture. By including such diverse perspectives in my study, I have been able to examine the interdisciplinary contributions of the rich field of feminist photography practices in Britain in the 1970s and 1980s, and to signal their ongoing significance.

Acknowledgments

I wish to extend my gratitude to the many people and institutions that assisted, encouraged, and supported the writing of this book. First and foremost, I am deeply indebted to John Tagg, my PhD adviser in the Art History Department at the State University of New York at Binghamton, for his intellectual guidance and generous support, and for inspiring this book. I am particularly thankful that he kindly gave me the space to examine issues with which he was personally involved. I also wish to express my gratitude to the brilliant teachers and scholars whom I was fortunate to work with during my graduate studies. Among them are Karen-edis Barzman, Kevin Hatch, Tom McDonough, Nancy Um, Benita Roth, and Julia Walker. I thank them for their intellectual insight, challenging questions, and genuine encouragement.

Next, I would like to thank my colleagues at Binghamton University for their friendship and continuing collegial support, among them Hala Auji, Chris Balsiger, Yuri Chang, Hye-ok Cho, Jeremy Culler, Josh Franco, Jessica Kaminski, Jennifer Kennedy, Phillip Kheller, Lalaine Little, Trista Mallory, Hye-ri Oh, Angelique Szymanek, Ariza Torres, Ya Ling Wang, and Deng Yan Zhou.

I am grateful for the Dissertation Year Fellowship and to the Rosa Colecchio Travel Award from Binghamton University that supported my invaluable research trip to London and Leeds.

A number of individuals have benevolently extended their comments and advice during the course of this book's development. I would like to acknowledge Kobena Mercer, Christopher Pinney, Hillary Robinson, and Laura Wexler. I must also thank this book's two anonymous readers for their insightful comments and suggestions, which enriched this project.

I also wish to extent my gratitude to Tel Aviv University and the Yad Hanadiv foundation for granting me postdoctoral fellowships in the Art History Department and the photography program at Tel Aviv University (2013–2015), during which I developed my research for publication. Numerous colleagues from Tel Aviv University deserve a warm thank-you for the fruitful conversations, sharp insights, and keen interest in my work. Among them are Tal Dekel, Vered Maimon, Assaf Pinkus, and, last but not least, Hana Taragan. A special t thank-you goes to Ruth Iskin and my colleagues Ayelet Carmi, Shira Gotlieb, Ori Levin, Osnat Rechter, and David Sperber for their friendship, wonderful ideas, and kind support during the period of this book's writing.

Research for this work would not have been possible without the assistance of numerous institutions, archives, and libraries. I would like to thank the late Terry Dennett, director of the Jo Spence Memorial Archive, London, for his generous assistance and for sharing his experiences, and Jalna Hanmer and Sandra McNeil, trustees of Feminist Archive North in Special Collections in the Brotherton Library at the University of Leeds, and staff for their kind assistance and benevolence, and for sharing their personal resources. I would also like to acknowledge the help of Emma Boyd, head of communications and events at Autograph ABP, London, as well as the staff of the Oral History of British Photography Sound Collection at the British Library; the British National Archives; the Tate Archive collections; the Women's Library Archives; London Metropolitan University; the Victoria and Albert Museum's Archive of Art and Design; Blythe House, London; the *Times* Archive, London; the Richard Saltoun Gallery, London; Julia Cahill and Amy Frost, trustees of the Alex Hunter Estate; and the Tamiment Library and Robert F. Wagner Labor Archives at the Elmer Holmes Bobst Library, New York University. I would also like to acknowledge Concha Calvo in the Collections Department of the National Museum Reina Sofia Center of Art.

In developing my research, I owe much to the kindness of individuals who shared with me their knowledge, experiences, and resources. I am grateful to Dinah Clark, Elizabeth Cowie, Anna Davin, Susan Greenberg, Liz Heron, Vanessa Jackson, Angela Kelly, Keith Kennedy, Yve Lomax, Julia Meadows, Michael Ann Mullen, Laura Mulvey, Maggie Murray, Joanne O'Brien, Pragna

Patel, Angela Phillips, Christine Roche, Val Wilmer, and the late Alexis Hunter, whom I am so fortunate to have met. Their contributions have been tremendously significant for the realization of this project. My thanks go also to Ofra Kaufman for her kind assistance and Marcos Klorman and Evelyn Velleman for their generous hospitality while I stayed in London.

I am very grateful to all of the photographers included in this book for their activity, courage, and determination, and to those who kindly extended their permission to use their work in this book. Every effort has been made to locate the copyright holders of works reproduced in this book, but if new information becomes available after publication of the book, please contact the author, and the publisher will correct the book files as needed.

I am particularly grateful to my late uncle Raphael Klorman for his generosity, genuine interest, and substantial involvement in this book, which he regretfully did not get to see published. I am also thankful to Edward Klorman for his substantial assistance and insightful comments.

Special thanks are owed to Kimberly Guinta at Rutgers University Press for identifying this book as a worthy project and for all her hard work. I also thank Jasper Chang for his efforts and assistance. Ashley Moore has done a wonderful and thorough job copy editing the manuscript, and I thank her for that.

I am indebted to my parents, Bat-Zion Eraqi Klorman and Alexander Klorman, for their unwavering support, love, and encouragement. I am also grateful for the benevolent cheering of my brother Haggai Klorman-Eraqi, Tamar Yaniv Klorman, and other family members, the Eraqis, the Jacksons, the Kanots, the Klormans, and the Rostamis.

A special thank-you goes to my partner in life, Mika Kanot, and to our daughter, Kadya, for their love, unwavering support, sense of humor, and endurance during this long journey. I am fortunate to have the two of them traveling beside me, and this book is dedicated to them.

Notes

Chapter 1 Introduction

1 As I mainly address feminist photography in London and in Leeds I use the term 'Britain'. Nevertheless, although not discussed in detail developments in feminist photography were happening elsewhere in the U.K.

2 Elizabeth Wilson and Angela Weir, "The British Women's Movement," *New Left Review* I/148 (November–December 1984): 76; Jonathan Harris, *The New Art History: A Critical Introduction* (London: Routledge, 2001).

3 Sirkka-Liisa Konttinen was, for example, a founding member of the Amber Collective who photographed working-class life in Northeast Britain in the 1970s, photographer Tish Murtha documented youth unemployment in Newcastle in the early 1980s, and Marketa Luskacova photographed street life in London. See Robert Hollands and John Vail, "The Art of Social Movement: Cultural Opportunity, Mobilisation, and Framing in the Early Formation of the Amber Collective," *Poetics* 40 (2012): 22–43; Alice Compton, "Waste of a Nation: Photography, Abjection and Crisis in Thatcher's Britain" (PhD diss., University of Sussex, 2016), 24, http://sro.sussex.ac.uk/65974/; and David Alan Mellor, "Ethnicity, Community and Street," in *No Such Thing as Society: Photography in Britain, 1967–87*, exhibition catalog (London: Hayward, 2008), 49–80.

4 In 2010 the National Museum Reina Sofia Center of Art purchased works by the socialist feminist photography collective the Hackney Flashers, which was active in London during the 1970s.

5 Geoffrey Batchen, *Burning with Desire: The Conception of Photography* (Cambridge, Mass.: MIT Press, 1999), 10; John Tagg, "Power and Photography—Part One: A Means of Surveillance: The Photograph as Evidence in Law," *Screen Education* 36 (Autumn 1980): 17–24; Allan Sekula, *Photography against the Grain: Essays and Photo Works, 1973–1983* (Halifax: Press of the Nova Scotia College of Art and Design, 1984); Victor Burgin, introduction to *Thinking Photography*, ed. Victor Burgin (London: Macmillan, 1982), 1–3.

6 Burgin, introduction, 1–3.

7 Burgin, 14.

8 For instance, Elizabeth Cowie drew on Claude Lévi-Strauss's work to examine how women are exchanged within patriarchal structures of kinship and to understand how "woman" functions as a sign communicated between men. While Cowie did not discuss photography, her essay influenced later discussions regarding the exchange of "woman as sign" in photographic representations. Furthermore, feminist theory and photography appeared alongside each other in publications such as the film journal *Screen*, which, for example, published Laura Mulvey's influential essay "Visual Pleasure and Narrative Cinema" (1975), as well as in the film and media journal *Screen Education*. See Elizabeth Cowie, "Woman as Sign," *m/f* 1 (January 1978): 49–64; and Laura Mulvey, "Visual Pleasure and Narrative Cinema," *Screen* 16, no. 3 (Autumn 1975): 6–18.

9 In addition to Spence, there were a number of other feminist writers and photographers who wrote about photography in 1970s Britain. See Liz Heron, "Hackney Flashers Collective: Who's Still Holding the Camera?," in *Putting Myself in the Picture: A Political, Personal and Photographic Autobiography*, by Jo Spence (London: Camden, 1986), 66–77; Jo Spence, "The Politics of Photography," in *Cultural Sniping: The Art of Transgression* (London: Routledge, 2007), 31–36, originally published in *Camerawork*, February 1976, 1–3; Yves Lomax, "Some Stories Which I Have Heard Some Questions Which I Asked," in *Three Perspectives on Photography: Recent British Photography*, exhibition catalog, by Paul Hill, Angela Kelly, and John Tagg (London: Hayward Gallery, 1979), 54–55; and Angela Kelly, "Feminism and Photography," in Hill, Kelly, and Tagg, *Three Perspectives on Photography*, 42–43.

10 See Elspeth H. Brown and Thy Phu, introduction to *Feeling Photography*, edited by Thy Phu and Elspeth H. Brown (Durham, N.C.: Duke University Press, 2014), 2.

11 See Elizabeth Meehan, "British Feminism from the 1960s to the 1980s," in *British Feminism in the Twentieth Century*, ed. Harold L. Smith (Amherst: University of Massachusetts Press, 1990), 194.

12 See Jessica Evans, "Photography," in *Feminist Visual Culture*, ed. Fiona Carson and Claire Pajaczkowska (New York: Routledge, 2001), 105–122.

13 In recent years, the term *performativity*, which originated in linguistic and gender theories, advanced into contemporary art and photography discourse. This term is often used in reference to works that in some formal, thematic, or structural way allude to notions of enactment, embodiment, and interactivity. See Dorothea von Hantelmann, "The Experiential Turn," in *On Performativity*, ed. Elizabeth Carpenter, Living Collections Catalogue 1 (Minneapolis: Walker Art Center, 2014), http://walkerart.org/collections/publications/performativity/experiential-turn.

14 See Vered Maimon, "Surviving Images and Images of Survival: On Activestills' Photographs of Protest," in *Activestills: Photography as Protest in Palestine/Israel*, ed. Vered Maimon and Shiraz Grinbaum (London: Pluto, 2016), 182–196; Sara Ahmed, "Affective Economies," *Social Text* 79, vol 22, no. 2 (Summer 2004): 117–139; Sara Ahmed, *The Cultural Politics of Emotion* (New York: Routledge, 2004); Thomas Keenan "Mobilizing Shame," *South Atlantic Quarterly* 103, no. 2/3 (Spring/Summer 2004): 435–449; and Marianne Hirsch, *Family Frames: Photography, Narrative, and Postmemory* (Cambridge, Mass.: Harvard University Press, 2012).

15 Elizabeth Edwards, "Objects of Affect: Photography Beyond the Image," *Annual Review of Anthropology* 41 (2012): 223; John Tagg, "A Means of Surveillance: The Photograph as Evidence in Law," in *The Burden of Representation: Essays on Photographies and Histories* (Minneapolis: University of Minnesota Press, 1988), 66–102.

16 This oversight is notable in Rozsika Parker and Griselda Pollock's anthology, *Framing Feminism: Art and the Women's Movement 1970–1985* (London: Pandora; New York: Routledge and Kegan Paul, 1987), which documents feminist art practices, exhibitions, art strategies, and writing produced in Britain in the 1970s and early 1980s. Few feminist photographic works are mentioned, as the book principally focuses on the emerging fields of feminist art and feminist art history, rather than on the particular relationship between feminist politics and feminist photographic activity.

17 Helen Reckit and Peggy Phelan, eds., *Art and Feminism* (London: Phaidon, 2001); Griselda Pollock, *Vision and Difference: Femininity, Feminism and Histories of Art* (London: Routledge, 1988); John A. Walker, *Left Shift: Radical Art in 1970s Britain* (London: I. B. Tauris, 2002), 5.

18 Kate Linker, "Representation and Sexuality," in *Art after Modernism: Rethinking Representation*, ed. Brian Wallis (New York: New Museum of Contemporary Art, 1984), 403.

19 Regarding "woman-centered" perspectives and "consciousness raising" as categories within the women's movement, see Sheila Rowbotham, "Introduction: Mapping the Women's Movement," in *Mapping the Women's Movement: Feminist Politics and Social Transformation in the North*, ed. Monica Threlfall (London: Verso, 1996), 6–7.

20 My inclusive approach to divergent definitions of "woman" among various feminist groups follows the work of Denise Riley, *"Am I That Name?": Feminism and the Category of "Women" in History* (Minneapolis: University of Minnesota Press, 1988), 1–6.

21 For an example of such a teleological view of the feminist movement, see Laura Mulvey's book *Visual and Other Pleasures*, which presents her articles written between 1971 and 1986 in a manner that suggests a narrative of "progression" from grassroots feminist activism to feminist theory. Like many of her contemporaries, Mulvey maintains that feminist theory can importantly influence feminist political practice. Nonetheless, the academic influence of her writings also begins to mark the detachment of feminist theory from the very grassroots activism she believes to have been superseded. See Laura Mulvey, introduction to *Visual and Other Pleasures* (Bloomington: Indiana University Press, 1989), vii, xv.

22 John Tagg, interview by Susan Bright, June 23 and 26, 2003, F14232A-B, Oral History of British Photography Sound Collection, British Library, London.

23 Rowbotham, "Introduction," 7–10.

24 Hazel V. Carby, "White Woman Listen! Black Feminism and the Boundaries of Sisterhood," in *The Empire Strikes Back: Race and Racism in 70s Britain*, ed. Centre for Contemporary Cultural Studies (London: Hutchinson, 1982), 211–212. This essay was published in the first volume of *Working Papers in Cultural Studies* in 1972, which addressed the question of race.

25 Rina Arya, "Rethinking Black Art as a Category of Experience," *Visual Culture in Britain* 18, no. 2 (June 2017): 164.

26 See Brixton Black Women's Group, "Black Women Organizing," *Feminist Review* 17 (Autumn 1984): 84–89; Southhall Black Sisters, *Against the Grain: A Celebration of Survival and Struggle, 1979–1989* (Nottingham: Russell, 1990); Gilane Tawadros, "Other Britains, Other Britons," in *British Photography: Towards a Bigger Picture*, ed. Mark Haworth-Booth (New York: Aperture Foundation, 1988), 41–46; and the journal *Black Phoenix*, which was edited by the Pakistani British artist Rasheed Araeen and first published in 1978.

27 Photography initiatives such as Autograph ABP (Association of Black Photographers) emerged in 1988. This initiative, which continues to operate today, was also invested in advocating for the inclusion of historically marginalized photographic practices and addressing issues of cultural identity and human rights. See Autograph, "Who We Are: About Autograph ABP," accessed August 10, 2017, http://autograph-abp.co.uk/who-we-are.

28 Many accounts of the history of black art, such as Rasheed Araeen's curatorial endeavors, attempted to counter the historiography of Western art but at the same time marginalized the contributions of black women artists. See Arya, "Rethinking Black Art," 169.

29 "Autograph Sees Light of Day," *British Journal of Photography*, August 4, 1988, available at Autograph, "Our History: Press," accessed August 10, 2018, http://autograph-abp.co.uk/history/all/press.

30 Mulvey, "Visual Pleasure."

31 Siona Wilson, *Art Labor, Sex Politics: Feminist Effects in 1970s British Art and Performance* (Minneapolis: University of Minnesota Press, 2015); Kathy Battista, *Renegotiating the Body: Feminist Art in 1970s London* (London: I. B. Tauris, 2013).

32 Andy Beckett, *When the Lights Went Out: What Really Happened to Britain in the Seventies* (London: Faber and Faber, 2009); Walker, *Left Shift*.

33 See Michel Foucault, *The Archaeology of Knowledge*, trans. A. M. Sheridan Smith (New York: Pantheon Books, 1972), 128–130.

34 Sarah Gamble, "Postfeminism," in *The Routledge Companion to Feminism and Postfeminism*, ed. Sarah Gamble (London: Routledge Taylor and Francis, 1998), 36; Susan Faludi, *Backlash: The Undeclared War against American Women* (New York: Three Rivers, 1991), 91.

35 Kira Cochrane, *All the Rebel Women: The Rise of the Fourth Wave of Feminism* (London: Guardian Books, 2013); Nina Power, *One Dimensional Woman* (Winchester, England: Zero Books, 2009); Bonnie J. Dow and Julia T. Wood, "Repeating History and Learning from It: What Can SlutWalks Teach Us about Feminism?," *Women's Studies in Communication* 37, no. 1 (2014): 22–43.

36 Elisa Adami, "How Do You Watch a Revolution? Notes from the 21st Century," *Journal of Visual Culture* 15, no. 1 (2016): 69–84; Derek Conrad Murray, "Notes to Self: The Visual Culture of Selfies in the Age of Social Media," *Consumption Markets and Culture* 18, no. 6 (2015): 490–516; #NotBuyingIt, Twitter, accessed December 3, 2018, https://twitter.com/hashtag/notbuyingit?lang=en.

Chapter 2 Feminist Photography and the Media

1 The term *women's liberation movement* was used by feminists in Britain between the late 1960s and the 1980s to refer to feminist activism.

2 An earlier Miss World demonstration was organized by the women's movement at the Royal Albert Hall on November 27, 1969, which was modeled on the U.S. women's liberation demonstration against the Miss America pageant in 1968 in Atlantic City, New Jersey. See *Shrew*, November/December 1969, 1.

3 Mick Hartey, "Video: From Art to Independence—a Short History of a New Technology," in *Diverse Practices: A Critical Reader on British Video Art*, ed. Julia Knight (Luton, England: Media Faculty of the Humanities, University of Luton, 1996), 28; Andy Beckett, *When the Lights Went Out: What Really Happened to Britain in the Seventies* (London: Faber and Faber, 2009), 224; Michelene Wandor, *Carry On, Understudies: Theatre and Sexuality* (London: Routledge and Kegan Paul, 1986), 25.

4 The Women's Liberation Workshop was one of the earliest networks of women's groups that were formed in London and Bristol in 1969. See Sonya Andermahr, "1970s Feminist Fiction," in *The 1970s: A Decade of Contemporary British Fiction*, ed. Nick Hubble, John McLeod, and Philip Tew (London: Bloomsbury, 2014), 70.

5 June Purvis, "Deeds Not Words: Emeline Pankhurst: Leader of the Militant Suffragettes," *History Today*, May 2002, 58.

6 Mary Chapman, *Making Noise, Making News: Suffrage Print Culture and U.S. Modernism* (New York: Oxford University Press, 2014), 34–36.

7 The year 1970 also saw other key events that gained ground for the British women's movement, such as the first National Women's Liberation Conference (held at Ruskin College, Oxford, and attended by four hundred women), demonstrations for various women's rights in London and Liverpool, and the passing of the Equal Pay Act. See Beckett, *When the Lights Went Out*, 224.

8 "Miss World," *Shrew*, December 1970, 16–19, was written by the protestors and was reprinted as Laura Mulvey and Margarita Jimenez, "The Spectacle Is Vulnerable: Miss World 1970," in *Visual and Other Pleasures*, by Laura Mulvey (London: Macmillan, 1989), 4–5. Among the other feminist writers and activists who participated in the Miss World action were Lynne Segal, Sheila Rowbotham, Susie Orbach, and Fey Weldon. See Andermahr, "1970s Feminist Fiction," 71.

9 James Penner, "Spectacular Disruptions: Situationism and the Terrorist Gesture in Howard Brenton's 'Skin Flicker' and 'Magnificence,'" *Spectator* 21, no. 1 (Spring 2001): 68–81.

10 Tom Vague, *Anarchy in the UK: The Angry Brigade* (London: AK, 1997), 33–34; Gordon Carr, *The Angry Brigade: A History of Britain's First Urban Guerilla Group* (Oakland, Calif.: PM, 2010), 33–34, 57.

11 Betty Friedan, *The Feminine Mystique* (Harmondsworth, England: Penguin, 1963), 63–64.

12 Veronica Beechy, "On Patriarchy," *Feminist Review* 3 (1979): 66–67.

13 Redstockings of the Women's Liberation Movement, *Feminist Revolution: An Abridged Edition with Additional Writings*, ed. Kathie Sarachild, Carol Hanisch, Faye Levine, Barbara Leon, and Colette Price (New York: Random House, 1978).

14 Sheila Jeffreys, "Kate Millett's *Sexual Politics*: 40 Years On," *Women's Studies International Forum* 34 (2011): 76.

15 This text critically examines works by male novelists active in the 1960s, such as Henry Miller and Norman Mailer, and challenges the manner in which they addressed women and sex. While their writing was considered sexually progressive, Millett argues

that it was patriarchal and oppressive toward women. Kate Millet, *Sexual Politics* (New York: Ballantine, 1970); in Britain this book was published in 1971.

16 Elizabeth Wilson and Angela Weir, "The British Women's Movement," *New Left Review* I/148 (November–December 1984): 77; Shulamith Firestone, *The Dialectic of Sex: The Case for a Feminist Revolution* (New York: Bantam Books, 1970).

17 Germain Greer, *The Female Eunuch* (London: MacGibbon and Kee, 1970).

18 Alice Ecols, *Daring to Be Bad: Radical Feminism in America, 1965–1975* (Minneapolis: University of Minnesota Press, 1989), 3–4.

19 Elizabeth Young-Bruehl and Laura Wexler, "On 'Psychoanalysis and Feminism,'" *Social Research* 2 (Summer 1992): 462; Juliet Mitchell, *Women: The Longest Revolution* (New York: Pantheon, 1984), 249.

20 Griselda Pollock, "What's Wrong with 'Images of Women'?" *Screen Education* 24 (1977): 25–34.

21 Laura Mulvey, "Visual Pleasure and Narrative Cinema," *Screen* 16, no. 3 (Autumn 1975): 14. Mulvey took a similar position in her critique of the Allen Jones exhibition at the Institute of Contemporary Arts, which included life-size sculptures of provocatively positioned pieces of furniture. See Laura Mulvey, "You Don't Know What Is Happening, Do You, Mr. Jones?," *Spare Rib*, February 1973, 13–16, 30, reprinted in *Framing Feminism: Art and the Women's Movement, 1970–1985*, ed. Rozsika Parker and Griselda Pollock (London: Pandora; New York: Routledge and Kegan Paul, 1987), 127–131.

22 Elizabeth Cowie and Rosalind Coward, who presented at the Papers on Patriarchy conference, were among the editors of *m/f*. See Parveen Adams, Rosalind Coward, and Elizabeth Cowie, "Editorial," *m/f* 1 (1978).

23 *Papers on Patriarchy: Conference, London, 1976* (London: Women's Publishing Collective, 1978).

24 Judy Chicago, *Through the Flower: My Struggle as a Woman Artist* (New York: Anchor Books, 1977), 103–104.

25 Miriam Schapiro, "The Education of Women as Artists: Project Womanhouse," *Art Journal* 3 (Spring 1972): 269.

26 Rozsika Parker and Griselda Pollock, "Fifteen Years of Feminist Action: From Practical Strategies to Strategic Practices," in Parker and Pollock, *Framing Feminism*, 11.

27 The student and worker uprising of May 1968 in Paris are among such movements. Like the women's movement, the Paris uprising consisted of a network of informal connections between its supporting groups, which functioned as a tool for political contestation. See Antigoni Memou, *Photography and Social Movements: From the Globalisation of the Movement (1968) to the Movement against Globalisation (2001)* (Manchester: Manchester University Press, 2013).

28 Suzanne Staggenborg and Amy Lang, "Culture and Ritual in the Montreal Women's Movement," *Social Movement Studies* 6, no. 2 (September 2007): 177.

29 David A. Snow et al., "Frame Alignment Processes, Micromobilization, and Movement Participation," *American Sociological Review* 51, no. 4 (August 1986): 464.

30 This crisis was attributed to various developments, such as Nikita Khrushchev's indictment of Stalinism, the purges executed under the latter regime, and the effects of the rise of consumption and commodification on the image of the working class. John Tagg, "Discipline and Protest: Thinking Photography after

Foucault," in *The (Un)becomings of Photography: On Reaggregating and Reassembling the Photographic and Its Institutions*, ed. Lars Willumeit (Krakow: Foundation for Visual Arts, 2016), 63.

31 John Tagg, *The Burden of Representation: Essays on Photographies and Histories* (Minneapolis: Univeristy of Minnesota Press, 1988), 22.

32 Louis Althusser, "Ideology and Ideological State Apparatuses," in *Lenin and Philosophy and Other Essays* (New York: Monthly Review Press, 1971), 127–188; cf. Tagg, introduction, 24–25.

33 Jo Spence, "The Politics of Photography," in *Cultural Sniping: The Art of Transgression* (London: Routledge, 2007), 31, originally published in *Camerawork*, February 1976, 1–3.

34 Victor Burgin, introduction to *Thinking Photography*, ed. Victor Burgin (London: Macmillan, 1982), 1–2.

35 Editorial, *Screen Education* 36 (Autumn 1980): 1–3.

36 John Tagg, "Power and Photography—Part One: A Means of Surveillance: The Photograph as Evidence in Law," *Screen Education* 36 (Autumn 1980): 17, 24.

37 Allan Sekula, "The Traffic in Photographs," *Art Journal* 41, no. 1 (Spring 1981): 15–16; Allan Sekula, "The Body and the Archive," *October* 39 (Winter 1986): 54–55; Geoffrey Batchen, *Burning with Desire: The Conception of Photography* (Cambridge, Mass.: MIT Press, 1999), 9.

38 Martha Rosler, "Around and After Thoughts," in *Decoys and Disruptions: Selected Writings, 1975–2001* (Cambridge, Mass.: MIT Press, 2004), 175–176 (first published 1981).

39 Edward Welch and J. J. Long, "A Small History of Photography Studies," introduction of *Photography: Theoretical Snapshots*, ed. J. J. Long, Andrea Noble, and Edward Welch (London: Routledge, 2009), 16–30.

40 Tagg, "Discipline and Protest," 58.

41 Dennett recalled that the idea for this undertaking was influenced by the American Floating Foundation of Photography project, which during the 1970s traveled on the Hudson River by barge and made stops along the way for lectures on photography. Terry Dennett, interview by the author, Jo Spence Memorial Archive, London, September 9, 2011.

42 Photography Workshop was mainly funded by donations but also by a grant from the Greater London Council. Jo Spence and Terry Dennett, "Ten Years of Photography Workshop," in *Jo Spence: Beyond the Perfect Image: Photography, Subjectivity, Antagonism* (Barcelona: Museu d'Art Contemporani, 2005), 136–137.

43 In 1975 Spence and Dennett were approached by photographers Mike Goldwater and Paul Trevor of the Half Moon Gallery and they became Half Moon Photography Workshop. Dennett, interview by the author.

44 Barbara Hunt, preface to *The Camerawork Essays: Context and Meaning in Photography*, ed. Jessica Evans (London: River Oram, 1997), 9.

45 Spence and Dennett were involved in the first seven issues of *Camerawork*; Spence was fired in 1977 due to ideological differences. See Dennett, interview by the author.

46 Trisha Ziff, "Working for the Council," in *Photography/Politics: One*, ed. Terry Dennett et al., (London: Photography Workshop, 1979), 165–170.

47 *The Pavilion*, booklet, Leeds, ca. 1984, 16–17, Pavilion Collection, Feminist Archive North, Special Collections, Brotherton Library, University of Leeds.

48 Shirley Moreno, "The Light Writing on the Wall: the Leeds Pavilion Project," in *Photographic Practices: Towards a Different Image*, ed. Stevie Bezencenet and Philip Corrigan (London: Comedia, 1986), 119. Maggie Murray recalled that when she started out as a photojournalist in the 1960s, she was rarely sent out on interesting assignments, as her employers thought that she was not capable of carrying heavy equipment. She also mentioned being patronized by male photographers who assumed that she did not know how to use a camera; these interactions led her to deliberately carry a large camera with impressive gadgets. See Helen Chappell, "Wednesday Women (Third Person): Macho but Not So Mucho," *Guardian*, July 26, 1989; and Val Wilmer and Maggie Murray, "Photography," *City Limits*, September 24–29, 1982, 48.

49 Stephanie Gilbert, "Spare Parts—How to Fix Your Own Fuses," *Spare Rib*, October 1972, 39; Stephanie Gilbert, "Spare Parts—Developing Your Own Films," *Spare Rib*, May 1974, 30–31.

50 Stevie Bezencenet, "Photography and Education," in Bezencenet and Corrigan, *Photographic Practices*, 6.

51 In 1982 Spence, Mary Ann Kennedy, Jane Munro, and Charlotte Pembrey (students in the photography program at the Polytechnic of Central London) produced an exhibition for the degree show. They called themselves the Polysnappers and staged and photographed dolls as a means to examine the family as a socially and ideologically produced unit. Some of the issues examined in this project were pornography and the de-eroticized representation of mothers. Moreover, in 1980 Prince produced an exhibition at the Polytechnic of Central London on lesbian mothers that consisted of interviews and photographs. Maggie Murray, interview by the author, Maggie Murray's home in London, October 19, 2011; Jo Spence, interview by Val Williams, March and April 1991, C459/13/1-7, Oral History of British Photography Sound Collection, British Library, London; Jo Spence, "Mature Student 1980 to 1982," in *Putting Myself in the Picture: A Political, Personal and Photographic Autobiography* (London: Camden, 1986), 134–141.

52 Murray, interview by the author.

53 This issue was produced by feminist photographers Angela Phillips, Val Wilmer, Liz Heron, Jo Spence, and Michael Ann Mullen, as well as Lesley Ruda, Carole Spedding, Sue Hobbs, Ruth Wallsgrove, Thalia Doukas, Jill Nicholls, Alison Fell (becoming Panama McAlister), Lucy Williams, Bee Tamarit, Pat Kahn, Janie Prince, Ruthie Petrie, Laura Margolis, Robyn Slovo, Penny Hallow, Jini Rawlings, Rozsika Parker, Susan Hemmings, Amanda Sebestyen, and Linda Phillips. See "Pictures Talk: Special Visual Issue," *Spare Rib*, July 1978, 3.

54 Marsha Rowe, introduction to *Spare Rib Reader*, ed. Marsha Rowe (Middlesex, England: Penguin Books, 1982), 13–15.

55 Katie Campbell, "Boning Up on *Spare Rib*," *Women's Review of Books* 9 (June 1984): 17.

56 Beckett, *When the Lights Went Out*, 226.

57 Editorial, in "Pictures Talk: Special Visual Issue," *Spare Rib*, July 1978, 3.

58 Ruth Wallsgrove, "Who Do I Think I Am?," in "Pictures Talk: Special Visual Issue," *Spare Rib*, July 1978, 31.

59 Challenges to cultural standards of femininity and of the female body also appeared in the time's feminist literature, including in Susie Orbach's *Fat Is a Feminist Issue*,

which examines eating disorders and being fat as feminist strategies for resisting expected female stereotypes. See Susie Orbach, *Fat Is a Feminist Issue: The Anti-diet Guide for Women* (London: Arrow Books, 1978).

60 As will be discussed in chapter 5, a feminist critique of media images continues to prevail in contemporary feminist photography practice. Thus, a recent parody of media images of female stars that is similar to Wallsgrove's exposure of advertising images' unattainable illusion of female beauty can be found in Australian comedian Celeste Barber's Instagram posts. In these posts, Barber photographs herself mimicking poses of female celebrities and in so doing exposes the extent of their distortion and the impossible beauty standards of the female body that they promote. See Celeste Barber (@celestebarber), Instagram, accessed October 1, 2017, https://www.instagram.com/celestebarber/; and "The Model World of Instagram Parody Star Celeste Barber—in Pictures," *Guardian*, June 29, 2017, https://www.theguardian.com/culture/2017/jun/30/the-model-world-of-instagram-parody-star-celeste-barber-in-pictures.

61 Rosita Brooks, "Through the Looking Glass Darkly," in *British Photography: Towards a Bigger Picture*, ed. Mark Haworth-Booth (New York: Aperture Foundation, 1988), 47.

62 Judith Williamson, *Decoding Advertisements: Ideology and Meaning in Advertising* (London: Marion Boyars, 1978), 12, 50.

63 Victor Burgin, "Photographic Practice and Art Theory," *Studio International* 190, no. 976 (1975), reprinted in Burgin, *Thinking Photography*, 82–83.

64 Victor Burgin, *Between* (London: Basil Blackwell, 1986), 17.

65 Liz Heron, "Getting on Top of the Job: Women in Manual Trades," in "Pictures Talk: Special Visual Issue," *Spare Rib*, July 1978, 43–46.

66 By 1984 the agency consisted of Maggie Murray, Val Wilmer, Pam Isherwood, Joanne O'Brien, Jenny Matthews, Raissa Page, Anita Corbin, and Sheila Gray. Two years later they were joined by Brenda Prince and three administrators. This agency would eventually end up representing up to twenty photographers. See Maggie Murray, "Format Photographers," talk at the National Portrait Gallery, May 25, 2010, private collection of Michael Ann Mullen.

67 Stevie Bezencenet, "Photography, Power and Responsibility: The Format Picture Agency," in Bezencenet and Corrigan, *Photographic Practices*, 74.

68 Sheila Gray et al., "Format Photographers," *Feminist Review* 18 (Winter 1984): 108.

69 Cf. John Tagg's analysis of Margaret Bourke White's photograph of the 1937 Louisville flood in "Melancholy Realism: Walker Evan's Resistance to Meaning," in *The Disciplinary Frame: Photographic Truths and the Capture of Meaning* (Minneapolis: University of Minnesota Press, 2009), 106–115.

70 Gray et al., "Format Photographers," 102.

71 Gray et al., 102; Murray, interview by the author.

72 The Hackney Flashers members were An Dekker, Helen Grace, Sally Greenhill, Liz Heron, Gerda Jager, Maggie Millman, Michael Ann Mullen, Maggie Murray, Jini Rawlings, Ruth Barrenbaum, Christine Roche, Annette Solomon, Jo Spence, Arlene Strasberg, Sue Treweek, and Julia Vellacott. Initially Terry Dennett and Neil Martinson were members, but they resigned in order to maintain it as an "all woman group." See "Photography Workshop—the Hackney Flashers Collective," [ca. 1981], Terry Dennett's collection, Jo Spence Memorial Archive, London; Terry

Dennett, "Jo Spence: Autobiographical Photography: Self, Class and Family," in *Jo Spence: Beyond the Perfect Image*, 20.

73 Terry Dennett, "Jo Spence: Autobiographical Photography: Self, Class and Family," in *Jo Spence: Beyond the Perfect Image*, 20.

74 Liz Heron, "Hackney Flashers Collective: Who's Still Holding the Camera?," in Spence, *Putting Myself in the Picture*, 67.

75 Michael Ann Mullen, interview by the author, British Library, London, October 31, 2011.

76 Hackney Flashers Collective, "The Hackney Flashers Collective," in *Three Perspectives on Photography: Recent British Photography*, by John Tagg, Angela Kelly, and Paul Hill, exhibition catalog (London: Hayward Gallery, 1979), 80.

77 Hackney Flashers Collective, 83.

78 Hackney Flashers Collective, 80; Liz Heron, *Domestic Labour and Visual Representation*, slide pack prepared by the Hackney Flashers (1980), 6–7, private collection of Michael Ann Mullen.

79 Heron, 18–19.

80 Hackney Flashers Collective, "The Hackney Flashers Collective," in Tagg, Kelly, and Hill, *Three Perspectives on Photography*, 83.

81 Jo Spence, "Women's Collective Work 1974 Onwards," in Spence, *Putting Myself in the Picture*, 72–74.

82 John Clarke et al., "Subcultures, Cultures and Class," *Working Papers in Cultural Studies*, no. 7/8 (1975): 274–285, reprinted in *Resistance through Rituals: Youth Subcultures in Post-war Britain*, ed. Stuart Hall and Tony Jefferson (London: Hutchinson, 1980), 9–74; Dick Hebdige, "Hiding in the Light," *Ten.8* 9 (1982): 4–19.

83 Stanley Mitchell, introduction to *Understanding Brecht*, by Walter Benjamin, trans. Anna Bostock (London: Verso, 1998), xiii.

84 See Peter Burger, *Theory of the Avant-Garde*, trans. Michael Shaw, foreword by Jochen Schulte-Sasse (Minneapolis: University of Minnesota Press, 1984), 75; and Jo Spence, "The Sign as a Site of Class Struggle: Reflections on Works by John Heartfield," *Block* 5 (1981): 7.

85 Spence, "Sign as a Site."

86 Toward the end of the 1970s, the issue of race was gaining visibility within the feminist movement. This was manifested, for example, in the foundation of the Asian and Afro-Caribbean feminist group Southall Black Sisters in 1979, which fought racism and challenged the patriarchy in its members' communities. This development could also be seen in publications. See Hazel V. Carby, "White Woman Listen! Black Feminism and the Boundaries of Sisterhood," in *The Empire Strikes Back: Race and Racism in 70s Britain*, by Centre for Contemporary Cultural Studies (London: Hutchinson, 1982), 211–234; and Southall Black Sisters, *Against the Grain: A Celebration of Survival and Struggle* (Southall, Middlesex: Southall Black Sisters, 1990).

87 Val Williams, "Celebration and Satire: Feminist Photography 1970–1986," in *Women Photographers: The Other Observers, 1900 to the Present* (London: Virago, 1986), 172.

88 Murray, interview by the author; Spence, interview by Williams.

89 Liz Heron, "Hackney Flashers Collective: Who's Still Holding the Camera?," in Dennett et al., *Photography/Politics: One*, 125. Also see "Hackney Flashers Photography

and Allied Media Workshop for Women," pamphlet, ca. 1975–1979, Jo Spence Memorial Archive.

90 Joanne O'Brien, interview by the author, Joanne O'Brien's London home, October 27, 2011.

91 Staggenborg and Lang, "Culture and Ritual," 178.

92 The Advertising Standards Association was a self-regulatory body for print advertisements in the United Kingdom.

93 Jon Savage, "London Subversive," in *Good Bye to London: Radical Art and Politics in the 70's*, ed. Astrid Proll in cooperation with curators Boris von Brauchitsch, Peter Cross, and Jule Reuter (Ostfildern, Germany: Hatje Cantz Verlag, 2010), 22.

94 Rosalind Coward, "Underneath We're Angry," *Time Out*, February 27, 1980, reprinted in Parker and Pollock, *Framing Feminism*, 144. Cf. discussion on Gigi ad in Na'ama Klorman-Eraqi, "Underneath We're Angry: Feminism and Media Politics in Britain in the Late 1970s and Early 1980s," *Feminist Media Studies* 17, no. 2 (April 2017): 231–247.

95 Jill Nicholls and Pat Moan, "'What Offends One of Us Won't Offend the Next Chap': The Advertising Standards Authority's Line on Sexism," in "Pictures Talk: Special Visual Issue," *Spare Rib*, July 1978, 18.

96 Jo Anna Isaak, *Feminism and Contemporary Art: The Revolutionary Power of Women's Laughter* (London: Routledge, 1996), 15–16.

97 Jill Posener, *Spray It Loud* (London: Pandora, 1982).

98 Posener, 20 (bottom).

99 Posener, 13.

100 Leeds Women's Fight Back Campaign, "Leeds Women Paint the Town!," *Outwrite*, December 1984, 1.

101 *Outwrite* was run by a feminist collective. Some of its early issues were dedicated to antiporn politics and actions by groups such as Angry Women. It also focused on intersections between gender and internationalist, antiracist, and anti-imperialist concerns. See "Women's Media Collectives," women's media panel at Zine Fest, with Melissa (Cherrybomb Comics), Jess Baines (See Red Poster Collective), and Rahila Gupta (*Outwrite*), January 24, 2009, Women's Library, London, audio recording, 1:06:42, http://.org/details/ZineFest09.

102 Patricia Holland, "The Page Three Girl Speaks to Women Too: A Sun-sational Survey," *Screen* 24, no. 3 (May 1983): 86.

103 *Outwrite*, December 1984, cover.

104 Leeds Women's Fight Back Campaign, "Paint the Town!," 1.

105 Tom McDonough, *"The Beautiful Language of My Century": Reinventing the Language of Contestation in Postwar France, 1945–1968* (Cambridge, Mass.: MIT Press, 2007), 44.

106 James Trier, introduction to *Detournement as Pedagogical Praxis*, ed. James Trier (Rotterdam: Sense, 2014), 16.

107 McDonough, *The Beautiful Language*, 44.

108 Leeds Women's Fight Back Campaign, "Paint the Town!," 1.

109 Christopher Miller, *Environmental Rights: A Critical Perspective* (New York: Routledge, 1995), 28.

110 Anna Coote and Beatrix Campbell, *Sweet Freedom: The Struggle for Women's Liberation* (Oxford: Basil Blackwell, 1987), 42, 224; Philip Jenkins, *Intimate*

Enemies: Moral Panics in Contemporary Great Britain (New York: Aldine de Gruyter, 1992), 52.

111 Jeska Rees, "'Are You a Lesbian?': Challenges in Recording and Analysing the Women's Liberation Movement in England," *History Workshop Journal* 69 (Spring 2010): 177–178.

112 Jeska Rees, "A Look Back at Anger: The Women's Liberation Movement in 1978," *Women's History Review* 3 (July 2010): 341.

113 Vanessa Engle, dir., *Lefties*, episode 2, "Angry Wimmin," aired February 15, 2006, on BBC 4, http://www.youtube.com/watch?v=Ap072n01ESI.

114 Carolyn Bronstein, "No More Black and Blue: Women against Violence against Women and the Warner Communications Boycott, 1976–1979," *Violence against Women* 14, no. 4 (April 2008): 419.

115 Carolyn Bronstein, *Battling Pornography: The American Feminist Anti-Pornography Movement, 1976–1986* (Cambridge: Cambridge University Press, 2011), 93–107.

116 "Reclaim the Night," *Spare Rib*, January 1978, 22–23.

117 Coote and Campbell, *Sweet Freedom*, 42, 224.

118 Nonetheless, the first Reclaim the Night march in Europe took place in Belgium in March 1976 and was organized by women who attended the International Tribunal on Crimes against Women. See Tony Campolo and Gordon Aeschliman, *Everybody Wants to Change the World: Practical Ideas for Social Justice* (Ventura, Calif.: Regal Books, 2006), 103.

119 Tacie Dejanikus and Janice Kelly, "Women Take Back the Night," *Off Our Backs*, December 31, 1977, 5, 7.

120 "Women, Angry at Male Violence, Say: 'Resist the Curfew!,' *Leeds Other Paper*, November 28, 1980, reprinted in *Women against Violence against Women*, ed. Dusty Rhodes and Sandra McNeill (London: Onlywomen, 1985), 12.

121 Rosalind Coward, "Sexual Violence and Sexuality," in "Sexuality," special issue, *Feminist Review* 11 (Summer 1982): 9.

122 Andrea Dworkin, *Pornography: Men Possessing Women* (New York: Putnam's Sons, 1981).

123 Susan Griffin, *Pornography and Silence: Culture's Revenge against Nature* (New York: Harper and Row, 1981).

124 Jeffreys, "Kate Millett's *Sexual Politics*," 76.

125 Fran, "Porn Not Art," *Outwrite*, December 1984, 7.

126 "What Fired Angry Women?," *Outwrite*, December 1988, 8. Posener mentioned that there was not only one Angry Women group but that it was rather an ad hoc name adopted by individuals or women's groups when performing illegal actions such as graffitiing, criminally damaging property, attacking sex shops, and producing stickers to put on sexist book covers, records, or posters. Posener, *Spray It Loud*, 30.

127 "What Fired Angry Women?," 8.

128 "What Fired Angry Women?," 8.

129 Judith R. Walkowitz, *City of Dreadful Delight: Narratives of Sexual Danger in Late-Victorian London* (Chicago: University of Chicago Press, 1992), 235.

130 "Arson Attacks at Video Shops," *Yorkshire Evening Post*, January 14, 1983, 1. Another Angry Women group operated in London. In 1982 they targeted Ann Summer's sex

shop on Edgeware Road by spray-painting it and destroying its video machines, magazines, and other materials. This group attested that they were responding to the positioning of the store on a main road, which they believed made porn and violence against women appear respectable. See "Angry Women Burn Sex Shop," *Off Our Backs*, November 1982, 11; "What Fired Angry Women?," 9.

131 "What Fired Angry Women?," 9.

132 Coward, "Sexual Violence and Sexuality."

133 Coward, 9.

134 Kobena Mercer, "Just Looking for Trouble: Robert Mapplethorpe and Fantasies of Race," in *Sex Exposed: Sexuality and the Pornography Debate*, ed. Lynne Segal and Mary McIntosh (New Brunswick, N.J.: Rutgers University Press, 1993), 92.

135 Rees, "'Are You a Lesbian?,'" 178.

136 Coward, "Sexual Violence and Sexuality," 19.

137 Kathy Myers, "Towards a Feminist Erotica," *Camerawork*, March 1982, reprinted in Evans, *Camerawork Essays*, 201–202.

138 Myers, 190–204. See Michel Foucault, *The History of Sexuality*, vol. 1, *An Introduction* (Harmondsworth, England: Penguin, 1978).

139 Carol S. Vance, "Pleasure and Danger: Towards a Politics of Sexuality," in *Pleasure and Danger: Exploring Female Sexuality*, ed. Carol S. Vance (Boston: Routledge and Kegan Paul, 1984), 1–25.

140 Carol S. Vance, "Petition in Support of the Scholar and Feminist IX Conference," in Vance, *Pleasure and Danger*, 451–453.

141 Vance, *Pleasure and Danger*.

142 Elizabeth Wilson, "The Context of 'Between Pleasure and Danger': The Barnard Conference on Sexuality," *Feminist Review* 13 (March 1983): 35–41.

143 Carol Avedon, "Don't Get Fooled Again: Assailed in Britain," *New York Law School Law Review* 38 (1993): 187.

144 Coward, "Sexual Violence and Sexuality," 20–21; Beckett, *When the Lights Went Out*, 286.

145 Walkowitz, *City of Dreadful Delight*, 235.

146 Maria Katyachild et al., "Pornography" (paper presented at the London Revolutionary Feminist Conference, February 1978, by the first antiporn group in the United Kingdom), reprinted in Rhodes and McNeill, *Women against Violence against Women*, 15.

147 Elizabeth Wilson, "Context of 'Between Pleasure and Danger,'" 36.

148 Deirdre English, Amber Hollibaugh, and Gayle Rubin, "Talking Sex: A Conversation on Sexuality and Feminism," in "Sexuality," special issue, *Feminist Review* 11 (Summer 1982): 40, 51.

149 "Sex Issue," special issue, *Heresies* 12 (1981).

150 Jayne Egerton, "The Goal of a Feminist Politics . . . the Destruction of Male Supremacy or the Pursuit of Pleasure? A Critique of the Sex Issue of *Heresies*," *Revolutionary and Radical Feminist Newsletter*, Autumn 1981, reprinted in *Sweeping Statements: Writings from the Women's Liberation Movement, 1981–83*, ed. Hannah Kanter et al. (London: Women's Press, 1984), 198–202.

151 Terry Lovell, introduction to pt. 3, "The Politics of Difference: Class, Race and Gender," in *British Feminist Thought: A Reader*, ed. Terry Lovell (Oxford: Basil Blackwell, 1990), 73.

152 Marc DiPaulo, *War, Politics, and Superheroes: Ethics and Propaganda in Comics and Film* (Jefferson, N.C.: McFarland, 2011), 175.

153 Sylvia Bashevkin, *Tales of Two Cities: Women and Municipal Restructuring in London and Toronto* (Vancouver: University of British Columbia Press, 2006), 56–57.

154 Bashevkin, 56–57.

155 Tagg, "Discipline and Protest," 63–64.

156 Holland, "The Page Three Girl Speaks to Women Too," 84–102.

157 Ros Ballaster, "Campbell, Beatrix," in *Encyclopedia of Feminist Literary Theory*, ed. Elizabeth Kowaleski-Wallace (New York: Routledge, 2009), 88.

158 Engle, "Angry Wimmin."

159 Sheila Rowbotham, "Introduction: Mapping the Women's Movement," in *Mapping the Women's Movement: Feminist Politics and Social Transformation in the North*, ed. Monica Threlfall (London: Verso, 1996), 9.

160 David Green and Joanna Lowry, "From Presence to the Performative: Rethinking Photographic Indexicallity," in *Where Is the Photograph?*, ed. David Green (Maidstone, England: Photoworks; Brighton, England: Photoforum, 2003), 47–48, 58.

161 *Affect* is often defined as distinct from *emotion*. Within a psychoanalytic model, emotions are often associated with first-person experience bound up with a subject. Affect, however, is associated with third-person perception that floats free of a particular subject. While this distinction is important, my analysis is similar to Siona Wilson's take on the film *Nightcleaners* (see chapter 3) in that I do not distinguish between these definitions in terms of first- and third-person modes of analysis but rather to emphasize their emotive qualities in terms of production and spectatorship. See Siona Wilson, *Art Labor*, 42–43.

162 Arguably, this is with the exception of the British Marxist literary theorist Raymond Williams, who developed the concept of "structures of feeling." See Wilson, 38.

163 Sianne Ngai, *Ugly Feelings* (Cambridge, Mass.: Harvard University Press, 2004), 24–25.

164 Staggenborg and Lang, "Culture and Ritual," 178.

165 Sara Ahmed, "Affective Economies," *Social Text* 79, vol. 22, no. 2 (Summer 2004): 119; Sara Ahmed, *The Cultural Politics of Emotion* (New York: Routledge, 2004), 1–4.

166 Robert Seyfert, "Beyond Personal Feelings and Collective Emotions: Towards a Theory of Social Affect," *Theory, Culture and Society* 29, no. 6 (2012): 27.

167 Ahmed, for example, illustrates how emotions such as love and hate are fundamental in the narrative found on the Aryan Nations' website and argues that they are employed to delineate the bodies of individual subjects within the nation. For instance, she draws attention to how the white nationalist is engendered as harboring a deep love for the nation and as endangered by imagined others who, driven by hate, threaten to take something away from the subject. While the stakes of feminist media intervention were substantially different from the Aryan Nations' website, their emotive affects are similarly employed to form an imagined feminist collectivity. Ahmed, "Affective Economies," 117–118.

168 Ahmed, *Cultural Politics of Emotion*, 58, 176–178.

Chapter 3 Photography and the Street

1 Since 1986, advance notice of a march needs to be given to the police, and the police have the right to impose conditions on marches. *The Governance of Britain: Managing Protest around Parliament* (Norwich: Stationery Office, 2007), 8–9.

2 "Picture Agencies," *Camerawork*, Winter 1983/1984, 8–9.

3 Richard Greenhill, Margaret Murray, and Jo Spence, *Photography* (Milwaukee: Ideals, 1980), 36–37; Russell Miller, *Magnum: Fifty Years at the Front Line of History* (New York: Grove, 1997), 50.

4 Angela Phillips, interview by the author, Angela Phillips's London home, October 26, 2011; Joanne Lukitsh, "Practicing Theories: An Interview with John Tagg," in *Grounds of Dispute: Art History, Cultural Politics, and the Discursive Field*, by John Tagg (Minneapolis: University of Minnesota Press, 1992), 78. Dephot's model also influenced the photography agency Magnum, formed in 1947 by Robert Capa, who was previously a photographer for Dephot. Report/IFL, [notes on photographs], in *Three Perspectives on Photography: Recent British Photography*, by Paul Hill, Angela Kelly, and John Tagg, exhibition catalog (London: Hayward Gallery, 1979), 90–91.

5 The people involved in the production of the Lewisham *Camerawork* issue were Ed Barber, Jan Clarke, Mike Goldwater, Ann Murphy, Sue Hobbs, Tom Picton, Richard Platt, Shirley Read, Swance Swanson, Paul Trevor, and Wendy Wallace. See *Camerawork*, November 1977.

6 Andy Becket, *When the Lights Went Out: What Really Happened to Britain in the Seventies* (London: Faber and Faber, 2009), 368, 444–445.

7 Mike Abrahams, who was a member of Report, formed Network Photographers with nine freelance photographers, among whom were John Sturrock, also a member of Report, and Mike Goldwater, a member of Camerawork. See Phillips, interview by the author. Peter Marlow would become associated with Magnum in the early 1980. See Miller, *Magnum*, 9.

8 "What Are You Taking Pictures For?," *Camerawork*, November 1977, 10–14.

9 John A. Walker, *Left Shift: Radical Art in 1970s Britain* (London: I. B. Tauris, 2002), 198. According to photographer Tom Picton, the national Sunday dailies reported that fifty policemen and one policewoman were injured at Lewisham but ignored all other concerns related to these events. Tom Picton, "What the Papers Said," in "Lewisham: What Are You Taking Pictures For?," special issue, *Camerawork*, November 1977, 7.

10 Stuart Hall et al., "The Politics of Mugging," in *Policing the Crisis: Mugging, the State, and Law and Order* (New York: Holmes and Meier, 1978), 349–350.

11 Ashley Dawson, "Linton Kwesi Johnson's Dub Poetry and the Political Aesthetics of Carnival in Britain," *Small Axe* 21 (October 2006): 62.

12 Hall et al., "Politics of Mugging," 349–350.

13 Beckett, *When the Lights Went Out*, 443–444, 448.

14 Beckett, 443–444, 448; Pratibha Parmar, "Gender, Race and Class: Asian Women in Resistance," in *The Empire Strikes Back: Race and Racism in 70s Britain*, ed. Centre for Contemporary Cultural Studies (London: Hutchinson, 1982), 240; Hall et al., " Politics of Mugging," 349–350.

15 Paul Gilroy, "Police and Thieves," in Centre for Contemporary Cultural Studies, *Empire Strikes Back*, 173–174.

16 "What Are You Taking Pictures For?," 14.
17 "What Are You Taking Pictures For?"
18 Tom Picton, "A Personal View," in "Lewisham: What Are You Taking Pictures For?," special issue, *Camerawork*, November 1977, 15.
19 Michael Warner, *Publics and Counterpublics* (New York: Zone Books, 2002), 56; Lauren Berlant and Michael Warner, "Sex in Public," *Critical Inquiry* 24, no. 2 (1998): 563; Katsuhiko Suganuma, "Ways of Speaking about Queer Space in Tokyo: Disorientated Knowledge and Counter-public Space," *Japanese Studies* 31, no. 3 (December 2011): 347–348.
20 Warner, *Publics and Counterpublics*, 57.
21 Ariella Azoulay, "Photography," *Mafte'akh* 2e (Winter 2011): 70–71.
22 Thomas Keenan, "Mobilizing Shame," *South Atlantic Quarterly* 103, no. 2/3 (Spring/Summer 2004): 447.
23 Kari Anden-Papadopoulos, "Citizen Camera-Witnessing: Embodied Political Dissent in the Age of 'Mediated Mass Self-Communication,'" *New Media Society* 16, no. 5 (2014): 754, 763.
24 "What Are You Taking Pictures For?"
25 Jack Dromey and Graham Taylor, *Grunwick: The Workers' Story* (London: Lawrence and Wishart, 1978), 112.
26 Judith Butler, "Bodies in Alliance and the Politics of the Street," in *Sensible Politics: The Visual Culture of Nongovernmental Activism*, ed. Meg McLagan and Yates McKee (New York: Zone Books, 2012), 119–120.
27 Participatory photography is often associated with the mobile camera phone, a device that has become an extension of the self and is intimately connected with global digital networks. This device enables ordinary citizens to bypass established editorial and censorial filters and turn their personal record of an event into a public testimony that might contradict "official" perspectives provided by the mainstream media. The 1970s was a different historical moment in terms of photographic technology and the available platforms for counterphotographic circulation, which were by far less immediate. Nonetheless, the participatory aspects of the photographic act and its circulation in networks other than the mainstream press allowed this work to be shared. See Anden-Papadopoulos, "Citizen Camera-Witnessing," 754, 764–763.
28 Val Wilmer, *Mama Said There'd Be Days like This: My Life in the Jazz World* (London: Women's Press, 1991), 268, 288.
29 Unlike white male and female demonstrators, black feminists were unwilling to expose themselves to police and state brutality, which they experienced as an everyday occurrence. See Valerie Amos and Pratibha Parmar, "Challenging Imperial Feminism," in "Reflections on 25 Years," special issue, *Feminist Review*, no. 80 (2005): 61.
30 Heron volunteered at the Half Moon gallery for about a year. The first piece she wrote for *Camerawork* was a feminist critique of George Brassai's photo book *The Secret Paris of the Thirties*. Heron suggested that her article's feminist perspective scandalized some of the magazine's male staff. Liz Heron, interview by the author, Liz Heron's London home, October 24, 2011.
31 In 1977, after being involved in the first seven issues of *Camerawork*, Spence was fired from her position as a paid administrator. Heron and Terry Dennett, who also worked as a volunteer, were also asked to leave. According to Dennett, differences

on theories of class and gender with the former Half Moon gallery directors were at the base of this dispute. Terry Dennett, "Jo Spence: Autobiographical Photography: Self, Class and Family," in *Jo Spence: Beyond the Perfect Image: Photography, Subjectivity, Antagonism* (Barcelona: Museu d'Art Contemporani, 2005), 20; Terry Dennett, interview by the author, Jo Spence Memorial Archive, London, September 9, 2011; Heron, interview by the author.

32 Joanne O'Brien, interview by the author, Joanne O'Brien's London home, October 27, 2011.

33 Wilmer, *Mama Said*, 268, 288.

34 Val Wilmer and Maggie Murray, "Photography," *City Limits*, September 24–29, 1982, 48–49.

35 Network Photographers was formed by photographers including Mike Goldwater, Mike Abrahams, and Sturrock (who was previously a member of Report). This agency shared Report's view regarding the political significance of photography. It also ran a photo library that consisted of a large collection of social documentary photos, and its members mostly took photographs on assignment for magazines with which the agency worked. See "Picture Agencies," 8.

36 Stevie Bezencenet, "Photography, Power and Responsibility: The Format Picture Agency," in *Photographic Practices: Towards a Different Image*, ed. Stevie Bezencenet and Philip Corrigan (London: Comedia, 1986), 74. Mike Abrahams, one of the founders of Network, was previously a photography student of Murray. Wilmer mentioned that Network asked her to join them but she refused since she had already committed to Format. Nonetheless, Network helped Format every step of the way. Val Wilmer, interview by the author, Val Wilmer's London home, October 20, 2011.

37 The initial Format collective consisted of photographers Murray, Wilmer, Pam Isherwood, O'Brien, Jenny Matthews, Raissa Page, Anita Corbin, Sheila Gray, and Brenda Prince, and three administrators. See Maggie Murray, "Format Photographers," talk at the National Portrait Gallery, March 25, 2010, private collection of Michael Ann Mullen.

38 Bezencenet, "Photography, Power and Responsibility," 74.

39 Janet Wolff criticized authors such as Charles Baudelaire, Georg Simmel, and Walter Benjamin for associating public space and the experience of the metropolis with men and for omitting women's experience of the city. Art historian Rosalyn Deutsche challenged the exclusion of feminism from various discourses in contemporary urban studies, and Griselda Pollock criticized a social, art-historical reading of modernity with a sexual-political reading of urban spaces in nineteenth-century French painting. Janet Wolff, "The Invisible Flâneuse: Women and the Literature of Modernity," *Theory, Culture, and Society* 3 (1985): 37; Rosalyn Deutsche, "Men in Space," in *Evictions: Art and Spatial Politics* (Cambridge, Mass.: MIT Press, 1996), 195–197; Griselda Pollock, "Modernity and the Spaces of Femininity," in *Vision and Difference: Femininity, Feminism and the Histories of Art* (London: Routledge, 1988), 50–90; Elizabeth Wilson, *The Sphinx in the City: Urban Life, the Control of Disorder, and Women* (Berkeley: University of California Press, 1991), 5–6; Elizabeth Wilson, "The Invisible Flâneur," *New Left Review* I/191 (January–February 1992): 90.

40 Elizabeth Wilson, *Sphinx in the City*, 5–6.

41 Elizabeth Wilson, "Invisible Flâneur," 90.

42 Elizabeth Wilson, *Sphinx in the City*, 10.

43 Walker, *Left Shift*, 5. Since the early 1970s, the film journal *Screen*, for instance, had published materials from the 1920s and 1930s by Russian formalists, as well as contemporary French writers, about film. *Screen* drew on sources in semiotics, Marxism, and Lacanian psychoanalysis that were otherwise unavailable in Britain. See Colin MacCabe, "Class of '68: Elements of an Intellectual Autobiography 1967–81," in *Tracking the Signifier: Theoretical Essays: Film, Linguistics, Literature* (Minneapolis: University of Minnesota Press, 1985), 7.

44 John Tagg, "Mindless Photography," in *Photography: Theoretical Snapshots*, ed. J. J. Long, Andrea Noble, and Edward Welch (London: Routledge, 2009), 17–24.

45 John Roberts, *The Art of Interruption: Realism, Photography and the Everyday* (Manchester: Manchester University Press, 1998), 145–148.

46 This talk was given as part of the series "Over-exposed: A Look at the Current Situation in Photography," organized by Sarah Kent to coincide with the exhibition *Photography as Art—Art as Photography*. See John Tagg, "Running and Dodging, 1943: The Breakup of the Documentary Moment," in *The Disciplinary Frame: Photographic Truths and the Capture of Meaning* (Minneapolis: University of Minnesota Press, 2009), 207.

47 Lukitsh, "Practicing Theories," 76–77.

48 John Tagg, *The Burden of Representation: Essays on Photographies and Histories* (London: Macmillan, 1988), 92–93.

49 Tagg, 92–95.

50 Harlesden Community Project, *Community Work and Caring for Children: A Community Project in an Inner City Local Authority by a Group of Workers from the Harlesden Community Project, 1971–1976* (Ilkley, England: Owen Wells, 1979), 23.

51 In the 1930s Willesden was known as Red Willesden, and it had a solid tradition of trade union organization. See Amrit Wilson, *Finding a Voice: Asian Women in Britain* (London: Virago, 1978), 59.

52 Homer Sykes, "Workers: Grunwick Was Different," in *Good Bye to London: Radical Art and Politics in the 70's*, ed. Astrid Proll in cooperation with curators Boris von Brauchitsch, Peter Cross, and Jule Reuter (Ostfildern, Germany: Hatje Cantz Verlag, 2010), 110.

53 Gijsbert Oonk, "Gujarati Asians in East Africa, 1880–2000: Colonization, De-colonization and Complex Citizenship Issues," *Diaspora Studies* 8 no. 1 (2015): 76.

54 The majority of the West Indian immigration was invited into Britain after the Second World War in order to fill shortages in the work force. See Huon Wardle and Laura Obermuller, "The Windrush Generation," *Anthropology Today* 34 no.4 (August 2018): 3–4; Beckett, *When the Lights Went Out*, 367.

55 Amrit Wilson, *Finding a Voice*, 55; Beckett, *When the Lights Went Out*, 359. Moreover, according to the Political and Economic Planning report of 1974, of all the immigrant groups in Britain, East Asian Africans had the highest qualifications and education but the lowest average income. See Dromey and Taylor, *Grunwick*, 21–24.

56 Dromey and Taylor, *Grunwick*, 43.

57 Sykes, "Workers," 110; Parmar, "Gender, Race and Class," 266.

58 Beckett, *When the Lights Went Out*, 402; Sykes, "Workers," 111.

59 Butler, "Bodies in Alliance," 118.
60 Butler, 117–118.
61 Butler, 118.
62 Warner, *Publics and Counterpublics*, 66.
63 Sykes, "Workers," 110; Parmar, "Gender, Race and Class," 266.
64 Dromey and Taylor, *Grunwick*, 59.
65 Dromey and Taylor, 59.
66 Dromey and Taylor, 25.
67 Amrit Wilson, *Finding a Voice*, 62.
68 Beckett, *When the Lights Went Out*, 365.
69 Amrit Wilson, *Finding a Voice*, 34.
70 Of the nine national dailies in Britain, three were uncompromisingly right wing: the *Daily Express*, the *Daily Mail*, and the *Daily Telegraph*. Of the three, the *Telegraph* aspired to be a "quality" newspaper containing the most facts. The *Sun* followed a conservative line, and its editorial positions were the most biased against the strikers and the least factual. The *Daily Mirror*, the *Financial Times*, the *Times*, and the *Guardian* made an effort to present both sides of the Grunwick strike. The *Morning Star* was the national daily with the smallest circulation and consistently supported the strikers and backed up its support with articles from a left-wing point of view. Dromey and Taylor, *Grunwick*, 128.
71 Sykes, "Workers," 111–113.
72 Dromey and Taylor, *Grunwick*, 129.
73 Parmar, "Gender, Race and Class," 267.
74 Val Wilmer, "The First Preference Is Pride," *Time Out*, September 1978, 16.
75 Parmar, "Gender, Race and Class," 264–267.
76 Dormey and Taylor, *Grunwick*, 96.
77 Poster Collective, "The Collective," accessed August 10, 2018, http://poster-collective.org.uk/historycollective.php.
78 Terry Dennett et al., "Film and Poster Collective: Interview," in *Photography/Politics: One*, ed. Terry Dennett et al., David Evans, Sylvia Gohl, and Jo Spence (London: Photography Workshop, 1979), 133–134.
79 Walker, *Left Shift*, 160.
80 Anna Coote, "Grunwick: The Lessons of the Bitter End," *New Statesman*, May, 19, 1978.
81 Amrit Wilson, *Finding a Voice*, 67–68.
82 Beckett, *When the Lights Went Out*, 402.
83 Amrit Wilson, *Finding a Voice*, 69.
84 Andrew Ward, "Drowning in Sympathy but Starving for Action," in "News Shorts," *Spare Rib* 78 (January 1978): 13; A similar photograph also appeared on the cover of the *Morning Star* on November 22, 1977.
85 Parmar, "Gender, Race and Class," 261, 267; Chris Thomas, dir., "Interview with Jayaben Desai," *The Great Grunwick Strike 1976–1978: A History* (London: Brent Trade Union Council, 2008), DVD.
86 Dromey and Taylor, *Grunwick*, 78.
87 Beckett, *When the Lights Went Out*, 359, 371.
88 Paula Bartely, *Emmeline Pankhurst* (London: Routledge, 2002), 114.
89 Wendy Webster, *Englishness and Empire, 1939–1965* (Oxford: Oxford University Press, 2005).

90 Camilla Schofield, *Enoch Powell and the Making of Postcolonial Britain* (New York: Cambridge University Press, 2013), 213–214.

91 John Street, *Music and Politics* (Cambridge, England: Polity, 2012), 80.

92 Beckett, *When the Lights Went Out*, 451–453. Throughout the late 1960s and 1970s, music had a central role in the black resistance culture that was forming in Britain, particularly among Afro-Caribbean groups. This took the shape of Anglo-Caribbean music such as ska and reggae, as well as a revival of the apocalyptic religio-politics of Rastafarianism. See Hall et al., "Politics of Mugging," 357.

93 Dromey and Taylor, *Grunwick*, 190.

94 Beatrix Campbell and Valerie Charlton, "Grunwick Women," *Spare Rib*, August 1977, 6–7.

95 Amrit Wilson, *Finding a Voice*, 70–71.

96 When the *Nightcleaners* project began, the Berwick Street Film Collective was an all-male group that included Marc Karlin, Humphrey Trevelyan, and Richard Moudaunt. The artist James Scott was also invited to contribute to the project. In order to make sure a feminist agenda was advocated, it was agreed that artist Mary Kelly would join the project. Kelly had also participated in the feminist action at Miss World mentioned in the previous chapter. *Nightcleaners* initially began as a straightforward agit prop film, but after four years in postproduction editing, it rather corresponded with Brechtian aesthetics. See Siona Wilson, *Art Labor, Sex Politics: Feminist Effects in 1970s British Art and Performance* (Minneapolis: University of Minnesota Press, 2015), 3–4, 24–25.

97 Siona Wilson, *Art Labor, Sex Politics*, 3; Claire Johnson and Paul Willemen, "Brecht in Britain: The Independent Political Film (on *The Nightcleaners*)," *Screen* 16, no. 4 (December 1975): 112, 115–116.

98 "London 'Reclaim the Night,'" *Women's Report: A Monthly Feminist News Magazine*, December 1978–January 1979, 2.

99 Campbell and Charlton, "Grunwick Women," 8.

100 Campbell and Charlton, 6–8, 46.

101 See Keenan's discussion of the wave gesture performed for a news camera by a Serb policeman looting a house in the Albanian Mijalic village. Keenan uses this example to demonstrate a contradiction of the human rights axiom of using photographic and video images for mobilizing shame. Nonetheless, I use his analysis to emphasize the performative aspects of 1970s street photography. See Keenan, "Mobilizing Shame," 445–446.

102 Campbell and Charlton, "Grunwick Women," 7, 46. According to a Wilsden doctor quoted in *Time Out* (August 12–18, 1977), some of the common injuries that the police inflicted on the strikers were a result of the their grabbing the strikers' testicles and breasts. Such injuries were generally unreported by the media. See Amrit Wilson, *Finding a Voice*, 67.

103 Dromey and Taylor, *Grunwick*, 112.

104 Avtar Brah and Ann Phoenix, "Ain't I a Woman? Re-visiting Intersectionality," in "Feminist Challenges: Crossing Boundaries," special issue, *Journal of International Women's Studies* 5, no. 3 (May 2004): 76.

105 Nonetheless, Desai mentioned that she was open to debating issues concerning abortion and contraception with the feminist supporters at the gate. Wilmer, "First Preference Is Pride," 16, 18.

106 Wilmer, 15.

107 Parmar, "Gender, Race and Class," 261. Desai and other women from the core group of strikers visited the homes of the women whose husbands, fathers, and fathers-in-law did not want them to participate in the strike. Desai's group tried to persuade these men that the women should take part in the struggle and urged the women to assert themselves against their families. Amrit Wilson, *Finding a Voice*, 63–64.

108 Dromey and Taylor, *Grunwick*, 41–42.

109 Beckett, *When the Lights Went Out*, 371; Thomas, "Interview with Jayaben Desai."

110 Alice Thorne and Maithreyi Krishnaraj, *Ideals Images and Real Lives: Women in Literature and History* (Mumbai: Orient Longman, 2000), 267–270.

111 Brixton Black Women's Group, "Black Women Organizing," *Feminist Review* 17 (Autumn 1984): 84–89.

112 Southall Black Sisters, *Against the Grain: A Celebration of Survival and Struggle, 1979–1989* (Southall, Middlesex: Southall Black Sisters, 1990), 3–4.

113 Gita Sahgal, "Fundamentalism and the Multi-culturalist Fallacy," in Southall Black Sisters, *Against the Grain*, 16–17.

114 Natalie Thomlinson, *Race, Ethnicity and the Women's Movement in England, 1968–1993* (Hampshire, England: Palgrave Macmillan, 2016), 2.

115 Cheryl Law, *Women: A Modern Political Dictionary* (London: I. B. Tauris, 2000), 237.

116 Reclaim the Night group, "Leeds," in "We Will Walk without Fear," *Spare Rib*, January 1978, 22.

117 Pat Moan, "London," in "We Will Walk without Fear,"; Soho had developed into a sex industry area beginning in the late nineteenth century. During the interwar period, it also developed into an artistic bohemian quarter. Since the 1960s, new forms of commercialized sex had proliferated in Soho, mainly in the form of strip clubs, theaters showing sex films, pornography shops, and sex shops. By the 1970s, aggressive touts, blaring music, and neon signs characterized this area. See John Eade, *Placing London: From Imperial Capital to Global City* (New York: Berghahn Books, 2000), 53–57; and Judith R. Walkowitz, *Night Out: Life in Cosmopolitan London* (New Haven, Conn.: Yale University Press, 2012), 295–296. The offices of the film and media journal *Screen Education*, in which various debates about photography developed in the 1970s, were located at 29 Old Compton Street, in the Soho area.

118 The national press gave the march some coverage, and the march's organizers also went on local radio and explained what they were doing. The BBC was contacted but was not interested. See "We Will Walk without Fear," 23.

119 "We Will Walk without Fear," 23.

120 Law, *Women*, 237.

121 Reclaim the Night group, "Leeds," in "We Will Walk without Fear," 22.

122 Pat Moan, "London," in "We Will Walk without Fear," 23.

123 Moan, 22.

124 Judith R. Walkowitz, *City of Dreadful Delight: Narratives of Sexual Danger in Late-Victorian London* (Chicago: University of Chicago Press, 1992), 234.

125 The first Reclaim the Night march took place in Belgium in March 1976 and was organized by women who attended the international Tribunal on Crimes against Women. See Tony Campolo and Gordon Aeschliman, *Everybody Wants to Change the World: Practical Ideas for Social Justice* (Ventura, Calif.: Regal Books, 2006), 103.

126 "Germany: Reclaiming the Night," *Spare Rib*, August 1977, 19.
127 Mikhail Mikhailovitz Bakhtin, *Rabelais and His World*, trans. Helene Iswolsky, (Bloomington: Indiana University Press, 1984), 10; Mikita Brottman, *High Theory/ Low Culture* (New York: Palgrave Macmillan, 2005), 10.
128 Brottman, *High Theory/Low Culture*, 10. In ancient Rome, the festival of Saturnalia was a precursor to early Christian medieval and Renaissance carnivals, which provided a brief window of opportunity to reverse hegemonic social roles and unusual restrictions on public behavior. See M. Lane Bruner, "Carnivalesque Protest and the Humorless State," *Text and Performance Quarterly* 25, no. 2 (April 2005): 138.
129 Mary Russo, *The Female Grotesque: Risk, Excess, and Modernity* (New York: Routledge, 1994).
130 Bruner, "Carnivalesque Protest," 139–140.
131 Beckett, *When the Lights Went Out*, 178.
132 Dick Hebdige, "Hiding in the Light," *Ten.8* 9 (1982): 13.
133 Beckett, *When the Lights Went Out*, 451–453.
134 Anna Poletti, "Self-Publishing in the Global and Local: Situating Life Writing in Zines," *Biography* 1 (Winter 2005): 184, 187.
135 This can be seen, for example, in a flyer from 1978 promoting the all-female punk band the Slits, which incorporates handwritten text, drawn stick figures presumably representing the band members, and a cut-and-pasted map indicating the performances' location in Acklam Hall. This venue also hosted a Rock against Racism benefit in June 1979, which included bands such as Beggar, Crisis, and the Samaritans. This overlap in performance sites might suggest another intersection between feminist punk cultural activity and antiracism politics. See Greil Marcus, *Lipstick Traces: A Secret History of the Twentieth Century* (Cambridge, Mass.: Harvard University Press, 1989), 38; and "Acklam Hall Riot: Beggar at the Acklam Rock against Racism Gig, 1979," Urban75, accessed August 10, 2017, http://www.urban75.org/music/beggar.html.
136 Cazz Blase, "A Woman Called Toothpaste: An Interview with Lucy Whitman," The F Word: Contemporary UK Feminism, May 20, 2011, http://www.thefword.org.uk/features/2011/05/Lucy_Whitman.
137 Blase, "A Woman Called Toothpaste."
138 "Rock against Sexism 1978," Women's Liberation Music Archive, accessed August 10, 2018, http://womensliberationmusicarchive.co.uk/s/.
139 Poletti, "Self-Publishing," 184.
140 Sue, *Penny Sillin*, *Shocking Pink* 2 (1981): 4.
141 Peter Jones, "Anxious Images: Linder's Fem-Punk Photomontages," *Women: A Cultural Review* 13, no. 2 (2002): 162–168; Lucy O'Brien, *She Bop II: The Definitive History of Women in Rock, Pop and Soul* (New York: Continuum, 2002), 167.
142 Jones, "Anxious Images"; Lucy O'Brien, *She Bop II*.
143 Julia Downes, "The Expansion of Punk Rock: Riot Grrrl Challenges to Gender Power Relations in British Indie Music Subcultures," *Women's Studies* 41, no. 2 (2012): 206.
144 Jones, "Anxious Images," 162–168; Lucy O'Brien, *She Bop II*, 163.
145 Moan, "London," in "We Will Walk without Fear," 22; "London 'Reclaim the Night,'" 2; "We Will Walk without Fear," 22. Nevertheless, according to Wilmer, in the first Reclaim the Night march, the police pushed photographer Angela Philips

to the ground. Wilmer, *Mama Said*, 288. The second march took place in London on July 7, 1978. See Law, *Women*, 237.

146 Second-wave feminists commonly dressed up as witches and self-identified as witches as a strategy of empowerment that referenced historical witch persecutions. This phenomenon was common in other locations as well, such as West Germany, France, and the United States. See Qinna Shen, "Shedding, Witchcraft, and the Romantic Subject: Feminist Appropriation of the Witch in Sarah Kirsch's *Zaubersprüche* (1973)," *Neophilologus* 93 (2009): 676.

147 "London 'Reclaim the Night,'" 2.

148 "London 'Reclaim the Night,'" 2.

149 Sally Collins, "Soho 16: 'Police Lied,'" *Spare Rib*, June 1978, 13.

150 Eileen Fairweather, "Leeds: Curfew on Men," *Spare Rib*, June 1979, 6.

151 "Women, Angry at Male Violence, Say: 'Resist the Curfew!,'" *Leeds Other Paper*, November 28, 1980, reprinted in *Women against Violence against Women*, ed. Dusty Rhodes and Sandra McNeill (London: Onlywomen, 1985), 12. According to the march's spokeswoman, *Dressed to Kill* was a misogynistic film that sexualized the act of killing. She mentioned that its screening was particularly infuriating since it took place at the time of Sutcliffe's attacks. The projection of the film was terminated when several dozen women threw rotten eggs and paint bombs on the screen. See Walkowitz, *City of Dreadful Delight*, 234–235.

152 "'Resist the Curfew!,'" 12.

153 Fairweather, "Leeds." In an email message to the author on March 27, 2018, John Tagg mentioned that at the time, a Yorkshire newspaper published a notorious front-page spread in which photographs of Sutcliffe's victims were divided into two sections: sex workers and "innocent women." This offensive division was frequent in other local newspapers and fueled much anger among the feminist community.

154 Fairweather, 6.

155 Walkowitz, *City of Dreadful Delight*, 229.

156 Hilary Robinson, ed., *Feminist Art Theory: An Anthology, 1968–2014* (Malden, Mass.: Blackwell, 2015), 91–93.

157 Peter Howard Selz, *The Art of Engagement: Visual Politics in California and Beyond*, with an essay by Susan Landauer (Berkeley: University of California Press, 2005), 194–195.

Chapter 4 Entering the Museum

1 Rozsika Parker and Griselda Pollock, "Fifteen Years of Feminist Action: From Practical Strategies to Strategic Practices," in *Framing Feminism: Art and the Women's Movement, 1970–1985*, ed. Rozsika Parker and Griselda Pollock (London: Pandora; New York: Routledge and Kegan Paul, 1987), 8–17.

2 The institutionalized spaces into which feminist activity entered also included the sphere of higher education; for instance, a full degree program in women's studies was established at the University of East London in 1983. See Maggie Humm, "Women's Studies at the University of East London," in "Women's Studies in Europe," special issue, *Women's Studies Quarterly* 20, no. 3/4 (Fall–Winter 1992): 38. Additionally, feminist art was also entering mainstream art publications; for instance, the modern art magazine *Studio International* dedicated an issue to women's art. See "Woman's Art," special issue, *Studio International*, 1977.

3 Donald Preziosi, "The Art of Art History," in *The Art of Art History: A Critical Anthology*, ed. Donald Preziosi (Oxford: Oxford University Press, 1998), 508.
4 Douglas Crimp, *On the Museum's Ruins* (Cambridge, Mass.: MIT Press, 1993), 48.
5 Carol Duncan, "The Art Museum as Ritual," in Preziosi, *Art of Art History*, 482.
6 Pierre Bourdieu, *The Field of Cultural Production: Essays on Art and Literature*, ed. Randal Johnson (New York: Columbia University Press, 1993), 36–37.
7 John Tagg, *The Disciplinary Frame: Photographic Truths and the Capture of Meaning* (Minneapolis: University of Minnesota Press, 2009), xxx–xxxii, 249.
8 Tagg, xxviii.
9 Theopisti Stylianou-Lambert and Elena Stylianou, "Editorial: Photography, Artists and Museums," *Photographies* 7, no. 2 (2014): 117.
10 Christopher Phillips, "The Judgment Seat of Photography," *October* 22 (1982): 30–32.
11 Phillips, 54.
12 Sean O'Hagan, "Was John Szarkowski the Most Influential Person in 20th-Century Photography?," *Guardian*, July 20, 2010.
13 Mark Haworth-Booth, "Where We've Come From: Aspects of Postwar British Photography," in *British Photography: Towards a Bigger Picture*, ed. Mark Haworth-Booth (New York: Aperture Foundation, 1988), 1–2. This committee was formed following the organization of an exhibition on the medium of photography, *From Today Painting Is Dead*, in 1972 at the Hayward Gallery. See Guy Lane, "The Photographer as Recorder: Daniel Meadows, Records, Discourse and Tradition in 1970s England," *Photographies* 4, no. 2 (2011): 157–173. The Hayward Gallery, initially operated by the Arts Council, opened in 1968 and exhibited modern and contemporary shows. See Peter Thomas, "The Struggle for Funding: Sponsorship, Competition and Pacification," *Screen* 47, no. 9 (Winter 2006): 461–467; Arts Council of Great Britain records, accessed April 6, 2016, http://www.vam.ac.uk/vastatic/wid/ead/acgb/acgb-121.html.
14 Barry Lane, interview by Shirley Read, December 13, 1999, C459/113/01-04, Oral History of British Photography Sound Collection, British Library, London.
15 According to Lane, supporting the publication of photography-related material was significant because book publishers were not interested in publishing photography at that time in Britain. Tom Picton, Barry Lane, and Bill Gaskin, "If It Is Art We Can Support It," *Camerawork*, February 1977, 1; Lane, interview by Read. Some of the photography galleries funded by the Arts Council included Half Moon Gallery founded in London in 1971 (later named Half Moon Photography Workshop and then Camerawork); Photographer's Gallery (founded 1971; a London gallery that traditionally featured documentary work), Impressions Gallery in York (founded 1972; one of the first photography galleries outside London), Ffotogallery in Cardiff (founded 1978), Stills Gallery in Edinburgh (founded 1977), and the Side Gallery (a photography and film cooperative in Newcastle upon Tyne). See "'70s/'90s: Notes for a Map of British Photography," in "British Photography: Towards a Bigger Picture," special issue, *Aperture* 113 (Winter 1988): 75–76.
16 Haworth-Booth, "Where We've Come From," 1–2.
17 Picton, Lane, and Gaskin, "If It Is Art," 2.
18 John Roberts, *The Impossible Document: Photography and Conceptual Art in Britain, 1966–1976* (London: Camerawords, 1997), 9. Conceptual art practices in Britain were initially viewed as an affront to established art values and were

often met with intense hostility. See Victor Burgin, "The Absence of Presence: Conceptualism and Postmodernisms," in *The End of Art Theory: Criticism and Postmodernity* (London: Macmillan Education, 1986), 29.

19 Anne Seymour, introduction to *The New Art*, exhibition catalog (London: Hayward Gallery, Arts Council of Great Britain, 1972), 6.

20 For instance, the workshop demonstrated at the National Conference on Art Education organized by the Artists Union in 1973 to demand that women comprise 50 percent of the faculty in art colleges, given that 50 percent of students were women. See Parker and Pollock, "Fifteen Years," 3, 8.

21 Parker and Pollock, 3.

22 Parker and Pollock, 11.

23 Parker and Pollock, 3.

24 Judy Chicago, *Through the Flower: My Struggle as a Woman Artist* (New York: Anchor Books, 1977), 103–104.

25 Miriam Schapiro, "The Education of Women as Artists: Project Womanhouse," *Art Journal* 3 (Spring 1972): 269.

26 Parker and Pollock, "Fifteen Years," 11. In Britain, as in the United States, the organization of feminist art shows was perceived as a form of activism associated with the larger women's movement and was initiated outside the established art institutions. See Ruth Iskin, "Feminism, Exhibitions and Museums in Los Angeles, Then and Now," *Women's Art Journal* 37, no. 1 (Spring/Summer 2016): 12.

27 Jacqueline Morreau, interview by Gillian Whiteley, artist's home, London, January 3, June 20, June 21, and December 16, 2002, F12409, F12412, NLSC: Artist's Lives Sound Collection, British Library, London.

28 *Men* and *Women* have been underresearched in exiting literature. My analysis is predominantly informed by my interview with the shows' organizer, Julia Meadows, and material from her private collection.

29 Wendy Ewald, interview by Shirley Read, October 23, 2006, and June 14, 2007, C459/191, Oral History of British Photography Sound Collection, British Library, London.

30 Julia Meadows, interview by the author, Julia Meadows's London home, November 3, 2011.

31 Wendy Ewald, founder and director of Half Moon Gallery, initially had the idea to organize a show of women photographing women. The idea was informed by similar contemporaneous exhibitions in the United States. Ewald ultimately returned to the United States and the project was taken over by Meadows. Meadows, interview by the author; and Ewald, interview by Read.

32 Meadows, interview by the author.

33 In an email message to the author on November 9, 2011, Meadows mentioned that other women who attended the planning meetings included Val Williams, Caroline Forbes, Angela Williams, Dorothy Bohm, and Fay Godwin.

34 Val Williams, *Women Photographers: The Other Observers, 1900 to the Present* (London: Virago, 1986), 172.

35 Meadows, interview by the author.

36 Val Wilmer, *Mama Said There'd Be Days like This: My Life in the Jazz World* (London: Women's Press, 1991), 270–271.

37 Meadows, interview by the author.

38 Wilmer, *Mama Said*, 270–271.

39 Wilmer, 270–271.
40 *Portrait of the Artist as Housewife* was exhibited at various provincial galleries in 1976, including the Chapter Arts Center in Cardiff, the Arnolfini Gallery in Bristol, the Blue Coat Gallery in Liverpool, Richard Demarco in Edinburgh, the Rochdale Gallery and the Midland Group Galley in Nottingham, and the London Institute of Contemporary Arts in 1977. Parker and Pollock, "Fifteen Years," 23.
41 Lee Comer, *Wedlocked Women* (Leeds: Feminist Books, 1974); Sandra Allen, Lee Sanders, and Jan Wallis, eds., *Conditions of Illusion* (Leeds: Feminist Books, 1974).
42 Eva Kaluzynska," Wiping the Floor with Theory: A Survey of Writings on Housework," *Feminist Review* 6 (1980): 37–38.
43 Meadows, interview by the author; Val Wilmer, interview by the author, Val Wilmer's London home, October 20, 2011.
44 Meadows, interview by the author.
45 Williams, *Women Photographers*, 172.
46 Wilmer, *Mama Said*, 271.
47 Meadows, interview by the author; Wilmer, *Mama Said*, 270–271.
48 Meadows, interview by the author.
49 Meadows, interview by the author.
50 Wilmer, *Mama Said*, 270–271.
51 This project was first exhibited at the New Zealand House in London in 1975. Alexis Hunter, *Radical Feminism in the 1970s* (Norwich: Norwich Gallery, 2006).
52 Hunter.
53 *Women Are Beautiful* was first exhibited in 1975 at the Light Gallery in New York. Garry Winogrand, *Women Are Beautiful* (New York: Light Gallery / Farrar, Straus and Giroux, 1975).
54 Alexis Hunter, interview by the author, café in London, October 18, 2011.
55 Jacqueline Morreau et al., introduction to *Women's Images of Men*, ed. Sarah Kent and Jacqueline Morreau, exhibition catalog (London: Institute of Contemporary Arts, 1980); Complete ICA Exhibitions list 1948–July 2017, accessed December 25 2018, https://archive.ica.art/sites/default/files/downloads/Complete%20ICA%20Exhibitions%20List%201948%20-%20Present%20-%20July%202017.pdf.
56 Morreau, interview by Whiteley.
57 Morreau et al., introduction.
58 Rozsika Parker, "Feminist Art Practices in 'Women's Images of Men,' 'About Time' and 'Issue,'" review of *Women's Images of Men*, *About Time*, and *Issue: Social Strategies by Women Artists*, exhibitions, *Art Monthly* 43 (1981): 16–19, reprinted in Parker and Pollock, *Framing Feminism*, 235. The show's focus on figurative work was perhaps also informed by a feminist opposition to the prevailing formalist abstraction, particularly in the early 1970s. See Parker and Pollock, "Fifteen Years," 5.
59 Morreau, interview by Whiteley.
60 "Women's Images of Men," review of *Women's Images of Men*, exhibition, Institute of Contemporary Arts, London, October 4–26, 1980, *Portfolio*, February 1981, 76, 79.
61 Parker and Pollock, "Fifteen Years," 41.
62 Philippa Beale, [notes on her work], in Kent and Morreau, *Women's Images of Men*.
63 Lill-Ann Chepstow-Lusty, [notes on her work], in Kent and Morreau, *Women's Images of Men*.

64 Catherine Elwes, Rose Garrard, and Sandy Nairne, *About Time: Video, Performance and Installation by 21 Women Artists*, exhibition catalog (London: Institute of Contemporary Arts, 1980).
65 Alexis Hunter moved to London in 1972 and worked there until her death in 2014. See Lynda Morris, "Alexis Hunter," obituary, *The Guardian,* Tuesday 11 March 2014, https://www.theguardian.com/artanddesign/2014/mar/11/alexis-hunter.
66 Lucy Lippard, "Issue and Tabu," in *Issue: Social Strategies by Women Artists*, curated by Lucy Lippard, exhibition catalog (London: Institute of Contemporary Arts, 1980).
67 Alexis Hunter, [notes on her photographs], in Kent and Morreau, *Women's Images of Men*.
68 Lippard, "Issue and Tabu."
69 Kate Linker, "Representation and Sexuality," in *Art after Modernism: Rethinking Representation*, ed. Brian Wallis (New York: New Museum of Contemporary Art, 1984), 403.
70 Loraine Leeson, "East London Health Project," in Lippard, *Issue*.
71 Alexis Hunter and Mary Kelly exhibited at the *Hayward Annual* exhibition in London in 1978. The Hayward was the main contemporary art gallery that was sponsored by the Arts Council at that time, and its 1978 annual exhibition was its first exhibition organized by women. Kelly had also exhibited *Post-partum Document* in a solo show at the Institute of Contemporary Arts in 1976. Margaret Harrison's work was exhibited in *Art for Society* at the White Chapel Gallery in London in 1978, and Adrian Piper exhibited her performance piece *Some Reflective Surfaces* at the Whitney Museum in New York in 1976. See Lippard, *Issue*.
72 Parker and Pollock, "Fifteen Years," 44; Fran Loyd, "Alison Wilding's Early Sculpture," *Secret Spaces, Forbidden Places: Rethinking Culture*, ed. Fran Loyd and Catherine O'Brien (New York: Berghahn Books), 239.
73 Griselda Pollock, "'Issue': An Exhibition of Social Strategies by Women Artists," review of *Issue: Social Strategies by Women Artists*, exhibition, *Spare Rib*, February 1981, 49–51, reprinted in Parker and Pollock, *Framing Feminism*, 233–234.
74 Parker and Pollock, "Fifteen Years," 45.
75 Parker and Pollock, 45.
76 John H. Hammond, "Viewed 'Women's Images of Men' at the ICA," review of *Women's Images of Men*, exhibition, Institute of Contemporary Arts, London, October 4–26, 1980, *British Journal of Photography* 26, no. 127 (December 26, 1980): 1315.
77 Rozsika Parker, "Portrait of the Artist as Housewife," review of *Portrait of the Artist as Housewife*, exhibition, Institute of Contemporary Arts, London, June 10–July 20, 1977, *Spare Rib*, July 1977, 5–8, reprinted in Parker and Pollock, *Framing Feminism*, 209–210.
78 Kenneth Robinson, *Punch*, September 6, 1978, quoted in Griselda Pollock, "Feminism and Modernism," in Parker and Pollock, *Framing Feminism*, 99.
79 The Women's Workshop of the Artists Union was a subgroup of the British Artists' Union formed in 1972 that addressed issues pertaining specifically to women artists, such as discrimination in the art world and childcare. Some of the artists active in this group were Kelly, Harrison, and Carol Kenna. See Parker and Pollock, "Fifteen Years," 7.
80 The women artists included in the show were Susan Derges, Ciobotaru, Donagh, Elisabeth Frink, Lilian Lijn, Deanna Petherbridge, Sandra Blow, Wendy Taylor,

Sue Beere, Kelly, Tess Jaray, Pamela Burns, Hunter, Susan Hiller, Edwina Leapman, and Julia Farrer. The male artists included in the show were Terry Pope, Leopoldo Maler, Marc Camille, Steve Fulonger, Stephen Cox, Michael Sandle, and Adrian Morris. See Griselda Pollock, "Feminism, Femininity and the Hayward Annual Exhibition 1978," *Feminist Review*, no. 2 (1979): 33–55.

81 Pollock, "Feminism, Femininity," 33–55; , eds., –;); John A. Walker, *Left Shift: Radical Art in 1970s Britain* (London: I. B. Tauris, 2002), 226–229.

82 Walker, *Left Shift*, 227.

83 David Bate, "Thirty Years: British Photography since 1979," *Portfolio*, November 2009, 5. In 1979 two major photography shows occurred in London, *People in Camera 1838–1914* at the National Portrait Gallery and *Atget's Gardens* at the Royal Institute of British Architects' Heinz Gallery. These shows were more historical in focus, whereas *Three Perspectives* centered on contemporary uses of photography. See "A Flash from the Past," review of *Three Perspectives on Photography*, *Evening Standard*, June 8, 1979.

84 The second photography show was planned for 1981; it was to continue exploration of the concept of different perspectives on photography and was to include an additional section on commercial photographic activity. See Barry Lane to John Taylor, August 21, 1979, in *Three Perspectives on Photography* exhibition, ACGB/121/1096, Archive of Art and Design, Victoria and Albert Museum, London.

85 Barry Lane to the director of the Australian Center of Photography, March 12, 1979; Barry Lane to Ake Sidwall, director of the Fotografiska Museet in Stockholm, Sweden, March 12, 1979; Barry Lane to Klaus Honnef, director of Rheunische Landesmuseum in Bonn, Germany, March 12, 1979; Barry Lane to Joe Deal, director of the California Museum of Photography at the University of California, San Francisco, March 12, 1979; Barry Lane to Cornell Capa, director of the International Center of Photography in New York, March 12, 1979, all in *Three Perspectives on Photography* exhibition, ACGB/121/1096, Archive of Art and Design, Victoria and Albert Museum, London.

86 Angela Kelly, interview by the author, Rochester Institute of Technology, May 19, 2010; Bate, "Thirty Years," 5.

87 Bate, "Thirty Years," 4–5.

88 John Tagg, interview by Susan Bright, June 23 and 26, 2003, F14232A–B, Oral History of British Photography Sound Collection, British Library, London; John Tagg, "A Socialist Perspective on Photographic Practice," in *Three Perspectives on Photography: Recent British Photography*, by Paul Hill, Angela Kelly. and John Tagg, exhibition catalog (London: Hayward Gallery, 1979), 71.

89 Kelly, interview by the author.

90 Bate, "Thirty Years," 5.

91 Kelly, interview by the author.

92 The feminist photographers included in Kelly's section were Aileen Ferriday, Christine Voge, Yve Lomax, Sarah McCarthy, Jo Spence, and Val Wilmer. Tagg's section also included feminist photographer Alexis Hunter and the all-female photography collective the Hackney Flashers.

93 Griselda Pollock, "Three Perspectives on Photography," review of *Three Perspectives on Photography*, *Screen Education* 31 (1979): 54.

94 Kelly, interview by the author.

95 Aileen Ferriday, "Aileen Ferriday," in Hill, Kelly, and Tagg, *Three Perspectives on Photography*, 44.
96 Kelly, interview by the author.
97 Yve Lomax, "Some Stories Which I Have Heard Some Questions Which I Asked," in Hill, Kelly, and Tagg, *Three Perspectives on Photography*, 54–55.
98 This book includes a different version of Spence's photograph from *Beyond the Family Album*. See Jo Spence, *Putting Myself in the Picture: A Political, Personal and Photographic Autobiography* (London: Camden, 1986).
99 John Tagg, "A Socialist Perspective on Photographic Practice," in Hill, Kelly, and Tagg, *Three Perspectives on Photography*, 70.
100 Report/I.F.L. "A Statistical Survey of Lost Working Days in 1978," *Three Perspectives on Photography*, 88–91; Hunter, interview by the author.
101 Kelly, interview by the author.
102 Hill, Kelly, and Tagg, "Catalog," *Three Perspectives on Photography*, 93–94.
103 Tagg, interview by Bright.
104 "Flash from the Past."
105 Richard Erlich, "Photography," review of *Three Perspectives on Photography*, *Art and Artists*, August 1979, 37.
106 Ian Jeffery, "Three Perspectives on Photography," review of *Three Perspectives on Photography*, *Artscribe*, July 1979, 49, 47.
107 Jeffery, 49; Erlich, "Photography," 37. It should be emphasized that the divisions proposed by the exhibition sections did not necessarily imply uniformity among its participating photographers; for example, various tensions emerged between the participating leftist documentary photographers and those who were more invested in theory. Yve Lomax, interview by the author, cafeteria of the Royal College of Art, London, October 20, 2011. Additionally, some presenters refused to have their work displayed in the vicinity of particular photographers; Burgin, for example, whose theoretically based work was included in Tagg's section, refused to have it hung opposite the Hackney Flashers'. Tagg, interview by Bright.
108 Waldemar Janusznack, "Though Talking in the Nursery," review of *Who's Holding the Baby?*, exhibition, *Guardian*, July 11, 1978.
109 Laura Margolis, review of *Three Perspectives on Photography: Recent British Photography*, exhibition, Hayward Gallery, London, June 1–June 8, 1979, *Spare Rib*, August 1979, 34–35.
110 Maggie Murray, interview by the author, Maggie Murray's London home, October 19, 2011; Jo Spence, interview by Val Williams, March and April 1991, Oral History of British Photography Sound Collection, British Library, London.
111 Michael Ann Mullen, interview by the author, October 31, 2011, British Library, London.
112 Tagg, interview by Bright.
113 Mullen, interview by the author.
114 Hackney Flashers Collective, "Who's Holding the Baby?," flyer for exhibition, Hayward Gallery, London, 1979, Visual Resources Collection, Department of Art History, Binghamton University, State University of New York. In an email message to the author on March 27, 2018, John Tagg mentioned that Nicki Road's and Linda Smith's talks on their involvement in the South London boroughs around the South Bank and the Hayward pointed to the Hayward Gallery's lack of connection to its own neighborhood.

115 Hackney Flashers Collective, "Who's Holding the Baby?"
116 Mullen, interview by the author. Maggie Murray recalls that the Hackney Flashers' events were well attended and that they mostly attracted "political" people who were predominantly interested in the "phenomenon" of the Hackney Flashers at the Hayward. She indicated that this crowd differed from the crowd at their previous interventions and was mainly interested in demanding a nursery. Murray, interview by the author.
117 Cunning Stunts was formed in 1977. Its shows combined music, dance, mime, magic, and acrobatics. It performed in locations such as community centers, housing centers, and the street. Carole Spedding, "Cunning Stunts," *Spare Rib*, September 1978, 39–40.
118 Tagg, interview by Bright; Bate, "Thirty Years," 5.
119 Bate, "Thirty Years," 5.
120 Mullen, interview by the author.
121 In an email message to the author on March 27, 2018, Tagg mentioned that contrary to *Three Perspectives*' reception as a face-off between aesthetic photography and socialist and feminist photography, there was not in fact any antagonism between Paul Hill, Angela Kelly, and himself. Tagg added that the three selectors were all supportive of each other's selections and that the spatial separation between the feminist and socialist sections in the large gallery and the aesthetic section in the lower-ceilinged side gallery was jointly determined by the selectors according to the scale of the works.
122 Sue Hollington, "The Pavilion," review of the Pavilion gallery, *Whippings and Apologies* 7 (January/February 1984): 11.
123 They were joined by Poppy Alexander, Rowena Jackson, Cathy Jacobs, Angie Kingston, Helen Kozich, and Sara Worall. Dinah Clark, phone interview by the author, October 31, 2011. Tagg was a lecturer in art history and the tutor in charge of the master's degree program in the social history of art in the Department of Fine Art at the University of Leeds between 1979 and 1984.
124 Shirley Moreno, "The Light Writing on the Wall: The Leeds Pavilion Project," in *Photographic Practices: Towards a Different Image*, ed. Stevie Bezencenet and Philip Corrigan (London: Comedia, 1986), 121.
125 Moreno, 121.
126 Parker and Pollock, "Fifteen Years," 33–34; Judy Chicago and eight of her students moved in 1971 from Fresno to Los Angeles where Chicago taught at Cal Arts and continued the concept of female education which began in Fresno. See Chicago, *Through the Flower*, 96.
127 Moreno, "Light Writing," 116; John Noble, "Arts Centre Challenges Divisions," review of the Pavilion, *Arts Yorkshire*, May 1982, 1; Pavilion's Women's Art Visual Center tenth anniversary conference draft transcript, ca. 1993, 104, Pavilion Collection, Feminist Archive North, Special Collections, Brotherton Library, University of Leeds.
128 Noble, "Arts Centre Challenges Divisions," 1.
129 Moreno, "Light Writing," 115, 119.
130 *The Pavilion*, booklet, Leeds, ca. 1984, 1, 19, Pavilion Collection, Feminist Archive North, Special Collections, Brotherton Library, University of Leeds.
131 The Pavilion's advisory committee members included Griselda Pollock, Tagg, Simon Watney, Spence, and Sarah McCarthy. See Pavilion's Women's Art Visual Center, 107–108.

132 Moreno, "Light Writing," 121.
133 Clark, phone interview by the author. In 1984 Tagg left for a position at the University of California, Los Angeles, and his position at the YAA, resulting in the council's withdrawal of funding for the Pavilion. Tagg, interview by Bright.
134 Penny Wark, "Art for Heart's Sake," *Yorkshire Post*, May 4, 1983, 5–6.
135 *Pavilion*, 16–17.
136 "Opening Space," review of the Pavilion gallery, *Leeds Other Paper*, April 29, 1983.
137 "Opening Space."
138 Wark, "Art for Heart's Sake," 6.
139 *Pavilion*, 20–21.
140 *Pavilion*, 122.
141 John Tagg, Skype interview by author, February 27, 2013.
142 Moreno, "Light Writing," 121.
143 Pavilion's Women's Art Visual Center, draft transcript, 113–115, 119.
144 Elizabeth Chaplin, *Sociology and Visual Representation* (London: Routledge, 1994), 113–114.
145 Clark, phone interview by the author.
146 Wells, "On and beyond the White Walls," 288–290.
147 Laura Mulvey, "Magnificent Obsession," in *Photography/ Politics: Two*, ed. Patricia Holland, Jo Spence, and Simon Watney (London: Comedia, 1986), 142.
148 Liz Wells, "On and beyond the White Walls: Photography as Art," in *Photography: A Critical Introduction*, 4th ed., ed. Liz Wells (London: Routledge, 2009), 288–290.
149 Bate, "Thirty Years," 6.
150 Knorr and Tabrizian studied photography with Burgin. During this time, the theoretical climate of their department was infused with psychoanalytic, linguistic, and feminist theory. See John Roberts, *The Art of Interruption: Realism, Photography and the Everyday* (Manchester: Manchester University Press, 1998), 154–155.
151 Karen Knorr, interview by Antonio Guzman, in *Karen Knorr: Marks of Distinction*, introduction by Patrick Mauries (London: Thames and Hudson, 1991), 124. Although perhaps not explicitly acknowledged, this outlook can also be identified in Burgin's photographic work since the 1970s, which emphasized image quality.
152 Knorr, 126.
153 Mrinalini Sinha, "Britishness, Clubbability, and the Colonial Public Sphere: The Genealogy of an Imperial Institution in Colonial India," in "At Home in the Empire," special issue, *Journal of British Studies* 40, no. 4 (October 2001): 490.
154 Gilane Tawadros, "Other Britains, Other Britons," in Haworth-Booth, *British Photography*, 46.
155 Mary Ann Doane, "Film and the Masquerade: Theorising the Female Spectator," *Screen* 23, no. 3–4 (September 1982): 74–88; Laura Mulvey, "Visual Pleasure and Narrative Cinema," *Screen* 16, no. 3 (Autumn 1975): 6–18.
156 Gerry Badger, "Through the Looking Glass: Photographic Art in Britain, 1945–1989," in *Through the Looking Glass: Photographic Art in Britain, 1945–1989*, by Gerry Badger, John Benton-Harris, and Michael Harris (London: Barbican Gallery, 1989), 23; cf. Martin Barnes, "One Perspective on Three Perspectives" *Portfolio*, November 2009, 9.
157 Susan Kismaric, *British Photography from the Thatcher Years* (New York: Museum of Modern Art, 1990), 10.

158 The photographers who participated in the show were Chris Killip, Graham Smith, John Davies, Martin Parr, and Paul Graham. Kismaric, *British Photography*.
159 Bate, "Thirty Years," 4–6.
160 Simon Watney, introduction to Bezencenet and Corrigan, *Photographic Practices*, 2.
161 Iskin, "Feminism, Exhibitions and Museums," 16–17.
162 Cornelia H. Butler and Lisa Gabrielle Mark, *WACK! Art and the Feminist Revolution* (Los Angeles: Museum of Contemporary Art, 2007).
163 Siona Wilson, "Destinations of Feminist Art: Past, Present and Future," *Women Studies Quarterly* 36, nos. 1 and 2 (Spring/Summer 2008): 324–325, 328.
164 In an email message to the author on April 24, 2014, Concha Calvo, employed at the Collections Department of the National Museum Reina Sofia Center of Art, mentioned that the exhibited *Who's Holding the Baby* panels were not the original version of the work made in 1978 but a later version that was made by Jo Spence around 1980. These were acquired by the museum in 2010 from Terry Dennett, but the complete set of original panels is held by the Arts Council Collection in Britain.
165 Museo Nacional Centro de Arte, "Collection 3: From Revolt to Postmodernity (1962–1982)," accessed November 29, 2018, http://www.museoreinasofia.es/en/collection/collection-3.
166 Museo Nacional Centro de Arte, "Room 104.07: The Feminist Revolution," accessed November 5, 2014, http://www.museoreinasofia.es/en/collection/room/room-10407.
167 David Alan Mellor, *No Such Thing as Society: Photography in Britain, 1967–87*, exhibition catalog (London: Hayward, 2008).
168 Siona Wilson, *Art Labor, Sex Politics: Feminist Effects in 1970s British Art and Performance* (Minneapolis: University of Minnesota Press, 2015); Kathy Battista, *Renegotiating the Body: Feminist Art in 1970s London* (London: I. B. Tauris, 2013).

Chapter 5 Conclusion and Afterthoughts

1 Victor Burgin, introduction to *Thinking Photography*, ed. Victor Burgin (London: Macmillan, 1982), 1–3.
2 The relationship between the Left and the women's movement was nonetheless ambivalent. The early British women's liberation movement was initially predominantly identified with socialism. Furthermore, feminists hoped to drag the labor movement and the working class in the direction of socialism and feminism, as well as to exert a feminist influence on the trades unions. Feminists were also recruited to the Communist Party of Great Britain, which was considered more open to the discussion of feminist ideas than other leftist groups. Feminist ideas were often marginalized or met with hostility by the labor movement, political parties, and the media, all of which denounced women's liberation as "middle class." See Elizabeth Wilson and Angela Weir, "The British Women's Movement," *New Left Review* I/148 (November–December 1984): 75–76.
3 Spence used photography for politicizing the personal, but her practice was not limited to this notion, as she also employed theory to contemplate the meaning of images and the different uses of photography. See Annette Kuhn, "Introduction," in *Cultural Sniping: The Art of Transgression*, by Jo Spence (London and New York: Routledge, 1995), xix—xxiv.

4 Geoffrey Batchen, *Burning with Desire: The Conception of Photography* (Cambridge, Mass.: MIT Press, 1999), 10. See also John Tagg, "Power and Photography—Part One: A Means of Surveillance: The Photograph as Evidence in Law," *Screen Education* 36 (Autumn 1980): 17–24; Allan Sekula, *Photography against the Grain: Essays and Photo Works 1973–1983* (Halifax: Press of the Nova Scotia College of Art and Design, 1984); and Burgin, introduction, 1–3.

5 Jo Anna Isaak, *Feminism and Contemporary Art: The Revolutionary Power of Women's Laughter* (London: Routledge, 1996), 14. See also Andrew Robertshaw, "'Irrepressible Chirpy Cockney Chappies'? Humour as an Aid to Survival," *Journal of European Studies* 3, no. 123 (September 2001): 277–278.

6 Isaak, *Feminism and Contemporary Art*, 14.

7 David Green and Joanna Lowry, "From Presence to the Performative: Rethinking Photographic Indexicality," in *Where Is the Photograph?*, ed. David Green (Maidstone, England: Photoworks; Brighton, England: Photoforum, 2003), 47–48, 58.

8 See Suzanne Staggenborg and Amy Lang, "Culture and Ritual in the Montreal Women's Movement," *Social Movement Studies* 6, no. 2 (September 2007): 178; Sara Ahmed, "Affective Economies," *Social Text* 79, vol. 22, no. 2 (Summer 2004): 119; Sara Ahmed, *The Cultural Politics of Emotion* (New York: Routledge, 2004), 1–4.

9 Vanessa Engle, dir., *Lefties*, episode 2, "Angry Wimmin," aired February 15, 2006, on BBC 4, http://www.youtube.com/watch?v=Ap072n01ESI.

10 James Penney, *After Queer Theory: The Limits of Sexual Politics* (London: Pluto, 2014), 1.

11 Feminist photographer Jill Posener changed her opinion on pornography as sexual violence against women after she moved to San Francisco in 1986. In San Francisco she encountered feminist sex-positive debates that explored libertarian sexual identities. The shift in Posener's perspective is manifested in her photography book *Nothing but the Girl: The Blatant Lesbian Image*, which features erotic images of lesbians photographed by lesbians. See Jill Posener, "Nothing but the Butch—Interview with Photographer Jill Posener," *ICON*, September 1996; Jill Posener, *Louder than Words* (London: Pandora, 1986); and Susie Bright and Jill Posener, *Nothing but the Girl: The Blatant Lesbian Image: A Portfolio and Exploration of Lesbian Erotic Photography* (New York: Freedom, 1996).

12 Rosalind Gill, "The Sexualization of Culture?," *Social and Personality Psychology Compass* 6, no. 7 (2012): 483–486, 493.

13 In *One Dimensional Woman*, Power invokes Herbert Marcuse's *One Dimensional Man* (1964) and its analysis of capitalism as granting the modern subject an illusion of freedom and happiness through the promises of consumerism and technological advancements. Power similarly suggests that, contemporary feminism, like capitalism, has devolved into a kind of consumerism that limits its political potential to purchasing particular products, to recreational activities, and to a concern with body image. Nina Power, *One Dimensional Woman* (Winchester, England: Zero Books, 2009), 1–3.

14 Pop stars such as Beyoncé associate feminism with sexual empowerment. This approach is manifested in Beyoncé's performances, where she employs her sexuality as a tool to culturally reclaim the black female body and sexuality. Her feminist arguments were also highlighted at the 2014 MTV Video Music Awards, where she performed her song "***Flawless" in front of the word *feminist* illuminated in bright capital letters. See Nathalie Weidhase, "'Beyoncé Feminism' and the

Contestation of the Black Feminist Body," *Celebrity Studies* 6, no. 1 (2015): 128–131; Linda M. Scott, *Fresh Lipstick: Redressing Fashion and Feminism* (New York: Palgrave Macmillan, 2005); and Dajanae Barrows, "In Search of Feminism: Fashion, My Body and Owning My Sexuality," *Campanil* (Mills College, Oakland, Calif.), September 15, 2015, http://www.thecampanil.com/in-search-of-feminism-fashion-my-body-and-owning-my-sexuality/.

15 Cheryl Wischhover, "Back Off, B*tches. There's Only One Butt Selfie Queen," Daily Beast, May 9, 2014, https://www.thedailybeast.com/back-off-btches-theres-only-one-butt-selfie-queen.

16 Tim Chester, "London Ad Asks If You're Beach Body Ready, and Everyone Says F*ck Off," Mashable, April 27, 2015, http://mashable.com/2015/04/27/protein-world-beach-body-advert-london/#pp4RZHAO2aqL.

17 Ramzi Alwakeel, "Protest over Protein World's 'Beach Body Ready' Advert Descends on Hyde Park," *Evening Standard*, May 2, 2015, https://www.standard.co.uk/news/london/protest-over-protein-world-s-beach-body-ready-advert-descends-on-hyde-park-10221028.html.

18 Rose Hackman, "Are You Beach Body Ready? Controversial Weight Loss Ad Sparks Varied Reactions," *Guardian*, June 27, 2015, https://www.theguardian.com/us-news/2015/jun/27/beach-body-ready-america-weight-loss-ad-instagram; Mark Sweney, "'Beach Body Ready' Ad Banned from Returning to Tube, Watchdog Rules," *Guardian*, April 29, 2015, https://www.theguardian.com/media/2015/apr/29/beach-body-ready-ad-faces-formal-inquiry-as-campaign-sparks-outrage.

19 Michael Warner, *Publics and Counterpublics* (New York: Zone Books, 2002), 56–57; Judith Butler, "Bodies in Alliance and the Politics of the Street," in *Sensible Politics: The Visual Culture of Nongovernmental Activism*, ed. Meg McLagan and Yates McKee (New York: Zone Books, 2012), 119–120.

20 Warner, *Publics and Counterpublics*, 57.

21 Ariella Azoulay, "What is Photography?," *Mafte'akh* 2 (2010): 118–119.

22 Thomas Keenan, "Mobilizing Shame," *South Atlantic Quarterly* 103, no. 2/3 (Spring/Summer 2004): 447.

23 Mary Russo, *The Female Grotesque: Risk, Excess, and Modernity* (New York: Routledge, 1994).

24 Durba Mitra, "Critical Perspectives on SlutWalks in India," *Feminist Studies* 38, no. 1 (Spring 2012): 254–255; Jessica Ringrose and Emma Renold, "Slut-Shaming, Girl Power and 'Sexualisation': Thinking through the Politics of the International SlutWalks with Teen Girls," *Gender and Education* 24, no. 3 (2012): 333–343.

25 Jo Reger, "Micro-cohorts, Feminist Discourse, and the Emergence of the Toronto SlutWalk," *Feminist Formations* 26, no. 1 (Spring 2014): 49.

26 Ringrose and Renold, "Slut-Shaming," 334.

27 Reger, "Micro-cohorts," 50.

28 Ringrose and Renold, "Slut-Shaming," 340; Bonnie J. Dow and Julia T. Wood, "Repeating History and Learning from It: What Can SlutWalks Teach Us about Feminism?," *Women's Studies in Communication* 37, no. 1 (2014): 23.

29 Reger, "Micro-cohorts," 50.

30 Reger, 61, 64.

31 Lilie Chouliaraki, "Digital Witnessing in War Journalism: The Case of Post-Arab Spring Conflicts," *Popular Communication* 13, no. 2 (2015): 106.

32 SlutWalk Toronto, Facebook page, accessed November 2017, https://www.facebook.com/SlutWalkToronto/; SlutWalk Johannesburg, Facebook page, accessed November 2017, https://www.facebook.com/slutwalkjhb/; SlutWalk Chicago, Facebook page, accessed November 2017, https://www.facebook.com/slutwalkchicago/; SlutWalk India, Facebook page, accessed November 2017, https://www.facebook.com/slutwalkindia/.

33 Dow and Wood, "Repeating History," 24; Madison Su, "SlutWalk or No SlutWalk: Examining Mainstream Media's Portrayal," Odyssey, December 12, 2016, https://www.theodysseyonline.com/slutwalk-examining-mainstream-medias-portrayal?altdesign=socialux.

34 Dow and Wood, "Repeating History," 24.

35 Terry Dennett and Jo Spence, "Photography Workshop 1974 Onwards," in *Putting Myself in the Picture: A Political Personal and Photographic Autobiography*, by Jo Spence (London: Camden, 1986), 62–65. Jo Spence and Terry Dennett's photography project *Remodelling Photo History* (1979–1982), for example, reappropriated established photography genres and subverted their representations of the female body. See Spence, *Putting Myself in the Picture*, 120–132.

36 Judy Harrison, "Absent Spaces: Histories, Empowerment and Representation," in *Our Faces, Our Spaces: Photography, Community and Representation*, ed. Judy Harrison (Southampton, England: John Hansard Gallery, University of Southampton, 2013), 9–10.

37 Shaila Waheed, in Harrison, *Our Faces, Our Spaces*, 71.

38 Val Williams, *Women Photographers: The Other Observers, 1900 to the Present* (London: Virago, 1986); *Spectrum Women's Photography Festival Exhibition Catalogue: A Collaboration with "Ten 8" International Photographic Magazine* (London: Spectrum, 1988).

39 Hackney Flashers, "Work of a Women's Collective 1974–1980," accessed December 20, 2018. https://hackneyflashers.com/exhibitions/.

40 "Feminist Avant-Garde of the 1970s: Works from the Verbund Collection," press release, July 18, 2016, for exhibition at the Photographers' Gallery, October 7, 2016–January 8, 2017. In the author's possession.

41 Astrid Proll, ed., *Good Bye to London: Radical Art and Politics in the 70's*, in cooperation with curators Boris von Brauchitsch, Peter Cross, and Jule Reuter (Ostfildern, Germany: Hatje Cantz Verlag, 2010).

42 Claire Bishop, "The Social Turn: Collaboration and Its Discontents," *Art Forum*, February 2006, 179–180.

43 Cf. Ruth Iskin's discussion of Huang Yong Ping's work *The History of Chinese Painting and the History of Modern Western Art Washed in the Washing Machine for Two Minutes*, Ruth Iskin, "Introduction: Re-envisioning the Canon: Are Pluriversal Canons Possible?," in *Re-envisioning the Contemporary Art Canon: Perspectives in a Global World*, ed. Ruth Iskin (London: Routledge, 2016), 2–6.

Bibliography

Published Sources

"Acklam Hall Riot: Beggar at the Acklam Rock against Racism Gig, 1979." Urban75, accessed August 10, 2017. http://www.urban75.org/music/beggar.html.

Adami, Elisa. "How Do You Watch a Revolution? Notes from the 21st Century." *Journal of Visual Culture* 15, no. 1 (2016): 69–84.

Adams, Parveen, Rosalind Coward, and Elizabeth Cowie. "Editorial." *m/f* 1 (1978).

Ahmed, Sara. "Affective Economies." *Social Text* 79, vol. 22, no. 2 (Summer 2004): 117–139.

———. *The Cultural Politics of Emotion.* New York: Routledge, 2004.

Allen, Sandra, Lee Sanders, and Jan Wallis, eds. *Conditions of Illusion.* Leeds: Feminist Books, 1974.

Althusser, Louis. *Lenin and Philosophy and Other Essays.* New York: Monthly Review Press, 1971.

Alwakeel, Ramzi. "Protest over Protein World's 'Beach Body Ready' Advert Descends on Hyde Park." *Evening Standard*, May 2, 2015. https://www.standard.co.uk/news/london/protest-over-protein-world-s-beach-body-ready-advert-descends-on-hyde-park-10221028.html.

Amos, Valerie, and Pratibha Parmar. "Challenging Imperial Feminism." In "Reflections on 25 Years." Special issue, *Feminist Review*, no. 80 (2005): 44–63.

Anden-Papadopoulos, Kari. "Citizen Camera-Witnessing: Embodied Political Dissent in the Age of 'Mediated Mass Self-Communication.'" *New Media Society* 16, no. 5 (2014): 754–769.

Andermahr, Sonya. "1970s Feminist Fiction." In *The 1970s: A Decade of Contemporary British Fiction*, edited by Nick Hubble, John McLeod, and Philip Tew, 69–92. London: Bloomsbury, 2014.

"Angry Women Burn Sex Shop." *Off Our Backs*, November 1982, 11.

"Arson Attacks at Video Shops." *Yorkshire Evening Post*, January 14, 1983.

Arts Council of Great Britain. *Hayward Annual: 1978.* London: Arts Council of Great Britain, 1978.

Arya, Rina. "Rethinking Black Art as a Category of Experience." *Visual Culture in Britain* 18, no. 2 (June 2017): 163–175.

Autograph. "Who We Are: About Autograph ABP." Accessed August 10, 2017. http://autograph-abp.co.uk/who-we-are.

"Autograph Sees Light of Day." *British Journal of Photography*, August 4, 1988. Available at "Our History: Press," Autograph, accessed August 10, 2018. http://autograph-abp.co.uk/history/all/press.

Avedon, Carol. "Don't Get Fooled Again: Assailed in Britain." *New York Law School Law Review* 38 (1993): 183–194.

Azoulay, Ariella. "What Is Photography?" *Mafte'akh* 2 (2010): 111–124.

Badger, Gerry, John Benton-Harris, and Michael Harris. *Through the Looking Glass: Photographic Art in Britain, 1945–1989*. London: Barbican Gallery, 1989.

Bakhtin, Mikhail Mikhailovitz. *Rabelais and His World*. Translated by Helene Iswolsky. Bloomington: Indiana University Press, 1984.

Ballaster, Ros. "Campbell, Beatrix." In *Encyclopedia of Feminist Literary Theory*, edited by Elizabeth Kowaleski-Wallace, 88. New York: Routledge, 2009.

Barnes, Martin. "One Perspective on Three Perspectives." *Portfolio*, November 2009, 8–11.

Barrows, Dajanae. "In Search of Feminism: Fashion, My Body and Owning My Sexuality." *Campanil* (Mills College, Oakland, Calif.), September 15, 2015. http://www.thecampanil.com/in-search-of-feminism-fashion-my-body-and-owning-my-sexuality/.

Bartely, Paula. *Emmeline Pankhurst*. London: Routledge, 2002.

Bashevkin, Sylvia. *Tales of Two Cities: Women and Municipal Restructuring in London and Toronto*. Vancouver: University of British Columbia Press, 2006.

Batchen, Geoffrey. *Burning with Desire: The Conception of Photography*. Cambridge, Mass.: MIT Press, 1999.

Bate, David. "Thirty Years: British Photography since 1979." *Portfolio*, November 2009, 4–7.

Battista, Kathy. *Renegotiating the Body: Feminist Art in 1970s London*. London: I. B. Tauris, 2013.

Beckett, Andy. *When the Lights Went Out: What Really Happened to Britain in the Seventies*. London: Faber and Faber, 2009.

Beechy, Veronica. "On Patriarchy." *Feminist Review* 3 (1979): 66–67.

Berlant, Lauren, and Michael Warner. "Sex in Public." *Critical Inquiry* 24, no. 2 (1998): 547–565.

Bezencenet, Stevie. "Photography and Education." In *Photographic Practices: Towards a Different Image*, edited by Stevie Bezencenet and Philip Corrigan, 6–12. London: Comedia, 1986.

———. "Photography, Power and Responsibility: The Format Picture Agency." In *Photographic Practices: Towards a Different Image*, edited by Stevie Bezencenet and Philip Corrigan, 71–78. London: Comedia, 1986.

Bishop, Claire. "The Social Turn: Collaboration and Its Discontents." *Art Forum*, February 2006, 178–183.

Blase, Cazz. "A Woman Called Toothpaste: An Interview with Lucy Whitman." The F Word: Contemporary UK Feminism, May 20, 2011. http://www.thefword.org.uk/features/2011/05/Lucy_Whitman.

Bourdieu, Pierre. *The Field of Cultural Production: Essays on Art and Literature*. Edited by Randal Johnson. New York: Columbia University Press, 1993.

Brah, Avtar, and Ann Phoenix. "Ain't I a Woman? Re-visiting Intersectionality." In "Feminist Challenges: Crossing Boundaries." Special issue, *Journal of International Women's Studies* 5, no. 3 (May 2004): 75–86.

Bright, Susie, and Jill Posener. *Nothing but the Girl: The Blatant Lesbian Image: A Portfolio and Exploration of Lesbian Erotic Photography*. New York: Freedom, 1996.

Brixton Black Women's Group. "Black Women Organizing." *Feminist Review* 17 (Autumn 1984): 84–89.

Bronstein, Carolyn. *Battling Pornography: The American Feminist Anti-Pornography Movement, 1976–1986*. Cambridge: Cambridge University Press, 2011.

———. "No More Black and Blue: Women against Violence against Women and the Warner Communications Boycott, 1976–1979." *Violence against Women* 14, no. 4 (April 2008): 418–436.

Brooks, Rosita. "Through the Looking Glass Darkly." In *British Photography: Towards a Bigger Picture*, edited by Mark Haworth-Booth, 47–51. New York: Aperture Foundation, 1988.

Brottman, Mikita. *High Theory/Low Culture*. New York: Palgrave Macmillan, 2005.

Brown, Elspeth H., and Thy Phu. Introduction to *Feeling Photography*, edited by Thy Phu and Elspeth H. Brown, 1–25. Durham, N.C.: Duke University Press, 2014.

Bruner, M. Lane. "Carnivalesque Protest and the Humorless State." *Text and Performance Quarterly* 25, no. 2 (April 2005): 136–155.

Burger, Peter. *Theory of the Avant-Garde*. Translated by Michael Shaw. Foreword by Jochen Schulte-Sasse. Minneapolis: University of Minnesota Press, 1984.

Burgin, Victor. "The Absence of Presence: Conceptualism and Postmodernisms." In *The End of Art Theory: Criticism and Postmodernity*, 29–50. London: Macmillan Education, 1986.

———. *Between*. London: Basil Blackwell, 1986.

———. Introduction to *Thinking Photography*, edited by Victor Burgin, 1–14. London: Macmillan, 1982.

———. "Photographic Practice and Art Theory." *Studio International* 190, no. 976 (1975). Reprinted in *Thinking Photography*, edited by Victor Burgin (London: Macmillan, 1982), 39–83.

Butler, Cornelia H., and Lisa Gabrielle Mark. *WACK! Art and the Feminist Revolution*. Los Angeles: Museum of Contemporary Art, 2007.

Butler, Judith. "Bodies in Alliance and the Politics of the Street." In *Sensible Politics: The Visual Culture of Nongovernmental Activism*, edited by Meg McLagan and Yates McKee, 117–137. New York: Zone Books, 2012.

Campbell, Beatrix, and Valerie Charlton. "Grunwick Women." *Spare Rib*, August 1977, 6–8, 46.

Campbell, Katie. "Boning Up on *Spare Rib*." *Women's Review of Books* 9 (June 1984): 17–18.

Campolo, Tony, and Gordon Aeschliman. *Everybody Wants to Change the World: Practical Ideas for Social Justice*. Ventura, Calif.: Regal Books, 2006.

Carby, Hazel V. "White Woman Listen! Black Feminism and the Boundaries of Sisterhood." In *The Empire Strikes Back: Race and Racism in 70s Britain*, edited by Centre for Contemporary Cultural Studies, 211–234. London: Hutchinson, 1982.

Carr, Gordon. *The Angry Brigade: A History of Britain's First Urban Guerilla Group*. Oakland, Calif.: PM, 2010.
Chaplin, Elizabeth. *Sociology and Visual Representation*. London: Routledge, 1994.
Chapman, Mary. *Making Noise, Making News: Suffrage Print Culture and U.S. Modernism*. New York: Oxford University Press, 2014.
Chappell, Helen. "Wednesday Women (Third Person): Macho but Not So Mucho." *Guardian*, July 26, 1989.
Chester, Tim. "London Ad Asks If You're Beach Body Ready, and Everyone Says F*ck Off." Mashable, April 27, 2015. http://mashable.com/2015/04/27/protein-world-beach-body-advert-london/#pp4RZHAO2aqL.
Chicago, Judy. *Through the Flower: My Struggle as a Woman Artist*. New York: Anchor Books, 1977.
Chouliaraki, Lilie. "Digital Witnessing in War Journalism: The Case of Post-Arab Spring Conflicts." *Popular Communication* 13, no. 2 (2015): 105–119.
Clarke, John, Stuart Hall, Tony Jefferson, and Brian Roberts. "Subcultures, Cultures and Class." *Working Papers in Cultural Studies*, no. 7/8 (1975). Reprinted in *Resistance through Rituals: Youth Subcultures in Post-war Britain*, edited by Stuart Hall and Tony Jefferson (London: Hutchinson, 1980), 9–74.
Cochrane, Kira. *All the Rebel Women: The Rise of the Fourth Wave of Feminism*. London: Guardian Books, 2013.
Collins, Sally. "Soho 16: 'Police Lied.'" *Spare Rib*, June 1978, 13.
Comer, Lee. *Wedlocked Women*. Leeds: Feminist Books, 1974.
Complete ICA Exhibitions List, 1948–July 2017. Accessed December 25 2018. https://archive.ica.art/sites/default/files/downloads/Complete%20ICA%20Exhibitions%20List%201948%20-%20Present%20-%20July%202017.pdf.
Compton, Alice. "Waste of a Nation: Photography, Abjection and Crisis in Thatcher's Britain." PhD diss., University of Sussex, 2016. http://sro.sussex.ac.uk/65974/.
Coote, Anna. "Grunwick: The Lessons of the Bitter End." *New Statesman*, May 19, 1978.
Coote, Anna, and Beatrix Campbell. *Sweet Freedom: The Struggle for Women's Liberation*. Oxford: Basil Blackwell, 1987.
Coward, Rosalind. "Sexual Violence and Sexuality." In "Sexuality." Special issue, *Feminist Review* 11 (Summer 1982): 9–22.
———. "Underneath We're Angry." *Time Out*, February 27, 1980. Reprinted in *Framing Feminism: Art and the Women's Movement, 1970–1985*, edited by Rozsika Parker and Griselda Pollock (London: Pandora; New York: Routledge and Kegan Paul, 1987), 144.
Cowie, Elizabeth. "Woman as Sign." *m/f* 1 (January 1978): 49–64.
Crimp, Douglas. *On the Museum's Ruins*. Cambridge, Mass.: MIT Press, 1993.
Dawson, Ashley. "Linton Kwesi Johnson's Dub Poetry and the Political Aesthetics of Carnival in Britain." *Small Axe* 21 (October 2006): 54–69.
Dejanikus, Tracie, and Janice Kelly. "Women Take Back the Night." *Off Our Backs*, December 31, 1977.
Dennett, Terry. "Jo Spence: Autobiographical Photography: Self, Class and Family." In *Jo Spence: Beyond the Perfect Image: Photography, Subjectivity, Antagonism*, 18–30. Barcelona: Museu d'Art Contemporani, 2005.
Dennett, Terry, David Evans, Sylvia Gohl, and Jo Spence. "Film and Poster Collective: Interview." In *Photography/Politics: One*, edited by Terry Dennett, David Evans, Sylvia Gohl, and Jo Spence, 133–138. London: Photography Workshop, 1979.

Deutsche, Rosalyn. "Men in Space." In *Evictions: Art and Spatial Politics*, 195–202. Cambridge, Mass.: MIT Press, 1996.

DiPaulo, Marc. *War, Politics, and Superheroes: Ethics and Propaganda in Comics and Film*. Jefferson, N.C.: McFarland, 2011.

Doane, Mary Ann. "Film and the Masquerade: Theorising the Female Spectator." *Screen* 23, no. 3–4 (September 1982): 74–88.

Dow, Bonnie J., and Julia T. Wood. "Repeating History and Learning from It: What Can SlutWalks Teach Us about Feminism?" *Women's Studies in Communication* 37, no. 1 (2014): 22–43.

Downes, Julia. "The Expansion of Punk Rock: Riot Grrrl Challenges to Gender Power Relations in British Indie Music Subcultures." *Women's Studies* 41, no. 2 (2012): 204–237.

Dromey, Jack, and Graham Taylor. *Grunwick: The Workers' Story*. London: Lawrence and Wishart, 1978.

Duncan, Carol. "The Art Museum as Ritual." In *The Art of Art History: A Critical Anthology*, edited by Donald Preziosi, 473–485. Oxford: Oxford University Press, 1998.

Dworkin, Andrea. *Pornography: Men Possessing Women*. New York: Putnam's Sons, 1981.

Eade, John. *Placing London: From Imperial Capital to Global City*. New York: Berghahn Books, 2000.

Ecols, Alice. *Daring to Be Bad: Radical Feminism in America, 1965–1975*. Minneapolis: University of Minnesota Press, 1989.

Edwards, Elizabeth. "Objects of Affect: Photography beyond the Image." *Annual Review of Anthropology* 41 (2012): 221–234.

Editorial. *Screen Education* 36 (Autumn 1980): 1–3.

Egerton, Jayne. "The Goal of a Feminist Politics . . . the Destruction of Male Supremacy or the Pursuit of Pleasure? A Critique of the Sex Issue of *Heresies*." *Revolutionary and Radical Feminist Newsletter*, Autumn 1981. Reprinted in *Sweeping Statements: Writings from the Women's Liberation Movement, 1981–83*, edited by Hannah Kanter, Sarah Lefanu, Shaila Shah, and Carole Spedding (London: Women's Press, 1984), 198–202.

Elwes, Catherine, Rose Garrard, and Sandy Nairne. *About Time: Video, Performance and Installation by 21 Women Artists*. London: Institute of Contemporary Arts, 1980. Exhibition catalog.

Engle, Vanessa, dir. *Lefties*. Episode 2, "Angry Wimmin." Aired February 15, 2006, on BBC 4. http://www.youtube.com/watch?v=Ap072n01ESI.

English, Deirdre, Amber Hollibaugh, and Gayle Rubin. "Talking Sex: A Conversation on Sexuality and Feminism." In "Sexuality." Special issue, *Feminist Review* 11 (Summer 1982): 40–52.

Erlich, Richard. "Photography." Review of *Three Perspectives on Photography* exhibition, Hayward Gallery, London, June 1–June 8, 1979. *Art and Artists*, August 1979, 36–41.

Evans, Jessica. "Photography." In *Feminist Visual Culture*, edited by Fiona Carson and Claire Pajaczkowska, 105–122. New York: Routledge, 2001.

Fairweather, Eileen. "Leeds: Curfew on Men." *Spare Rib*, June 1979, 6.

Faludi, Susan. *Backlash: The Undeclared War against American Women*. New York: Three Rivers, 1991.

"Feminist Avant-Garde of the 1970s: Works from the Verbund Collection." Press release, July 18, 2016, for exhibition at the Photographers' Gallery, October 7, 2016–January 8, 2017. In the author's possession.

Ferriday, Aileen. "Aileen Ferriday." In *Three Perspectives on Photography: Recent British Photography*, by Paul Hill, Angela Kelly, and John Tagg, 44–47. London: Hayward Gallery, 1979. Exhibition catalog.

Firestone, Shulamith. *The Dialectic of Sex: The Case for a Feminist Revolution*. New York: Bantam Books, 1970.

"A Flash from the Past." Review of *Three Perspectives on Photography* exhibition, Hayward Gallery, London, June 1–June 8, 1979. *Evening Standard*, June 8, 1979.

Foucault, Michel. *The Archaeology of Knowledge*. Translated by A. M. Sheridan Smith. New York: Pantheon Books, 1972.

———. *The History of Sexuality*. Vol. 1, *An Introduction*. Harmondsworth, England: Penguin, 1978.

Fran. "Porn Not Art." *Outwrite*, December 1984, 7.

Friedan, Betty. *The Feminine Mystique*. Harmondsworth, England: Penguin, 1963.

Gamble, Sarah. "Postfeminism." In *The Routledge Companion to Feminism and Postfeminism*, edited by Sarah Gamble, 36–46. London: Routledge Taylor and Francis, 1998.

"Germany: Reclaiming the Night." *Spare Rib*, August 1977, 19.

Gilbert, Stephanie. "Spare Parts—Developing Your Own Films." *Spare Rib*, May 1974, 30–31.

———. "Spare Parts—How to Fix Your Own Fuses." *Spare Rib*, October 1972, 39.

Gill, Rosalind. "The Sexualization of Culture?" *Social and Personality Psychology Compass* 6, no. 7 (2012): 483–498.

Gilroy, Paul. "Police and Thieves." In *The Empire Strikes Back: Race and Racism in 70s Britain*, edited by Centre for Contemporary Cultural Studies, 141–182. London: Hutchinson, 1982.

The Governance of Britain: Managing Protest around Parliament. Norwich: Stationery Office, 2007.

Gray, Sheila, Pam Isherwood, Joanne O'Brien, Jenny Matthews, Maggie Murray, Raissa Page, Brenda Prince, and Val Wilmer. "Format Photographers." *Feminist Review* 18 (Winter 1984): 102–108.

Green, David, and Joanna Lowry. "From Presence to the Performative: Rethinking Photographic Indexicality." In *Where Is the Photograph?*, edited by David Green, 47–60. Maidstone, England: Photoworks; Brighton, England: Photoforum, 2003.

Greenhill, Richard, Margaret Murray, and Jo Spence. *Photography*. Milwaukee: Ideals, 1980.

Greer, Germaine. *The Female Eunuch*. London: MacGibbon and Kee, 1970.

Griffin, Susan. *Pornography and Silence: Culture's Revenge against Nature*. New York: Harper and Row, 1981.

Guardian. "The Model World of Instagram Parody Star Celeste Barber—in Pictures." June 29, 2017. https://www.theguardian.com/culture/2017/jun/30/the-model-world-of-instagram-parody-star-celeste-barber-in-pictures.

Hackman, Rose. "Are You Beach Body Ready? Controversial Weight Loss Ad Sparks Varied Reactions." *Guardian*, June 27, 2015. https://www.theguardian.com/us-news/2015/jun/27/beach-body-ready-america-weight-loss-ad-instagram.

Hackney Flashers Collective. "The Hackney Flashers Collective." In *Three Perspectives on Photography: Recent British Photography*, by John Tagg, Angela Kelly, and Paul Hill, 80–83. London: Hayward Gallery, 1979. Exhibition catalog.

———. "Work of a Women's Collective 1974–1980." Accessed December 20, 2018. https://hackneyflashers.com/exhibitions/.

Hammond, John H. "Viewed *Women's Images of Men* at the ICA." Review of *Women's Images of Men*, exhibition, Institute of Contemporary Arts, London, October 4–26, 1980. *British Journal of Photography* 26, no. 127 (December 26, 1980): 1315.

Hall, Stuart, Chas Critcher, Tony Jefferson, John Clarke, and Brian Roberts. "The Politics of Mugging." In *Policing the Crisis: Mugging, the State, and Law and Order*, 327–401. New York: Holmes and Meier, 1978.

Harlesden Community Project. *Community Work and Caring for Children: A Community Project in an Inner City Local Authority by a Group of Workers from the Harlesden Community Project, 1971–1976*. Ilkley, England: Owen Wells, 1979.

Harris, Jonathan. *The New Art History: A Critical Introduction*. London: Routledge, 2001.

Harrison, Judy. "Absent Spaces: Histories, Empowerment and Representation." In *Our Faces, Our Spaces: Photography, Community and Representation*, edited by Judy Harrison, 9–13. Southampton, England: John Hansard Gallery, University of Southhampton, 2013.

Hartey, Mick. "Video: From Art to Independence—a Short History of a New Technology." In *Diverse Practices: A Critical Reader on British Video Art*, edited by Julia Knight, 21–58. Luton, England: Media Faculty of the Humanities, University of Luton, 1996.

Haworth-Booth, Mark. "Where We've Come From: Aspects of Postwar British Photography." In *British Photography: Towards a Bigger Picture*, edited by Mark Haworth-Booth, 1–9. New York: Aperture Foundation, 1988.

Hebdige, Dick. "Hiding in the Light." *Ten.8* 9 (1982): 4–19.

Heron, Liz. *Domestic Labour and Visual Representation*. Slide pack prepared by the Hackney Flashers. 1980.

———. "Getting on Top of the Job: Women in Manual Trades." In "Pictures Talk: Special Visual Issue." *Spare Rib*, July 1978, 43–46.

———. "Hackney Flashers Collective: Who's Still Holding the Camera?" In *Photography/Politics: One*, edited by Terry Dennett, David Evans, Sylvia Gohl, and Jo Spence, 124–132. London: Photography Workshop, 1979.

———. "Hackney Flashers Collective: Who's Still Holding the Camera?" In *Putting Myself in the Picture: A Political, Personal and Photographic Autobiography*, by Jo Spence, 66–77. London: Camden, 1986.

Hirsch, Marianne. *Family Frames: Photography, Narrative, and Postmemory*. Cambridge, Mass.: Harvard University Press, 2012.

Holland, Patricia. "The Page Three Girl Speaks to Women Too: A Sun-sational Survey." *Screen* 24, no. 3 (May 1983): 84–102.

Hollands, Robert, and John Vail. "The Art of Social Movement: Cultural Opportunity, Mobilisation, and Framing in the Early Formation of the Amber Collective." *Poetics* 40 (2012): 22–43.

Hollington, Sue. "The Pavilion." Review of the Pavilion gallery. *Whippings and Apologies* 7 (January/February 1984): 11, 15.

Humm, Maggie. "Women's Studies at the University of East London." In "Women's Studies in Europe." Special issue, *Women's Studies Quarterly* 20, no. 3/4 (Fall–Winter 1992): 38–43.

Hunt, Barbara. Preface to *The Camerawork Essays: Context and Meaning in Photography*, edited by Jessica Evans, 9–10. London: River Oram, 1997.

Hunter, Alexis. *Radical Feminism in the 1970s*. Norwich: Norwich Gallery, 2006.

Isaak, Jo Anna. *Feminism and Contemporary Art: The Revolutionary Power of Women's Laughter*. London: Routledge, 1996.

Iskin, Ruth. "Feminism, Exhibitions and Museums in Los Angeles, Then and Now." *Women's Art Journal* 37, no. 1 (Spring/Summer 2016): 12–20.

———. "Introduction: Re-envisioning the Canon: Are Pluriversal Canons Possible?" In *Re-envisioning the Contemporary Art Canon: Perspectives in a Global World*, edited by Ruth Iskin, 1–42. London: Routledge, 2016.

Jeffery, Ian. "Three Perspectives on Photography." Review of *Three Perspectives on Photography* exhibition, Hayward Gallery, London, June 1–June 8, 1979. *Artscribe*, July 1979, 37–49.

Jeffreys, Sheila. "Kate Millett's *Sexual Politics*: 40 Years On." *Women's Studies International Forum* 34 (2011): 76–84.

Jenkins, Philip. *Intimate Enemies: Moral Panics in Contemporary Great Britain*. New York: Aldine de Gruyter, 1992.

Johnson, Claire, and Paul Willemen. "Brecht in Britain: The Independent Political Film (on *The Nightcleaners*)." *Screen* 16, no. 4 (December 1975): 101–118.

Jones, Peter. "Anxious Images: Linder's Fem-Punk Photomontages." *Women: A Cultural Review* 13, no. 2 (2002): 161–178.

Kaluzynska, Eva. "Wiping the Floor with Theory: A Survey of Writings on Housework." *Feminist Review* 6 (1980): 27–54.

Keenan, Thomas. "Mobilizing Shame." *South Atlantic Quarterly* 103, no. 2/3 (Spring/Summer 2004): 435–449.

Kelly, Angela. "Feminism and Photography." In *Three Perspectives on Photography: Recent British Photography*, by Paul Hill, Angela Kelly and John Tagg, 42–43. London: Hayward Gallery, 1979. Exhibition catalog.

Kismaric, Susan. *British Photography from the Thatcher Years*. New York: Museum of Modern Art, 1990.

Klorman-Eraqi, Na'ama. "Underneath We're Angry: Feminism and Media Politics in Britain in the Late 1970s and Early 1980s." *Feminist Media Studies* 17, no. 2 (April 2017): 231–247.

Knorr, Karen. Interview by Antonio Guzman. In *Karen Knorr: Marks of Distinction*, 124–131. With an introduction by Patrick Mauries. London: Thames and Hudson, 1991.

Kuhn, Annette. "Introduction." In *Cultural Sniping: The Art of Transgression*, by Jo Spence, xix–xxiv, (London and New York: Routledge, 1995).

Lane, Guy. "The Photographer as Recorder: Daniel Meadows, Records, Discourse and Tradition in 1970s England." *Photographies* 4, no. 2 (2011): 157–173.

Law, Cheryl. *Women: A Modern Political Dictionary*. London: I. B. Tauris, 2000.

Leeds Women's Fight Back Campaign. "Leeds Women Paint the Town!" *Outwrite*, December 1984, 1.

Linker, Kate. "Representation and Sexuality." In *Art after Modernism: Rethinking Representation*, edited by Brian Wallis, 391–415. New York: New Museum of Contemporary Art, 1984.

Lippard, Lucy. "Issue and Tabu." In *Issue: Social Strategies by Women Artists*, curated by Lucy Lippard. London: Institute of Contemporary Arts, 1980. Exhibition catalog.

Lomax, Yve. "Some Stories Which I Have Heard Some Questions Which I Asked." In *Three Perspectives on Photography: Recent British Photography*, by Paul Hill, Angela Kelly, and John Tagg, 54–55. London: Hayward Gallery, 1979. Exhibition catalog.

"London Reclaim the Night." *Women's Report: A Monthly Feminist News Magazine*, December 1978–January 1979, 2.

Lovell, Terry. Introduction to pt. 3, "The Politics of Difference: Class, Race and Gender." In *British Feminist Thought: A Reader*, edited by Terry Lovell, 71–75. Oxford: Basil Blackwell, 1990.

Loyd, Fran. "Alison Wilding's Early Sculpture." In *Secret Spaces, Forbidden Places: Rethinking Culture*, edited by Fran Loyd and Catherine O'Brien, 231–246. New York: Berghahn Books.

Lukitsh, Joanne. "Practicing Theories: An Interview with John Tagg." In *Grounds of Dispute: Art History, Cultural Politics, and the Discursive Field*, by John Tagg, 62–96. Minneapolis: University of Minnesota Press, 1992.

MacCabe, Colin. "Class of '68: Elements of an Intellectual Autobiography 1967–81." In *Tracking the Signifier: Theoretical Essays: Film, Linguistics, Literature*, 1–32. Minneapolis: University of Minnesota Press, 1985.

Maimon, Vered. "Surviving Images and Images of Survival: On Activestills' Photographs of Protest." In *Activestills: Photography as Protest in Palestine/Israel*, edited by Vered Maimon and Shiraz Grinbaum, 182–196. London: Pluto, 2016.

Marcus, Greil. *Lipstick Trace: A Secret History of the Twentieth Century.* Cambridge, Mass.: Harvard University Press, 1989.

Margolis, Laura. Review of *Three Perspectives on Photography: Recent British Photography* exhibition, Hayward Gallery, London, June 1–June 8, 1979. *Spare Rib*, August 1979, 34–35.

McDonough, Tom. *"The Beautiful Language of My Century": Reinventing the Language of Contestation in Postwar France, 1945–1968.* Cambridge, Mass.: MIT Press, 2007.

Meehan, Elizabeth. "British Feminism from the 1960s to the 1980s." In *British Feminism in the Twentieth Century*, edited by Harold L. Smith, 189–204. Amherst: University of Massachusetts Press, 1990.

Mellor, David Alan. "Ethnicity, Community and Street." In *No Such Thing as Society: Photography in Britain, 1967–87*, 49–80. London: Hayward, 2008. Exhibition catalog.

———. *No Such Thing as Society: Photography in Britain, 1967–87.* London: Hayward, 2008. Exhibition catalog.

Memou, Antigoni. *Photography and Social Movements: From the Globalisation of the Movement (1968) to the Movement against Globalisation (2001).* Manchester: Manchester University Press, 2013.

Mercer, Kobena. "Just Looking for Trouble: Robert Mapplethorpe and Fantasies of Race." In *Sex Exposed: Sexuality and the Pornography Debate*, edited by Lynne Segal and Mary McIntosh, 92–110. New Brunswick, N.J.: Rutgers University Press, 1993.

Miller, Christopher. *Environmental Rights: A Critical Perspective*. New York: Routledge, 1995.

Miller, Russell. *Magnum: Fifty Years at the Front Line of History*. New York: Grove, 1997.

Millet, Kate. *Sexual Politics.* New York: Ballantine, 1970.

Mitchell, Juliet. *Women: The Longest Revolution.* New York: Pantheon, 1984.

Mitchell, Stanley. Introduction to *Understanding Brecht*, by Walter Benjamin, vii–xix. Translated by Anna Bostock. London: Verso, 1998.

Mitra, Durba. "Critical Perspectives on SlutWalks in India." *Feminist Studies* 38, no. 1 (Spring 2012): 254–261.
Moreno, Shirley. "The Light Writing on the Wall: The Leeds Pavilion Project." In *Photographic Practices: Towards a Different Image*, edited by Stevie Bezencenet and Philip Corrigan, 111–123. London: Comedia, 1986.
Morreau, Jacqueline, Joyce Agee, Catherine Elwes, and Pat Whiteread. Introduction to *Women's Images of Men*. London: Institute of Contemporary Arts, 1980. Exhibition catalog.
Morris, Lynda. "Alexis Hunter obituary." *Guardian*, March 11, 2014. https://www.theguardian.com/artanddesign/2014/mar/11/alexis-hunter.
Mulvey, Laura. "Magnificent Obsession." In *Photography/Politics: Two*, edited by Patricia Holland, Jo Spence, and Simon Watney, 142–151. London: Comedia, 1986.
———. *Visual and Other Pleasures*. Bloomington: Indiana University Press, 1989.
———. "Visual Pleasure and Narrative Cinema." *Screen* 16, no. 3 (Autumn 1975): 6–18.
———. "You Don't Know What Is Happening, Do You, Mr. Jones?" *Spare Rib*, February 1973, 13–16, 30. Reprinted in *Framing Feminism: Art and the Women's Movement, 1970–1985*, edited by Rozsika Parker and Griselda Pollock (London: Pandora; New York: Routledge and Kegan Paul, 1987), 127–131.
Mulvey, Laura, and Margarita Jimenez. "The Spectacle Is Vulnerable: Miss World 1970." In *Visual and Other Pleasures*, by Laura Mulvey, 4–5. London: Macmillan, 1989.
Murray, Derek Conrad. "Notes to Self: The Visual Culture of Selfies in the Age of Social Media." *Consumption Markets and Culture* 18, no. 6 (2015): 490–516.
Museo Nacional Centro de Arte. "Collection 3: From Revolt to Postmodernity (1962–1982)." Accessed November 29, 2018. http://www.museoreinasofia.es/en/collection/collection-3.
———. "Room 104.07: The Feminist Revolution." Accessed November 5, 2014. http://www.museoreinasofia.es/en/collection/room/room-10407.
Myers, Kathy. "Towards a Feminist Erotica." *Camerawork*, March 1982. Reprinted in *The Camerawork Essays: Context and Meaning in Photography*, edited by Jessica Evans (London: Rivers Oram, 1997), 188–204.
Ngai, Sianne. *Ugly Feelings*. Cambridge, Mass.: Harvard University Press, 2004.
Nicholls, Jill, and Pat Moan. "'What Offends One of Us Won't Offend the Next Chap': The Advertising Standards Authority's Line on Sexism." In "Pictures Talk: Special Visual Issue." Special issue, *Spare Rib*, July 1978, 18–19.
Noble, John. "Arts Centre Challenges Divisions." Review of the Pavilion gallery. *Arts Yorkshire*, May 1982, 1.
O'Brien, Lucy. *She Bop II: The Definitive History of Women in Rock, Pop and Soul*. New York: Continuum, 2002.
O'Hagan, Sean. "Was John Szarkowski the Most Influential Person in 20th-Century Photography?" *Guardian*, July 20, 2010.
Oonk, Gijsbert. "Gujarati Asians in East Africa, 1880–2000: Colonization, Decolonization and Complex Citizenship Issues." *Diaspora Studies* 8, no. 1 (2015): 66–79.
"Opening Space." Review of the Pavilion gallery. *Leeds Other Paper*, April 29, 1983.
Orbach, Susie. *Fat Is a Feminist Issue: The Anti-diet Guide for Women*. London: Arrow Books, 1978.
Outwrite. "What Fired Angry Women?" December 1988, 8–9.

Papers on Patriarchy: Conference, London, 1976. London: Women's Publishing Collective, 1978.

Parker, Rozsika. "Feminist Art Practices in 'Women's Images of Men,' 'About Time' and 'Issue.'" Review of *Women's Images of Men, About Time*, and *Issue: Social Strategies by Women Artists*, exhibitions. *Art Monthly* 43 (1981): 16–19. Reprinted in *Framing Feminism: Art and the Women's Movement, 1970–1985*, edited by Rozsika Parker and Griselda Pollock (London: Pandora; New York: Routledge and Kegan Paul, 1987), 235–237.

———. "Portrait of the Artist as Housewife." Review of *Portrait of the Artist as Housewife*, exhibition, Institute of Contemporary Arts, London, June 10–July 20, 1977. *Spare Rib*, July 1977, 5–8. Reprinted in *Framing Feminism: Art and the Women's Movement, 1970–1985*, edited by Rozsika Parker and Griselda Pollock (London: Pandora; New York: Routledge and Kegan Paul, 1987), 207–210.

Parker, Rozsika, and Griselda Pollock. "Fifteen Years of Feminist Action: From Practical Strategies to Strategic Practices." In *Framing Feminism: Art and the Women's Movement, 1970–1985*, edited by Rozsika Parker and Griselda Pollock, 3–78. London: Pandora; New York: Routledge and Kegan Paul, 1987.

———, eds. *Framing Feminism: Art and the Women's Movement, 1970–1985*. London: Pandora; New York: Routledge and Kegan Paul, 1987.

———. *Old Mistresses: Women, Art and Ideology*. London: Routledge and Kegan Paul, 1981.

Parmar, Pratibha. "Gender, Race and Class: Asian Women in Resistance." In *The Empire Strikes Back: Race and Racism in 70s Britain*, edited by Centre for Contemporary Cultural Studies, 236–275. London: Hutchinson, 1982.

Penner, James. "Spectacular Disruptions: Situationism and the Terrorist Gesture in Howard Brenton's 'Skin Flicker' and 'Magnificence.'" *Spectator* 21, no. 1 (Spring 2001): 68–81.

Penney, James. *After Queer Theory: The Limits of Sexual Politics*. London: Pluto, 2014.

Phillips, Christopher. "The Judgment Seat of Photography." *October* 22 (1982): 27–63.

Picton, Tom. "A Personal View." In "Lewisham: What Are You Taking Pictures For?" Special issue, *Camerawork*, November 1977, 15.

———. "What the Papers Said." In "Lewisham: What Are You Taking Pictures For?" Special issue, *Camerawork*, November 1977, 7.

Picton, Tom, Barry Lane, and Bill Gaskin. "If It Is Art We Can Support It." *Camerawork*, February 1977, 1–3.

"Picture Agencies." *Camerawork*, Winter 1983/1984, 8–9.

Poletti, Anna. "Self-Publishing in the Global and Local: Situating Life Writing in Zines." *Biography* 1 (Winter 2005): 183–192.

Pollock, Griselda. "Feminism and Modernism." In *Framing Feminism: Art and the Women's Movement, 1970–1985*, edited by Rozsika Parker and Griselda Pollock, 79–122. London: Pandora; New York: Routledge and Kegan Paul, 1987.

———. "Feminism, Femininity and the Hayward Annual Exhibition 1978." *Feminist Review*, no. 2 (1979): 33–55.

———. "'Issue': An Exhibition of Social Strategies by Women Artists." Review of *Issue: Social Strategies by Women Artists*, exhibition. *Spare Rib*, February 1981, 49–51. Reprinted in *Framing Feminism: Art and the Women's Movement, 1970–1985*, edited by Rozsika Parker and Griselda Pollock (London: Pandora; New York: Routledge and Kegan Paul, 1987), 232–237.

———. "Three Perspectives on Photography." Review of *Three Perspectives on Photography* exhibition, Hayward Gallery, London, June 1–June 8, 1979. *Screen Education* 31 (1979): 49–54.

———. *Vision and Difference: Femininity, Feminism and Histories of Art*. London: Routledge, 1988.

———. "What's Wrong with 'Images of Women'?" *Screen Education* 24 (1977): 25–34.

Posener, Jill. *Louder than Words*. London: Pandora, 1986.

———. "Nothing but the Butch: Interview with Photographer Jill Posener." *ICON*, September 1996.

———. *Spray It Loud*. London: Pandora, 1982.

Poster Collective. "The Collective." Accessed August 10, 2018. http://poster-collective.org.uk/historycollective.php.

Power, Nina. *One Dimensional Woman*. Winchester, England: Zero Books, 2009.

Preziosi, Donald. "The Art of Art History." In *The Art of Art History: A Critical Anthology*, edited by Donald Preziosi, 507–525. Oxford: Oxford University Press, 1998.

Proll, Astrid, ed. *Good Bye to London: Radical Art and Politics in the 70's*. In cooperation with curators Boris von Brauchitsch, Peter Cross, and Jule Reuter. Ostfildern, Germany: Hatje Cantz Verlag, 2010.

Purvis, June. "Deeds Not Words: Emeline Pankhurst: Leader of the Militant Suffragettes." *History Today*, May 2002, 56–63.

Reckit, Helen, and Peggy Phelan, eds. *Art and Feminism*. London: Phaidon, 2001.

Redstockings of the Women's Liberation Movement. *Feminist Revolution: An Abridged Edition with Additional Writings*. Edited by Kathie Sarachild, Carol Hanisch, Faye Levine, Barbara Leon, and Colette Price. New York: Random House, 1978.

Rees, Jeska. "'Are You a Lesbian?': Challenges in Recording and Analysing the Women's Liberation Movement in England." *History Workshop Journal* 69 (Spring 2010): 177–187.

———. "A Look Back at Anger: The Women's Liberation Movement in 1978." *Women's History Review* 3 (July 2010): 337–356.

Reger, Jo. "Micro-cohorts, Feminist Discourse, and the Emergence of the Toronto SlutWalk." *Feminist Formations* 26, no. 1 (Spring 2014): 49–69.

Report/IFL. "A Statistical Survey of Lost Working Days in 1978." In *Three Perspectives on Photography: Recent British Photography*, by Paul Hill, Angela Kelly, and John Tagg, 88–91. London: Hayward Gallery, 1979. Exhibition catalog.

Rhodes, Dusty, and Sandra McNeill, eds. *Women against Violence against Women*. London: Onlywomen, 1985.

Riley, Denise. *"Am I That Name?": Feminism and the Category of "Women" in History*. Minneapolis: University of Minnesota Press, 1988.

Ringrose, Jessica, and Emma Renold. "Slut-Shaming, Girl Power and 'Sexualisation': Thinking through the Politics of the International SlutWalks with Teen Girls." *Gender and Education* 24, no. 3 (2012): 333–343.

Roberts, John. *The Art of Interruption: Realism, Photography and the Everyday*. Manchester: Manchester University Press, 1998.

Robertshaw, Andrew. "'Irrepressible Chirpy Cockney Chappies'? Humour as an Aid to Survival." *Journal of European Studies* 31, no. 123 (September 2001): 277–287.

Robinson, Hilary, ed. *Feminist Art Theory: An Anthology, 1968–2014*. Malden, Mass.: Blackwell, 2015.

Rosler, Martha. *Decoys and Disruptions: Selected Writings, 1975–2001*. Cambridge, Mass.: MIT Press, 2004.

Rowbotham, Sheila. "Introduction: Mapping the Women's Movement." In *Mapping the Women's Movement: Feminist Politics and Social Transformation in the North*, edited by Monica Threlfall, 1–16. London: Verso, 1996.

Rowe, Marsha. Introduction to *Spare Rib Reader*, edited by Marsha Rowe, 13–22. Middlesex, England: Penguin Books, 1982.

Russo, Mary. *The Female Grotesque: Risk, Excess, and Modernity*. New York: Routledge, 1994.

Sahgal, Gita. "Fundamentalism and the Multi-culturalist Fallacy." In *Against the Grain: A Celebration of Survival and Struggle, 1979–1989*, by Southall Black Sisters, 16–24. Southall, Middlesex: Southall Black Sisters, 1990.

Savage, Jon. "London Subversive." In *Good Bye to London: Radical Art and Politics in the 70's*, edited by Astrid Proll in cooperation with curators Boris von Brauchitsch, Peter Cross, and Jule Reuter, 14–31. Ostfildern, Germany: Hatje Cantz Verlag, 2010.

Schapiro, Miriam. "The Education of Women as Artists: Project Womanhouse." *Art Journal* 3 (Spring 1972): 268–270.

Schofield, Camilla. *Enoch Powell and the Making of Postcolonial Britain*. New York: Cambridge University Press, 2013.

Scott, Linda M. *Fresh Lipstick: Redressing Fashion and Feminism*. New York: Palgrave Macmillan, 2005.

Sekula, Allan. "The Body and the Archive." *October* 39 (Winter 1986): 3–64.

———. *Photography against the Grain: Essays and Photo Works, 1973–1983*. Halifax: Press of the Nova Scotia College of Art and Design, 1984.

———. "The Traffic in Photographs." *Art Journal* 41, no. 1 (Spring 1981): 15–25.

Selz, Peter Howard. *The Art of Engagement: Visual Politics in California and Beyond*. With an essay by Susan Landauer. Berkeley: University of California Press, 2005.

"'70s/'90s: Notes for a Map of British Photography." In "British Photography: Towards a Bigger Picture." Special issue, *Aperture* 113 (Winter 1988): 75–76.

"Sex Issue." Special issue, *Heresies* 12 (1981).

Seyfert, Robert. "Beyond Personal Feelings and Collective Emotions: Towards a Theory of Social Affect." *Theory, Culture and Society* 29, no. 6 (2012): 27–46.

Seymour, Anne. *The New Art*. London: Hayward Gallery, Arts Council of Great Britain, 1972. Exhibition catalog.

Shen, Qinna. "Shedding, Witchcraft, and the Romantic Subject: Feminist Appropriation of the Witch in Sarah Kirsch's *Zaubersprüche* (1973)." *Neophilologus* 93, no. 4 (2009): 675–689.

Sinha, Mrinalini. "Britishness, Clubbability, and the Colonial Public Sphere: The Genealogy of an Imperial Institution in Colonial India." In "At Home in the Empire." Special issue, *Journal of British Studies* 40, no. 4 (October 2001): 489–521.

Snow, David A., E. Burke Rochford Jr., Steven K. Worden, and Robert D. Benford. "Frame Alignment Processes, Micromobilization, and Movement Participation." *American Sociological Review* 51, no. 4 (August 1986): 464–481.

Southall Black Sisters. *Against the Grain: A Celebration of Survival and Struggle, 1979–1989*. Southall, Middlesex: Southall Black Sisters, 1990.

Spare Rib. "Pictures Talk: Special Visual Issue." July 1978.

Spectrum Women's Photography Festival, Exhibition Catalogue: A Collaboration with "Ten 8" International Photographic Magazine. London: Spectrum, 1988.

Spedding, Carole. "Cunning Stunts." *Spare Rib*, September 1978, 30–40.

Spence, Jo. "The Politics of Photography." In *Cultural Sniping: The Art of Transgression*, 31–36. London: Routledge, 2007. Originally published in *Camerawork*, February 1976,.

———. *Putting Myself in the Picture: A Political, Personal and Photographic Autobiography*. London: Camden, 1986.

———. "The Sign as a Site of Class Struggle: Reflections on Works by John Heartfield." *Block* 5 (1981): 2–13.

Spence, Jo, and Terry Dennett. *Jo Spence: Beyond the Perfect Image: Photography, Subjectivity, Antagonism*. Barcelona: Museu d'Art Contemporani, 2005.

Staggenborg, Suzanne, and Amy Lang. "Culture and Ritual in the Montreal Women's Movement." *Social Movement Studies* 6, no. 2 (September 2007): 177–194.

Street, John. *Music and Politics*. Cambridge, England: Polity, 2012.

Studio International. "Women's Art." Special issue. 1977.

Stylianou-Lambert, Theopisti, and Elena Stylianou. "Editorial: Photography, Artists and Museums." *Photographies* 7, no. 2 (2014): 117–129.

Su, Madison. "SlutWalk or No SlutWalk: Examining Mainstream Media's Portrayal." Odyssey, December 12, 2016. https://www.theodysseyonline.com/slutwalk-examining-mainstream-medias-portrayal?altdesign=socialux.

Suganuma, Katsuhiko. "Ways of Speaking about Queer Space in Tokyo: Disorientated Knowledge and Counter-public Space." *Japanese Studies* 31, no. 3 (December 2011): 345–358.

Sweney, Mark. "'Beach Body Ready' Ad Banned from Returning to Tube, Watchdog Rules." *Guardian*, April 29, 2015. https://www.theguardian.com/media/2015/apr/29/beach-body-ready-ad-faces-formal-inquiry-as-campaign-sparks-outrage.

Sykes, Homer. "Workers: Grunwick Was Different." In *Good Bye to London: Radical Art and Politics in the 70's*, edited by Astrid Proll in cooperation with curators Boris von Brauchitsch, Peter Cross, and Jule Reuter, 110–127. Ostfildern, Germany: Hatje Cantz Verlag, 2010.

Tagg, John. *The Burden of Representation: Essays on Photographies and Histories*. Minneapolis: University of Minnesota Press, 1988.

———. *The Disciplinary Frame: Photographic Truths and the Capture of Meaning*, Minneapolis: University of Minnesota Press, 2009.

———. "Discipline and Protest: Thinking Photography after Foucault." In *The (Un) becomings of Photography: On Reaggregating and Reassembling the Photographic and Its Institutions*, edited by Lars Willumeit, 57–71. Krakow: Foundation for Visual Arts, 2016.

———. "Mindless Photography." In *Photography: Theoretical Snapshots*, edited by J. J. Long, Andrea Noble, and Edward Welch, 17–24. London: Routledge, 2009.

———. "Power and Photography—Part One: A Means of Surveillance: The Photograph as Evidence in Law." *Screen Education* 36 (Autumn 1980): 17–55.

———. "A Socialist Perspective on Photographic Practice." In *Three Perspectives on Photography: Recent British Photography*, by Paul Hill, Angela Kelly, and John Tagg, 70–73. London: Hayward Gallery, 1979. Exhibition catalog.

Tawadros, Gilane. "Other Britains, Other Britons." In *British Photography: Towards a Bigger Picture*, edited by Mark Haworth-Booth, 41–66. New York: Aperture Foundation, 1988.

Thomas, Chris, dir. "Interview with Jayaben Desai." *The Great Grunwick Strike 1976–1978: A History*. London: Brent Trade Union Council, 2008. DVD.

Thomas, Peter. "The Struggle for Funding: Sponsorship, Competition and Pacification." *Screen* 47, no. 9 (Winter 2006): 461–467.

Thomlinson, Natalie. *Race, Ethnicity and the Women's Movement in England, 1968–1993*. Hampshire, England: Palgrave Macmillan, 2016.

Thorne, Alice, and Maithreyi Krishnaraj. *Ideals Images and Real Lives: Women in Literature and History*. Mumbai: Orient Longman, 2000.

Trier, James. Introduction to *Detournement as Pedagogical Praxis*, edited by James Trier, 1–38. Rotterdam: Sense, 2014.

Vague, Tom. *Anarchy in the UK: The Angry Brigade*. London: AK, 1997.

Vance, Carol S. "Petition in Support of the Scholar and Feminist IX Conference." In *Pleasure and Danger: Exploring Female Sexuality*, edited by Carol S. Vance, 451–454. Boston: Routledge and Kegan Paul, 1984.

———. "Pleasure and Danger: Towards a Politics of Sexuality." In *Pleasure and Danger: Exploring Female Sexuality*, edited by Carol S. Vance, 1–25. Boston: Routledge and Kegan Paul, 1984.

Von Hantelmann, Dorothea. "The Experiential Turn." In *On Performativity*, edited by Elizabeth Carpenter. Living Collections Catalogue 1. Minneapolis: Walker Art Center, 2014. http://walkerart.org/collections/publications/performativity/experiential-turn.

Waheed, Shaila. In *Our Faces, Our Spaces: Photography, Community and Representation*, edited by Judy Harrison, 71–96. Southampton, England: John Hansard Gallery, University of Southhampton, 2013.

Waldemar, Janusznack. "Though Talking in the Nursery." Review of *Who's Holding the Baby?*, exhibition. *Guardian*, July 11, 1978.

Walker, John A. *Left Shift: Radical Art in 1970s Britain*. London: I. B. Tauris, 2002.

Walkowitz, Judith R. *City of Dreadful Delight: Narratives of Sexual Danger in Late-Victorian London.* Chicago: University of Chicago Press, 1992.

———. *Night Out: Life in Cosmopolitan London.* New Haven, Conn.: Yale University Press, 2012.

Wallsgrove, Ruth. "Who Do I Think I Am?" In "Pictures Talk: Special Visual Issue." *Spare Rib*, July 1978, 31.

Wandor, Michelene. *Carry On, Understudies: Theatre and Sexuality.* London: Routledge and Kegan Paul, 1986.

Wardle, Huon, and Laura Obermuller, "The Windrush Generation," *Anthropology Today*, 34 no.4 (August 2018):3–4

Wark, Penny. "Art for Heart's Sake." *Yorkshire Post*, May 4, 1983, 5–6.

Warner, Michael. *Publics and Counterpublics.* New York: Zone Books, 2002.

Watney, Simon. Introduction to *Photographic Practices: Towards a Different Image*, edited by Stevie Bezencenet and Philip Corrigan, 1–3. London: Comedia, 1986.

Webster, Wendy. *Englishness and Empire, 1939–1965*. Oxford: Oxford University Press, 2005.

Weidhase, Nathalie. "'Beyoncé Feminism' and the Contestation of the Black Feminist Body." *Celebrity Studies* 6, no. 1 (2015): 128–131.

Welch, Edward, and J. J. Long. "Introduction: A Small History of Photography Studies." In *Photography: Theoretical Snapshots*, edited by J. J. Long, Andrea Noble, and Edward Welch, 16–30. London: Routledge, 2009.

Wells, Liz. "On and beyond the White Walls: Photography as Art." In *Photography: A Critical Introduction*, 4th ed., edited by Liz Wells, 257–303. London: Routledge, 2009.

"We Will Walk without Fear." *Spare Rib*, January 1978, 22–23.

"What Are You Taking Pictures For?" *Camerawork*, November 1977, 10–14.

Williams, Val. *Women Photographers: The Other Observers, 1900 to the Present.* London: Virago, 1986.

Williamson, Judith. *Decoding Advertisements: Ideology and Meaning in Advertising.* London: Marion Boyars, 1978.

Wilmer, Val. "The First Preference Is Pride." *Time Out*, September 1978, 15–21.

———. *Mama Said There'd Be Days like This: My Life in the Jazz World.* London: Women's Press, 1991.

Wilmer, Val, and Maggie Murray. "Photography." *City Limits*, September 24–29, 1982, 47–52.

Wilson, Amrit. *Finding a Voice: Asian Women in Britain.* London: Virago, 1978.

Wilson, Elizabeth. "The Context of 'Between Pleasure and Danger': The Barnard Conference on Sexuality." *Feminist Review* 13 (March 1983): 35–41.

———. "The Invisible Flâneur." *New Left Review* I/191 (January–February 1992): 90–110.

———. *The Sphinx in the City: Urban Life, the Control of Disorder, and Women.* Berkeley: University of California Press, 1991.

Wilson, Elizabeth, and Angela Weir. "The British Women's Movement." *New Left Review* I/148 (November–December 1984): 74–103.

Wilson, Siona. *Art Labor, Sex Politics: Feminist Effects in 1970s British Art and Performance.* Minneapolis: University of Minnesota Press, 2015.

———. "Destinations of Feminist Art: Past, Present and Future." *Women Studies Quarterly* 36, nos. 1 and 2 (Spring/Summer 2008): 324–330.

Winogrand, Garry. *Women Are Beautiful.* New York: Light Gallery / Farrar, Straus and Giroux, 1975.

Wischhover, Cheryl. "Back Off, B*tches. There's Only One Butt Selfie Queen." Daily Beast, May 9, 2014. https://www.thedailybeast.com/back-off-btches-theres-only-one-butt-selfie-queen.

Wolff, Janet. "The Invisible Flâneuse: Women and the Literature of Modernity." *Theory, Culture, and Society* 3 (1985): 37–46.

"Women, Angry at Male Violence, Say: 'Resist the Curfew!'" *Leeds Other Paper*, November 28, 1980. Reprinted in *Women against Violence against Women*, edited by Dusty Rhodes and Sandra McNeill (London: Onlywomen, 1985), 12.

"Women's Images of Men." Review of *Women's Images of Men*, exhibition, Institute of Contemporary Arts, London, October 4–26, 1980. *Portfolio*, February 1981, 76, 79.

"Women's Media Collectives." Women's media panel at Zine Fest, with Melissa (Cherrybomb Comics), Jess Baines (See Red Poster Collective), and Rahila Gupta (*Outwrite*), January 24, 2009, Women's Library, London. Audio recording, 1:06:42. http://archive.org/details/ZineFest09.

Young-Bruehl, Elizabeth, and Laura Wexler. "On 'Psychoanalysis and Feminism.'" *Social Research* 2 (Summer 1992): 453–483.

Ziff, Trisha. "Working for the Council." In *Photography/Politics: One*, edited by Terry Dennett, David Evans, Sylvia Gohl, and Jo Spence, 165–170. London: Photography Workshop, 1979.

Archived Interviews

Ewald, Wendy. Interview by Shirley Read, October 23, 2006, and June 14, 2007. C459/191, Oral History of British Photography Sound Collection, British Library, London.
Lane, Barry. Interview by Shirley Read, December 13, 1999. C459/113/01-04, Oral History of British Photography Sound Collection, British Library, London.
Morreau, Jacqueline. Interview by Gillian Whiteley, artist's home, London, January 3, June 20, June 21, and December 16, 2002. F12409, F12412, NLSC: Artist's Lives Sound Collection, British Library, London.
Spence, Jo. Interview by Val Williams, March and April 1991. C459/13/1-7, Oral History of British Photography Sound Collection, British Library, London.
Tagg, John. Interview by Susan Bright, June 23 and 26, 2003. F14227, F14230–F14234, Oral History of British Photography Sound Collection, British Library, London.

Interviews by the Author

Clark, Dinah. Phone interview, October 31, 2011.
Dennett, Terry. Interview, Jo Spence Memorial Archive, London, September 9, 2011.
Heron, Liz. Interview, Liz Heron's London home, October 24, 2011.
Hunter, Alexis. Interview, café in London, October 18, 2011.
Lomax, Yve. Interview, cafeteria of the Royal College of Art, London, October 20, 2011.
Meadows, Julia. Interview, Julia Meadows's London home, November 3, 2011.
Mullen, Michael Ann. Interview, British Library, London, October 31, 2011.
Murray, Maggie. Interview, Maggie Murray's London home, October 19, 2011.
Kelly, Angela. Interview, Rochester Institute of Technology, May 19, 2010.
O'Brien, Joanne. Interview, Joanne O'Brien's London home, October 27, 2011.
Phillips, Angela. Interview, Angela Phillips's London home, October 26, 2011.
Tagg, John. Skype interview, February 27, 2013.
Wilmer, Val. Interview, Val Wilmer's London home, October 20, 2011.

Index

About the Author

NA'AMA KLORMAN-ERAQI obtained her PhD in the Art History Department at the State University of New York at Binghamton and is currently a lecturer in the Art History Department at Tel Aviv University. She has published articles in the journals *Photography and Culture* and *Feminist Media Studies*.